Financing New Ventures

Financing New Ventures

An Entrepreneur's Guide to
Business Angel Investment

Geoffrey Gregson

First published in 2014 by
Business Expert Press, LLC
222 East 46th Street, New York, NY 10017
www.businessexpertpress.com

ISBN-13: 978-1-60649-472-1 (paperback)
ISBN-13: 978-1-60649-473-8 (e-book)

Business Expert Press Babson College Entrepreneurship Research Conference Collection

Collection ISSN: Forthcoming (print)
Collection ISSN: Forthcoming (electronic)

Cover and interior design by Exeter Premedia Services Private Ltd., Chennai, India

First edition: 2014

10 9 8 7 6 5 4 3 2 1

Printed in the United States of America.

Abstract

This book provides guidance on what makes a new venture more likely to attract external financing, with an emphasis on business angel investment. The author incorporates the views of business angels, venture capitalists, entrepreneurs, and legal advisors; draws upon the latest academic thinking on financing new ventures; and provides comparisons between business angel and venture capital investing to further inform the reader. The concepts, principles, and guidelines presented in *Financing New Ventures: An Entrepreneur's Guide to Business Angel Investment* will be relevant to entrepreneurs and investors, business support agencies, business students, and others interested in raising external investment and in developing an "investable" business.

The book is organized into seven chapters, with Chapter 1 introducing key topics. Chapter 2 covers fundamental concepts of entrepreneurial venturing and finance. Chapter 3 discusses the market conditions from which "investable" businesses emerge and provides guidelines for building an investable business case, which considers business models and plans. Chapter 4 describes the investment process and guides the reader through the stages leading to an investment deal. Chapter 5 examines deal negotiation between entrepreneur and investor and the common provisions contained in an investment deal agreement. Chapter 6 examines the relationship between entrepreneur and investor *post investment* and the different strategies by which investment returns are realized (e.g., trade sale, merger, initial public offering). Chapter 7 discusses recent trends affecting how entrepreneurs raise finance that include strategic exits, "super angels," and the emergence of "crowdfunding."

Keywords

business angel, entrepreneur, private equity investment, new venture

Contents

Preface

Welcome to *Financing New Ventures: An Entrepreneur's Guide to Business Angel Investment.* This book provides a practical guide—informed by contemporary academic thinking—for the entrepreneur seeking to raise business angel (BA) investment. The book also provides an informed perspective for entrepreneurs seeking to understand how an investor might see their business.

The decision to raise external equity financing is a significant step for any entrepreneur and requires careful consideration of the advantages as well as the trade-offs. The entrepreneur or founders will be required to give up ownership stakes in their business and may give up full autonomy over business decisions. In return, they are able to access financing to fuel business development and growth and to receive business and mentoring related support that is not possible with other funding sources.

If you are an entrepreneur, you have a much better chance of raising investment from a BA than from a venture capitalist (VC). The high investment returns demanded of VCs, combined with the high risk and uncertainty in financing a new, unproven business, has seen VCs move away in recent years from the early-stage market, leaving this space open for a flourishing of BA activity.

At the same time, entrepreneurs need to be realistic when raising BA investment. Only a small percentage of new ventures successfully raise investment—many simply don't meet basic BA investment criteria. Sometimes entrepreneur aspirations and investor expectations don't align because the value of the business is perceived differently. A commonly observed challenge is the entrepreneur's uncertainty over what constitutes an *investable* business and what will be required in the process of raising private equity investment.

The book provides guidance on what makes a new venture more likely to attract BA investment and presents this within a wider discussion of contemporary academic thinking on financing new ventures. Comparisons between BA and VC investing are provided throughout the book to further inform the discussion.

Key topic areas covered in the book include the following: how to develop an investable business; how to develop a compelling business plan; how to approach and pitch to BAs; how BAs evaluate opportunities; the investment deal process and deal negotiation; managing the entrepreneur–investor relationship; and investment exit strategies. Foundational concepts of entrepreneurial venturing and entrepreneurial finance are covered early in the book to inform subsequent topics. Later in the book, we discuss emerging trends, including the rise of crowdfunding and "super angels."

The concepts, principles, and guidelines presented in *Financing New Ventures: An Entrepreneur's Guide to Business Angel Investment* will be relevant to entrepreneurs and investors, business support agencies, business students, and others interested in raising external investment and in developing an "investable" business.

The book draws upon the author's academic and practitioner background in entrepreneurship, new venture creation, and entrepreneurial finance. Relevant academic research is drawn into the discussion, along with contributions from a number of BAs, VCs, entrepreneurs, and others.

The aspiration for this book, indeed, the motivation behind writing it, is to enhance reader understanding on raising BA investment and on developing an investable business that will stimulate more entrepreneurs receiving financing for their high-growth businesses.

Acknowledgments

I am grateful to the following people who have contributed their insights to the book: Juliana Iarossi of Coalesce Capital, Paul Atkinson of Par Equity, David Grahame of LINC Scotland, business angel Nelson Gray, entrepreneur Martin Avison, and Sandy Finlayson, senior partner of MBM Commercial LLP.

I would like to acknowledge Archangel Informal Investment, Ltd., based in Edinburgh, United Kingdom, who has generously shared their approach to business angel investing with me and with many others. I would also like to express my thanks to the Canadian Environmental Technology Advancement Corporation based in Calgary, Alberta.

I am grateful to Andrew Zacharakis of Babson College as the commissioning editor of this book and would like to express my appreciation to David Parker, Destiny Hadley, and Cindy Durand of Business Expert Press for their support.

Finally, I would like to express my gratitude to my partner Marion Lamb and daughter Alaina Eloise for their considerable patience and unwavering support while I completed this project.

CHAPTER 1

Introduction

Each year, millions of aspiring entrepreneurs around the globe make the decision to start their own ventures. The majority of these new ventures are *lifestyle* or *necessity-driven* businesses, as much as 90% by some estimates.[1] Funding will come primarily from the *founders* themselves, supplemented by *family* and *friends*, the aptly named "3F" funding source.

Lifestyle or necessity-driven ventures are less likely to face high start-up capital requirements. Many will be service based, typically employ only the founder or a small number of employees, and remain small. New ventures that can generate early sales and free cash flow (e.g., cash left over after expenses are paid) are not likely to require any external investment.

A smaller proportion of new ventures will be growth oriented, more innovative, and led by visionary and ambitious entrepreneurs. These ventures are market *catalysts* that in time will contribute disproportionately to economic development and future prosperity for the global economy. Such firms have become known as "gazelles."[2] Their early funding requirements will typically take them beyond the limits of 3F sources and to seek external sources of investment.

Sourcing adequate capital is a major obstacle to early-stage growth-oriented ventures—particularly seed capital for product development, prototyping, and testing the idea in the market. Many early-stage ventures are not yet profitable—some have yet to make their first sale. For those ventures led by nascent (i.e., new) entrepreneurs, the absence of a business track record—along with an unproven product or service or market need—makes these risky investments.[3]

Debt financing from banks is usually not an option, given the lack of built-up assets to offer as collateral against the debt. So, although the entrepreneur has identified a promising new business opportunity and is passionate about pursuing it, the dream may not become a reality because of a lack of funding or difficulty in accessing capital markets.[4]

These early-stage growth-oriented ventures—the "baby gazelles" if you will—and their desire to raise external financing through business angels (BAs) is a central focus of this book.

Rise of Business Angels

Business angels (BAs) have become a predominant investment source for growth-oriented ventures and are recognized as the "entrepreneurial financiers" of many western economies.[5] BAs refer to high-net-worth individuals who invest their own funds in support of promising, early-stage ventures.

BAs invest in significantly more new ventures than venture capitalists (VCs) despite the high profile of venture capital in the media and in the aspirations of many entrepreneurs seeking investment. In the United States, BAs are estimated to fund up to ten times more ventures than VCs and globally, it is suggested the BAs fund one hundred times more seed-stage high-technology ventures than VCs.

There are various explanations as to why BAs have become a more prevalent early-stage funding source. One explanation involves the significant changes that the VC market has undergone in recent years. Since 2009, global VC has declined by 20% year on year, influenced by the absence of investment exits under global economic uncertainty, which has in turn slowed the flow of capital back to VC investors.

One consequence of the VC downturn has been a major reduction in early-stage investments—particularly for product development, "pre-revenue" ventures that carry high risks but offer potentially high returns. Another consequence has been tougher investment deal terms, as VCs establish stricter time frames and development milestones in an attempt to stimulate exits and to minimize losses from poorly performing investments.[6]

The gap left in the early-stage market has provided new opportunities for BA investors—as well as for emerging *crowdfunding* platforms (which we discuss in Chapter 7). BA investors have also been organizing themselves into groups and syndicates, where the pooling of individual BA investments has extended investment capabilities to finance larger deals. This allows BA investors to "follow their money" and to fund new investments to exit—without recourse to VC funding in many cases. The result has been new investment opportunities across a broader range of sectors and a wide and growing geographical spread of BAs, groups, and syndicates across different regions.

Increased BA activity in the early-stage market has coincided with new trends in entrepreneurial venturing. The costs to start a new business, such as a consumer web-based business, have decreased dramatically in recent years, allowing entrepreneurs to prove their products and engage with customers using far less initial capital.

The "lean start-up" concept, which we discuss in Chapter 3, also provides opportunities for BA investors who seek earlier exits from their investments. This has led to the rise of the "super angel," a term coined to refer to BAs who raise an investment fund, invest in early-stage ventures, and attempt an early exit. The acquisition of BA-funded ventures by larger firms, known as a "strategic exit," is also occurring in sectors that require longer time horizons, more investment, and specialized BAs with value-adding experiences and domain expertise. We discuss "strategic exits" in Chapter 6.

The rise of BAs is also being facilitated by public policies in some countries. In Europe, for example, strong tax incentives—that offset potential losses and protect capital gains—have been used to stimulate high-net-worth individuals to become BAs and to invest their own wealth in higher-risk, early-stage ventures. This has contributed to releasing personal wealth and stimulating flows of equity finance for early-stage ventures in regions where this level of activity may not have otherwise occurred.

Challenges in Raising BA Investment

Although BA activity has grown in the early-stage market, only a small percentage of business proposals submitted to BAs attract investment; some studies suggest less than 5%.[7] The reality is that few entrepreneurs are offered the opportunity to pitch for investment—most business proposals are rejected upon first review by investors.[8] Many business proposals are rejected because they do not offer a foreseeable profitable exit for the investor. Most BA investors expect a healthy return on their investment and seek new ventures that can build enough value over a reasonable time period to generate above-average investment returns.

Experienced BA investors and the larger BA syndicates and groups will favor opportunities where exit options are evident at initial investment. BA investors only make money when the value of the "investee" venture increases and they are able to liquidate their shares and exit the business. Some profitable BA investments, if providing regular dividends to investors, may reduce the pressure for an exit.

Entrepreneurs raising BA investment should be aware that developing a new business is not an end in itself, but rather a means to an exit. Many entrepreneurs view BA investment as "growth capital," to be invested in extending capabilities in management, sales, distribution, product development, and so forth. Less attention is paid to building market value or determining strategies for share liquidation and exiting the business.

Most BAs are not interested in funding a lifestyle business. Lifestyle businesses are often driven by the entrepreneur's desire to be self-employed or to satisfy an unmet personal need—and usually less so to grow a highly profitable business. Financial objectives for a lifestyle business are typically modest, and the business is unlikely to offer a healthy return for an investor or a clear path to investment exit.

We should be cautious, however, in suggesting that lifestyle businesses will not attract the interest of some BAs. Because they invest their own money, BAs remain free to determine who and what to invest in. As discussed in this book, it remains difficult to predict how BA investors make their investment decisions, given the wide range of personal motivations for investing. A lifestyle business seeking a modest level of financing might be attractive to a BA who wishes to work with the entrepreneur as mentor and business advisor.

Other business plans (BPs) are rejected because the business opportunity does not fit the investor's particular investment criteria, which may include preference for a particular market sector, business model, makeup of the founding team, and so forth. Because BAs are not identical in how they make investment decisions, there is no definitive set of BA investment criteria. This requires that entrepreneurs carefully assess an investor's profile to ensure that the opportunity aligns with the investor's investment criteria and preferences.

Another reason for rejection occurs when BA investors perceive that the investment requirements to achieve an exit are beyond their ability to finance it. Early-stage ventures may require multiple rounds of investment to further develop the capabilities required to grow the business and position it for a profitable exit. Some BAs will pass on an opportunity if they cannot support the investment themselves, while others may seek other BA investors to co-invest or join BA networks or syndicates where investments are pooled. The arrival of later investors, particularly VCs, can dilute the share value of existing shareholders, challenging co-investment between BAs and VCs. Dilution of investment is discussed in Chapter 5.

Focus of the Book

A central theme for this book is: *How can the entrepreneur more positively influence an investor's perception of their business opportunity that makes investment more likely?* The concept of "investor readiness" refers to a business proposition that fulfills the key investment criteria of the BA investor enough to be considered for investment, rather than be rejected. This suggests that entrepreneurs carefully assess their business opportunities for their "investable" qualities, a theme that dominates Chapter 3.

The dynamic, evolving, and difficult-to-plan operating environment for the new venture makes raising investment a challenge. Entrepreneurs will be required to revise original plans a large number of times during the start-up journey and be flexible and adaptive in aligning their business with the right market opportunity. Some new ventures may not be prepared to raise or receive BA finance initially but may have the potential to develop into an investable business.

The book aspires to facilitate better alignment between entrepreneurial aspirations and investor expectations by equipping the entrepreneur with a better understanding of the particulars of raising investment and engaging with investors, covered in Chapters 4, 5, and 6. The book suggests that this "common ground" between well-informed and well-prepared entrepreneurs and receptive and willing investors is where successful investments are more likely to occur.

The book attempts to address some common misperceptions about raising BA finance and about private equity (PE) investment more generally. One misconception is that BA investors seek to control the business and will manage the entrepreneur or founding team through restrictive deal terms and contractual arrangements.

Most BA investors seek confidence in their decision to risk their personal wealth for an uncertain future benefit. An unproven product or service, uncertain market demand, and untested entrepreneur or founding team presents a high-risk proposition for any investor. A BA's willingness to invest his/her own personal wealth should be interpreted as a sign of trust in the business opportunity and a commitment to share the risk with the entrepreneur and team.

At the same time, legal and contractual arrangements are required to cover potential downside risks—such as the investor losing all their money—while ensuring upside benefits that are fair and equitable to both investor and entrepreneur. Deal negotiation is typically investor driven; in other words, investors usually only write a check when the terms and conditions of an investment deal are right for them. We discuss this in detail in Chapter 5.

Book Outline

The book is organized into seven chapters which are described below. First, it is worth explaining how the book is presented to make it easier to follow. The term "entrepreneur" as used throughout the book also refers to the founder or founders of the new venture. The term "new venture" is used throughout the book and can also refer to an "early-stage company," a "new business," or a "start-up."

Although the focus of the book is on BA investment, there are extensive references to VC. This comparative approach allows us to highlight the distinctive as well as the salient features of BA investing while informing about VC at the same time.

There are inserts that are highlighted throughout the book and designed to complement the main discussion. They represent four different themes and are described as follows:

    ✓ *Case insights*: lessons from a company or example of a business scenario

✓ *Research notes*: summary of research results that inform a particular topic

✓ *Clarifying concepts*: discussion around a key concept or term

✓ *Views from practice*: captured thoughts and interviews from practitioners that inform a particular topic

The book attempts to integrate the author's perspective, experiences, and observations with an extensive supportive literature on the related topics and with the views of practitioners who have generously contributed their insights. As such, the book is not written in the first person but instead uses a third-person narrative. We will now consider the book's content.

Chapter 1 is an introduction to the book, describing the rise of BAs and challenges to raising BA investment and explaining the book's focus.

Chapter 2: "Entrepreneurial Venturing and Financing" begins with a discussion of fundamental concepts of entrepreneurial venturing and entrepreneurial finance that lays the foundation for subsequent chapters. Five key entrepreneurial activities for developing the new venture are described—in which the entrepreneur plays the central role. Entrepreneurial finance is then introduced, followed by a description of sources of entrepreneurial finance, which include personal sources, public sources, and private equity (PE).

Key PE concepts are then described, which include risk and return; information asymmetries; adverse selection; and moral hazard. We then examine VC finance in more detail and consider the things an entrepreneur should know about raising VC. We also briefly discuss PE funds.

Chapter 2 then presents a discussion of BA finance, the BA market, types of BAs, groups, and syndicates, followed by a comparative assessment of BA and VC financing. Initial public offerings (IPOs) are discussed (and revisited in Chapter 6 in our discussion on investment exit options). A series of questions are then posed for the entrepreneur considering raising PE investment. In the final section of Chapter 2, we consider the "funding escalator" concept to describe entrepreneurial finance and consider the critical market conditions that affect access to PE investment.

Chapter 3: "What Makes a Compelling Business Angel Investment Opportunity?" considers some common characteristics of an "investable business," emphasizing that there is no standard, validated set of business characteristics that if met, will assure an investment offer. Different types of markets that provide opportunities for entrepreneurial venturing and BA investment are described, which include understood, new, and service-based markets.

Chapter 3 then offers guidelines for building an investable business case—which discusses the business model, competitive advantages, business planning, and approaches for crafting a business plan (BP). The chapter concludes with a discussion of common pitfalls in business planning.

Chapter 4: "Understanding the Business Angel Investment Process" examines investment processes and the steps that a business opportunity will progress through to a final investment deal agreement. The five steps include deal origination; deal screening; deal evaluation; deal structure; and deal agreement. We discuss deal agreement—the final stage of the process—in Chapter 5. Next, guidelines are suggested for the entrepreneur in choosing an appropriate investor, preparing to raise investment and presenting the opportunity to investors.

We also consider some distinctions between BAs and VCs in the investment deal process and particularly in how due diligence and valuation is undertaken. We examine factors affecting the decision to invest and consider recent research that identifies investor intuition and empathy as factors influencing the investment decision. The raising of a term sheet and initial structuring of a deal are also described.

Chapter 4 then provides an assessment of common valuation methods used by BAs and VCs. Although these valuation methods are inappropriate for early-stage valuations for the most part, they are nevertheless relevant to discuss, as different investors will deploy a combination of valuation methods. These include discounted cash flow; the "comparables" method; the VC method; the asset-based method, and *rule of thumb*. Market effects on valuation are discussed to conclude the chapter.

Chapter 5: "Deal Negotiation and the Deal Agreement" looks at deal negotiation between entrepreneur and investor and the common provisions contained in an investment deal agreement. We examine the shareholder's agreement and the various provisions that attempt to reduce different types of risk exposure for the investor common to PE investing, as discussed in Chapter 2. We consider the role of legal intermediation and how it may influence the negotiation and deal-making processes. We also consider how deal pricing and equity stakes are determined.

Chapter 6: "Investment Management, Staged Financing and Exits" examines the relationship between entrepreneur and investor in growing the business once investment is secured—which we refer to as the "post-investment" stage. Typical processes by which "investee" ventures are monitored are considered, including the distinctions between BA and VC post-investment management. The terms and conditions on which "staged" or follow-on funding occurs is discussed. We consider the potentially contentious issue of BA–VC co-investment and discuss the different classes of shares and preferential provisions that will affect follow-on funding for the venture.

Chapter 6 then examines the options by which shareholders liquidate fully or partially their shareholdings, beginning with how investors determine exit value. The vast majority of BA exits occur through a trade sale, where the business is sold to another business. We discuss two types of trade sales: financial sales and strategic sales. We also discuss the IPO, which is a much less common exit option for BA-financed ventures. Nevertheless, it is worthwhile to discuss as the IPO is becoming more common as an exit strategy in emerging markets.

Chapter 7: "Summary and Future Trends" provides a summary of some key concepts discussed in the book, which include the notion of an investable business, market effects on raising equity investment, and the effects of policy and regulations on accessing investment. We revisit the lean start-up concept and consider some current trends in BA investing: the emphasis on early exits, "super angels," and "crowdfunding" and its emergence as an alternative equity funding source. We postulate on the potential effects of crowdfunding on the early-stage financing market. The book then finishes with some final thoughts.

The book includes five appendices. Appendix A provides an overview of the United Kingdom's "Enterprise Investment Scheme" to give the reader an understanding of the criteria required to become a business angel investor. The regulations for becoming an accredited investor in both the United Kingdom and the United States are noted. Appendix B provides an outline of the key sections of a traditional BP, while Appendix C briefly describes the essential documents that should be included in the financial section of a BP.

Appendix D provides a comprehensive summary of the investment screening criteria used by the largest BA group in the United States, the Tech Coast Angels. Finally, Appendix E provides a sample outline of a *Preferred* Investment Term Sheet.

CHAPTER 2

Entrepreneurial Venturing and Financing

Pursuit of a life less ordinary.

Introduction

This chapter discusses fundamental concepts of entrepreneurial venturing and entrepreneurial finance that inform our discussion in subsequent chapters. While these two topics are often discussed separately, for our purposes, they are complementary. Entrepreneurs express their business ideas by forming new ventures, with the venture also a legal entity for attracting and receiving private equity (PE) investment.

The chapter describes the sources of entrepreneurial finance available to the entrepreneur: bootstrapping, 3F (founder, family, and friends) funding, public sources, and PE, and then examines in more detail the two primary sources of PE we will consider throughout the book, namely, business angel (BA) investment and venture capital (VC). The chapter also considers the implications for the entrepreneur in deciding whether or not to raise PE investment.

Entrepreneurial Venturing

Introduction

Entrepreneurial venturing refers to the creation and formation of a new business entity—in which the entrepreneur plays the central role. The new venture entrepreneur must overcome a different set of challenges compared to established ventures. New resources must be secured, new employees recruited, advisory and board members appointed, and

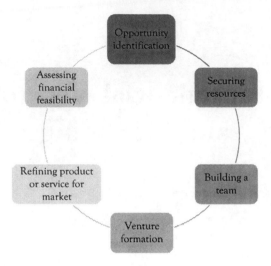

Figure 2.1 Key entrepreneurial venturing activities

investment raised. The new business is unknown and its market value unproven, making its survival, let alone growth, highly uncertain.

Different market conditions will influence the entrepreneur's ability to develop a new venture—and to raise external investment. Entrepreneurial venturing tends to be concentrated in locations where there is an abundance of talent, related services, large markets to sell products and services, less barriers to do business, and access to different sources of finance. This usually favors large metropolitan cities as hotbeds for entrepreneurial activity, but there are exceptions—no better illustrated than by Internet-based start-ups which can be launched into the World Wide Web from almost anywhere.

Six key entrepreneurial venturing activities are suggested in Figure 2.1: opportunity identification; securing resources; team building; venture formation; refining product/service for market; and financial feasibility. Each is described further below.

Opportunity Identification

The ideas behind new ventures are as varied as the entrepreneurs who create them, from social media sites to medical devices, to speech and language recognition software, to new distribution platforms, new value chains, new linkages between consumer markets, and so forth. New ventures are typically formed when an entrepreneur or founding team applies personal know-how to better solve an existing problem in the market or to offer a novel product or service.

The majority of new venture opportunities are identified through an individual's previous experience and his/her domain expertise in a particular field. In these cases, a trigger event may compel the individual to leave a salaried position and venture out on his/her own. This trigger event could include a desire to work for oneself or to pursue an opportunity that might not otherwise be developed.

Some opportunities are based on a particular vision or set of values that shape the subsequent venture. For example, Anita Roddick, founder of the Body Shop, established a clear set of values that defined her company and attracted customers who shared these values. They included no animal testing on products; support for community fair trade; defending human rights; and protecting the planet.[1]

Alternatively, opportunities may emerge through research or academic study, where recognition of the commercial potential of research results stimulates the formation of a new business to exploit the results. Academic entrepreneurship, as it is commonly referred to, often involves postgraduates and early career researchers/faculty forming a new venture rather than senior or tenured professors.

While web-based and Internet start-up ventures suggest a bias toward younger founders, certain specialized high-technology ventures are more likely to involve senior faculty, upon whose knowledge and intellectual property (IP) the opportunity is based. However, research-based opportunities pose certain risks for investors, as discussed in "Research Notes" on the following page.

Whether or not an individual decides to pursue an identified opportunity will be influenced by various factors, including a personal assessment of career alternatives and trade-offs, a personal reflection on costs and benefits, and some consideration of risks and rewards. We discuss the concept of risk–reward later in the chapter, as it is also a key concept in the raising of PE investment.

Research Notes

Opportunities From the Science Base

Scientific research can form the basis for highly innovative solutions to previously unsolved problems and for radical new technologies. However, a common complaint of business angels and venture capitalists seeking to fund academic ventures is their lack of investor readiness compared to other early-stage ventures. Investor readiness may include generating a prototype technology, securing an experienced management team, and demonstrating early sales. Particular characteristics of research-based opportunities can pose different investment risks, with three mentioned here:

✓ Most academics are not obsessed with commercial value creation but seek to contribute new knowledge to their field of study, through publications, conferences, and teaching. Restricting release of scientific results, if they form the basis of a new venture's proprietary market advantage, may be an issue.

✓ Academic inventors may seek "creative control" over their knowledge and are known to accept lower pay to maintain autonomy of their research. An important question for an investor is the following: How willing is the academic to relinquish full control over the innovation or to be flexible in its "commercial interpretation"?

✓ Transforming science into a customer value proposition (i.e., marketable product/service) can be a lengthy and costly process. How much capital is required, and for how long, before revenue is generated?

The predominance of academics in a founding team may raise concerns with external investors, particularly regarding incentives or motivations to undertake "reduction to practice" of research to commercial outcomes that may become far removed from their academic research. We discuss the issue of business validation of research further on pp. 86–87.

Academic founders keen to raise external investment are encouraged to seek experienced legal intermediation to ensure that intellectual property (IP) is secured cleanly from the host institution, proper governance and company formation structures are put in place, and the role of the academic(s) in pursuing the commercial opportunity is made clear.

Sources: Branscomb and Auerswald, 2002; Stern, 2004; Wright et al., 2004; Gregson, 2011.

Entrepreneurs have been shown to spend little time actually researching and analyzing opportunities; rather, entrepreneurs screen opportunities quickly, focus on a few important issues, and are ready to adapt original plans, even when they are not entirely sure of the outcomes.[2] Flexibility and acceptance of the need to adapt original plans will be expected of entrepreneurs by most investors. However, this will vary, depending on the type of business. Forming a medical device venture, for example, will require more considered planning compared to a web-based start-up.

Securing Resources

The willingness of the entrepreneur to take on personal risk and to demonstrate an almost evangelical passion for the opportunity will be key factors in securing resources from others, including investment.[3] New ventures are challenged by a lack of legitimacy in the market, referred to as the "liability of newness,"[4] which makes securing resources challenging. The role of third-party referrals is particularly important in raising investment and discussed further in Chapter 4. Other key resource requirements include skilled people, specialized equipment to develop the product or service, business support facilities, and advisors (e.g., legal, accounting, etc.).

Building a Team

The quality of the entrepreneur and founding team is consistently rated by BA investors (and VCs) as among the top criterion in decisions to invest. New ventures founded by a team are shown to be more successful than those founded by a sole entrepreneur. A complementary balance of people skill sets, capabilities, and experiences determines the knowledge or "intellectual" base of the business from which competitive advantages arise.

The entrepreneur must identify key people, if not already founders, and attract them into the business with a compelling vision of opportunity that secures their services and commitment. Cofounders or key individuals joining a founding team usually receive part ownership (e.g., equity) in the new venture to incentivize commitment and to compensate for a typically lower salary common with new venture teams.

Forming the Venture

Venture formation refers to formal registration of a company in a particular jurisdiction for legal and tax purposes. In this process, rights are allocated to a new venture, and founders of the venture receive shares or an ownership stake to compensate them for the knowledge and IP brought in to the venture. Referred to as "founder shares," subsequent investors represent another type of share—"financial shares," which are directly related to the capital invested. Share equity is discussed further in "Clarifying Concepts" on p. 22.

Refining Product or Service for Market

Some new ventures do not yet have a market-ready product or service upon formation. Refining, fine-tuning, and adapting the product/service for the appropriate market segment usually occurs as teams are formed and resources acquired.

The entrepreneur's vision, passion, and business ethos are often reflected in the products and services offered and how the venture is run, but not all ventures or particular products and services will be attractive to external investors. New ventures seeking BA or VC investment need to offer products or services that have high potential to build business value, which often equates to market growth. As we will discuss in Chapter 3, investors seek businesses with strong "value propositions" that meet a clearly defined market need and can expand beyond a single product or service.

Assessing Financial Feasibility

Entrepreneurial venturing, as any experienced entrepreneur will acknowledge, is a highly personal career choice. Entrepreneurs must make a personal case for themselves in deciding to pursue a new business opportunity or not. For some, it is the logical choice, but for others, it is a much more measured decision. An objective assessment of the feasibility of a new business concept is often difficult, given the level of emotional, intellectual, and often financial capital committed. Some common questions that may inform the decision include the following: What are the financial goals for the business? Is it to replace a salaried position (i.e., suggesting a lifestyle business) or to achieve significant financial reward, suggesting a high-growth business? What outcome do I want to achieve?

It is often the case that the process of generating a business plan, requiring more formal financial data, clarifies the financial feasibility of the opportunity, as discussed in Chapter 3.

Determining Seed-Funding Requirements

Entrepreneurs usually need to spend money before they make money, to cover expenses required to sell a product or deliver a service in the absence of any sales revenues (referred to as "pre-revenue"). The investment required to form and launch the business is known as start-up capital or seed funding. Such expenses may include registering the business, renting or leasing office space, purchasing computers, mobile phones, and business-related software, refining the product or service to be sold, paying suppliers, paying staff salaries, and so forth.

The level of seed or start-up capital required will also be influenced by the nature of the market and industry, which may include the following:

1. *Capital intensity* of the particular business sector. Capital costs to launch a software firm or computer support service will be significantly less than starting a biotechnology firm, which has longer product development lead times—or a microbrewery, which has high plant and equipment costs. High start-up costs, along with the need for specialized know-how, can be significant entry barriers for new ventures attempting to enter certain sectors.

2. *Size and growth of the market.* A large market of customers with a similar profile may allow a new venture to gain rapid market share; however, this usually requires a highly innovative product or service, secured channels to sell to customers, and strong sales support and marketing spend.

The market and industry factors noted in the preceding text will also affect the level of external financing sought from BAs (or VC). Some investors will provide seed funding, but others will expect entrepreneurs to fund early-venture development themselves. Most investors will require the entrepreneur to treat their investment as growth capital rather than business development funding. Chapter 4 further discusses funding requirements and approaches for raising external investment.

Summarizing Entrepreneurial Venturing

The entrepreneurial venturing process, shown in Figure 2.1, is *iterative in nature* rather than linear or sequential, reflecting the fact that there is no "one best method" for creating a new venture. Although opportunity identification is likely a first step in the process, some entrepreneurs may form a company prior to building a team or refine a technology for the market after securing resources.

Entrepreneurial venturing is a learning process, particularly for first-time entrepreneurs (referred to as "nascent" entrepreneurs). Each of the activities in Figure 2.1 generates new information and insights that informs the viability of the opportunity. If the perception of risk by the entrepreneur exceeds their personal threshold of "bearable risk," then the opportunity may not be perceived as viable, and the entrepreneur may abandon pursuit of the opportunity. Different personal circumstances, career alternatives, and perceptions of opportunity by an entrepreneur make each new venture's formation profile different.

There are also different approaches for the entrepreneur in pursuing market opportunity. For example, the entrepreneur may identify a market opportunity and configure resources and capabilities to exploit the opportunity, or the entrepreneur may possess resources and capabilities and *configure an opportunity* that leverages these. A "resource-based view" (RBV) of ventures suggests that entrepreneurs assemble a bundle of resources, in comparison to others, that creates value and contributes to competitive advantage.[5] Presenting a sustainable competitive advantage is a requirement for an investable business and is discussed further in Chapter 3.

Even if an entrepreneur assembles appropriate resources, determines financial feasibility as positive and makes the decision to pursue an opportunity, he/she may still be constrained in realizing the opportunity if there is a lack of capital, collateral, or access to capital markets, which we discuss next.[6]

Entrepreneurial Financing

Introduction

Entrepreneurial financing refers to the different sources of funding available for entrepreneurial or early-stage ventures. Entrepreneurs are generally unable to secure bank loans as a source of financing, given the lack of collateral that can be offered to the bank to secure the loan (i.e., in the event the new business fails, there are few tangible assets for the bank to liquidate to offset their loss on the loan). Therefore, bank debt financing is not included as a source of early-stage finance, although it is a critical source of funding for established ventures.

Figure 2.2 identifies three common sources of entrepreneurial finance: personal, public, and PE. We discuss each source in the following text and include a discussion of initial public offering (IPO) which may follow PE investment.

Figure 2.2 Sources of entrepreneurial finance
3F = founder, friends, and family; IPO = initial public offering; PE = private equity.

Personal Sources

Personal sources refer to personal, readily accessible finance available to the entrepreneur to fund the new venture. In the United Kingdom, it is estimated that 85% of new business start-ups rely on internal finance.[7] Personal sources, it is safe to say, are the most significant sources of new venture finance in any country.

Bootstrapping

The term "bootstrapping" is used to describe all personal means available to the entrepreneur to fund the business without resorting to (external) PE finance. Bootstrapping sources include personal capital of the entrepreneur such as personal savings, extending overdrafts on bank accounts, and use of credit cards (extending credit limits on existing credit cards and securing new credit cards).

Bootstrapping also refers to all available options undertaken by the entrepreneur to *minimize the costs* of starting the business. Bootstrapping activities include:

- ✓ working from home or accessing rent-free office space;
- ✓ borrowing or leasing equipment;
- ✓ seeking free support and advice from individuals, institutions, and other sources (e.g., Internet resources, free public programs, open-access courses);
- ✓ leveraging personal networks of contacts—and those of others—to gain access to resources and capabilities to start the business.

The primary advantage of bootstrapping is that the entrepreneur usually does not give up any ownership or equity of the venture in return for such funds. One limitation of bootstrapping is that venture growth must be held in check, to avoid expanding beyond what the entrepreneur can afford and control.[8] Bootstrapping can also be a risky (and expensive) approach to starting a new venture, as suggested below:

- ✓ Debt can build up quickly using credit cards and overdraft facilities—that typically incur high interest rates.

✓ Default on monthly payments can have a damaging effect on credit ratings that may constrain the entrepreneur's ability to secure bank debt financing as a potential source of growth financing in the future.

Founder, Family, and Friends (3F) Funding

Personal sources of finance are also available from family, friends, or colleagues. Such sources can complement the entrepreneur's personal capital and increase the overall amount of funds available. This combined source of personal funding is referred to as "3F funding" (founder, family, and friends). It is difficult to establish the true extent of 3F investment in the economy, but one estimate suggests that 3F funding is as much as three to five times more than either VC or BA investment.[9]

Much 3F financing is informal and unstructured. The motivation for such funding is usually to support the entrepreneur *unequivocally*; hence, the term "love money" is commonly associated with 3F funding. Parents or close family members are more likely to provide funding without expectations that the money will be repaid.

However, 3F investment from friends or colleagues may be in the form of a personal loan to the entrepreneur, where repayment is expected. This might include repaying the principal only within an agreed-upon time period, or include the principal plus an agreed-upon rate of interest to be paid back.

An entrepreneur should be cautious about 3F financing when considering the consequences of not paying back family or friends, particularly when there is an expectation of repayment. An important question for the entrepreneur is "If my business fails and I cannot pay back this money, what effect will this have on these relationships?" For some entrepreneurs, the trade-off is too high, and other sources of funding should be sought.

The entrepreneur should also consider the implications of 3F funding on the business itself. For example, are friends and family members expecting to have a position within the management team? What level of influence will they have on negotiations with potential PE investors? PE investors may require that these questions be addressed as a condition for investment, requiring the entrepreneur to re-evaluate the roles of 3F investors in the management team or how the financial agreements are structured. This is particularly important if friends or colleagues demand an "equity stake" in the fledgling venture in return for 3F funding. An equity stake refers to an ownership stake in the venture and is discussed in "Clarifying Concepts" in the following text.

Clarifying Concepts

Share Equity

Share equity, or equity stake, refers to the proportional share of ownership (i.e., out of 100%) of a company. The proportional share usually, but not always, provides the shareholder with a proportionate degree of control over the decisions to be made regarding the company. With company success, the shareholders will see an increase in the value of their shares and potentially receive dividends, but they will also bear the greatest risk should the company fail. We discuss shareholder control more in Chapter 5.

There are two types of shares. "Founder shares" refers to those shares provided to venture founder(s) in recognition of the contribution of the original idea, concept, or intellectual property (IP) upon which the new venture is based. It can be difficult to assign values to founder contributions, as some ventures will be much more valuable than others, based on the original idea, concept or IP. Some founders have invested life savings and personal time to launch their ventures. Others have contributed to a business idea while fully employed and have little personal savings committed. Financial shares, on the other hand, are directly related to the capital invested in the venture.

The term "sweat equity" refers to ownership shares provided to the entrepreneur and founding team and key people recruited onto the management team in exchange for the future value of their contributions to increase the value of the business. Known as an "option pool," a proportion of equity is set aside to incentivize key individuals to join the original founding team. The amount of share equity required by a business angel (or venture capitalist) in exchange for the investment will be influenced by valuation of the venture, the expected investment return, and other factors, discussed further in Chapters 4 and 5.

Entrepreneurs intending to raise PE should be aware that most PE investors are not keen to see friends and family members receive equity stakes in exchange for small amounts of funding. Such funders are identified as "noncontributing owners." For example, offering $10k for a 5% equity stake to a 3F funder represents a significant give-away of equity for a promising new venture, when that 5% equity stake may attract anywhere from $25k to $150k from a BA, depending on the type of business and venture's stage of development.

Some PE investors will require the entrepreneur to simplify the shareholding, particularly if there are many small shareholders or noncontributing owners. In some cases, investors may be willing to buy out early shareholders to simplify the shareholdings.

As suggested earlier, the majority of new ventures globally are launched with 3F funding with entrepreneurs owning 100% of the equity. Many of these are lifestyle businesses or "necessity" businesses, where founders are compelled to venture to make a living. Profits are typically reinvested to fund additional working capital that supports the growing business, and the venture grows "organically," with the entrepreneur or cofounders fully owning and controlling the business.

However, for entrepreneurs with high ambitions, who identify growth opportunities and have developed novel products or new technologies, 3F funding will not be sufficient. The ability to finance the transformation of new technologies into marketable products, build outstanding management teams, or support high business growth require levels of risk capital only available through PE investors.

Public Sources

Public funding sources are available to support very early-stage commercial application of new technologies. In promising new sectors such as renewable energy or translational medicine, for example, technical uncertainties and unproven market applications make these markets unattractive for PE investment. Such early-stage markets typically incur high costs over long time horizons with uncertain commercial outcomes.

Public funding is prominent in the phase between invention and innovation (defined here as new market applications) along with large corporation funding that supports collaborative applied research with leading research institutions, universities, and other partners. As some of these publically funded projects begin to show promising commercial applications, BA activity can be observed. However, much of this activity that remains "pre-revenue" remains unattractive to VCs.[10]

Public sources include funds available through research councils, investment grants, and public loans (from enterprise agencies, business incubators, charities, etc.). Smaller public funding is used to support "proof-of-concept" activities and initial start-up activity that may include marketing and promotion activity or funding for office space. In some regions and countries, public funds are available that provide grants or interest-free loans to support company formation activities.

Availability of public sources of finance appears to positively influence entrepreneurial venturing decisions. In the United States, public funding (in the form of Small Business Innovation Research [SBIR] grants), along with credit cards and earnings from a salaried job are among the most important sources of funds for entrepreneurs in their decision to start up a new venture.[11]

Seed Capital

Seed capital is a term commonly used to describe the funding necessary to start a business but also refers to the capital required for testing the feasibility of a commercial concept or a product prototype prior to market exposure. Seed capital may also be used to support product development but is rarely used for production or marketing. Such activity is seen by investors and most industry specialists as embracing the highest level of risk and uncertainty, given that the market acceptance remains uncertain. Moreover, pilot or beta testing and proof-of-concept projects commonly supported by seed capital are very difficult to conduct or assess as an exclusively commercial activity.[12]

Investors also use the term seed capital to refer to the funding that precedes first, second, third, and so forth, rounds of PE funding. Gaining access to seed capital from PE sources may substitute for the need to access 3F funding, but many PE investors are cautious about funding such pre-commercial activities unless the technology appears exceptionally innovative. Some VCs have seed funds that invest in such innovations, as discussed later in the chapter.

Private Equity Investment

Private equity (PE) refers to various forms of independent investments that are provided by BAs, VCs, and PE funds. PE investments are into companies that are not listed on a public exchange, meaning that shares are not freely traded, and no established markets exist for the shares. In the absence of a public market for stock, a PE investment is generally "illiquid," which means that a PE investor needs to wait for a "liquidity event" such as a trade sale or public listing. PE investments are therefore considered to be longer-term investments.

In exchange for PE investment, the entrepreneur or cofounders of the venture offer up a portion of company ownership or equity stake. PE investors, notably BAs and VCs, negotiate the terms and conditions under which the investment will be made and take an active role with the entrepreneur in formulating an investment strategy. This is not possible in public company investments.

By comparison, **PE funds** focus on existing and mature businesses and attract large institutional investors, such as pension funds and corporate investment. PE fund investments are significantly larger than VC or BA investments and use a combination of equity and debt financing, whereas VCs and BAs are primarily focused on equity financing (although "convertible debt" is also used, discussed in Chapter 5). PE funds typically invest across all types of industries, whereas VCs and BAs usually focus on a narrower range of sectors where they have expertise and experience.

PE funds are typically used to reintroduce value into a mature business and generate a profit from "rightsizing" the *investee* business. This may include buying out original owners, introducing a new management team, reengineering the business and positioning it for a public listing (e.g., IPO), reducing company debt load to stimulate reinvestment and growth and so forth.

Unlike BAs or VCs, who generally take a minority (i.e., less than 50%) investment in a company and support rather than control the entrepreneur and team, many PE funds take a 100% or majority stake, allowing them to control the company, manage a quick turnaround in performance, and generate an attractive return. PE funds seek companies with proven markets and products but have management, strategic, or other challenges—which have reduced performance and thus attracted PE fund interest.

All forms of PE seek investment return opportunities well above what an average *public* equity investment would achieve. This expectation makes the vast majority of new ventures started each year in the economy unattractive to PE investors. Most new ventures forecast modest sales and profit returns and display low-to-moderate ambitions for profit and growth. Further, most new ventures do not possess the quality of management required by PE investors. However, BAs and VCs can differ substantially in their investment criteria and what they chose to invest in, as discussed later in the chapter.

Key Investment Concepts in PE

The entrepreneur will benefit from familiarity with some investment concepts that influence PE investment decisions and deal terms. These include risk–return criteria, information asymmetry, adverse selection, and moral hazard. Although these concepts have origins in the study of VC, they have relevance in understanding BA investing and the distinctions between BA and VC investment.

Risk and Return

All PE investment decisions will be influenced by a particular *risk–reward assessment* of the opportunity. Every investment requires the expenditure of a known sum of money today in anticipation of uncertain benefits in the future. For some PE investors, the risk and uncertainty need to be formally calculated—in determining whether or not the opportunity matches an explicit return on investment requirement, as is the case with most VC. If PE investors cannot assess the level of risk, then they are not likely to invest.

The assessment of risk and reward is ultimately an "informed prediction" based on the investor's interpretation of available information on the opportunity. The more uncertain the prediction, the more the investor will expect to be compensated for assuming a higher risk. BA investors—who invest their personal money—will also assess their own personal threshold of bearable risk compared to VCs who invest other peoples' money.

Experienced PE investors recognize that some of their predictions of investment returns are not likely to be achieved. Such investors manage such risk by following an **"investment portfolio"** approach, where smaller investments are placed across a number of companies to "spread" the risk and reduce their exposure to losing all their investment in a single investment.

Information Asymmetry

Information asymmetry refers to the entrepreneur's ability to withhold or misrepresent important information from the investor or where the investor is constrained from directly observing the entrepreneur or team's activities or capabilities. This makes it difficult for the investor to ascertain the actual quality and potential value of the business, technology, or product.

> **Example:** An entrepreneur possesses superior knowledge of the science behind a new medical device but fails to disclose that further development is required that will take longer than outlined in the business plan. The investor is reliant on reports and data generated by the entrepreneur and team but is not involved in day-to-day activities to observe or pick up potential delays.

PE investment is highly unlikely if investors cannot ascertain the quality and potential of a business. However, if information is withheld or misrepresented, investment may occur based on asymmetrical information, contributing to an adverse selection problem or moral hazard problem for the investor, described in the following text.

Adverse Selection

Adverse selection would refer to a situation where the investor selects a weak business or overvalues the business because its quality has not been adequately "signaled" by the entrepreneur. This could result from the entrepreneur not accurately revealing all that he/she knows about the business or the entrepreneur withholding or misrepresenting information (i.e., one party in a transaction knows more than the other).

In theory, if quality of the business opportunity is adequately signaled by the entrepreneur, then costly due diligence by the investor may be unnecessary as all information would be disclosed.[13] In reality, investors will still undertake a level of due diligence to assess the business even if a more accurate level of risk is known. However, investors may not have the same incentive to have a high-risk premium on the venture and may lower their demand on equity ownership share.

Moral Hazard

Moral hazard is defined as a situation where one person makes a risky decision but someone else bears the cost when the decision goes wrong.[14] If a PE investor invests a significant amount into a new venture, the question is how much risk is carried by the entrepreneur and who bears more cost if the business fails. This is often why investors expect the entrepreneur or founding team to demonstrate a strong commitment to the venture by committing personal savings, referred to as "putting skin in the game."

Moral hazard can also arise when investment funds are misallocated by the entrepreneur or the use of funds deviates from an agreed strategy with the investor. A moral hazard problem typically occurs after the investment has been made.

> **Example:** An academic entrepreneur has raised funds from a PE investor but investment appears to be spent disproportionately on further research activities that bring notoriety to scientific achievements but for which there is little progress on product development, as expected by the investor.

Moral hazard is more likely if investors fail to adequately monitor and evaluate the ongoing decisions of the entrepreneur and team following the investment or if incentives are not adequate for the entrepreneur or misaligned with those of the investor.

Moral hazard may be reduced in the case of investors who "specialize" in the sector and have deep domain knowledge and experience. Such investors are less likely to make risky decisions on the technology or product. Specialist VCs have been shown to achieve greater investment performance than "generalist" VCs.[15] Choosing the right investor is discussed further in Chapter 4.

For the PE investor, information asymmetries, adverse selection, and moral hazard are addressed by due diligence and contractual arrangement that set out obligations for the entrepreneur and team receiving the investment. Staged financing is commonly used, where investment is tied to achieving shorter-term milestones that can be monitored more closely by investors (and will be discussed further in Chapter 6).

VCs are more inclined to establish stringent measures to counter the possibility of these problems emerging, including replacing the entrepreneur or founding team, compared with BAs; who rely more on interpersonal trust with the entrepreneur—facilitated by close, regular, face-to-face contact. This explains why BA investors favor close proximity with their "investee" companies.

Entrepreneurs can reduce information asymmetries by disclosing as much about the business as possible to the investor. Open and honest disclosure of all available information may offer three potential benefits:

- ✓ Establishes trust and credibility between investor and entrepreneur.
- ✓ Generates discussion between entrepreneur and investor on where and how to overcome certain deficiencies or gaps in the business:
  - ○ If the investor does not perceive that these deficiencies can be overcome—or that they cannot contribute relevant experience, expertise, or contacts to strengthen an otherwise promising investment opportunity—then the entrepreneur may benefit from finding a more suitable investor.
- ✓ May reduce the investment risk, potentially reducing the equity stake demanded by the investor or their expected rate of return.

Reducing information asymmetries can also involve the entrepreneur verifying information and data about the business from highly credible sources, including customers. Further, having introductions from trustworthy sources can reduce the potential concerns by investors over adverse selection. Such information from high-value sources may also reduce the perceived need for some investors to undertake comprehensive and costly due diligence. This is more often the case with BAs than with VCs and will be discussed in more detail in Chapter 4.

Venture Capital

Introduction

Venture capital (VC) has a high profile reputation in the media and among many entrepreneurs seeking to raise external finance. VC has been described as the engine of American ingenuity and has played a predominant role in the success of Silicon Valley and in financing many globally recognized businesses, such as Twitter, Skype, Facebook, and Google. In countries such as India and China, VC is rising as a percentage of PE investment, as new sectors emerge with promising, high-growth opportunities.

How difficult is it to raise VC investment? It is estimated that of approximately 600,000 businesses started each year in the United States, approximately 1,000 receive their first VC funding each year. This equates to 1/6th of 1% of new businesses each year in the United States that successfully secure VC funding.[16]

VC refers to companies that specialize in investing in "unquoted" companies (e.g., companies that are not listed on a public exchange). VC is a more formalized and regulated form of PE investment than that of BAs. VC has been described as a "hits-driven" business, as investments are typically into high-risk–high-return ventures, where a few significant returns can offset losses from the majority of other VC investments.

A defining characteristic of VC is its limited partnership (LP) structure, which is prevalent in the United States, Canada, Europe, and a number of other countries. The partnership structure provides a formal, legal vehicle for bringing together different investors to share in the economic gains (or losses) of pooled investment. Investors are known as limited partners (LPs) and include wealthy individuals, pension funds, institutional funds, and so forth. LPs provide most of the money in VC funds but take no role in investment management; they are also not legally liable for debts arising from the partnership.

Each VC firm has an investment manager, known as a general partner (GP), who finds investors (LPs) and organizes a partnership. GPs will invest in a fund themselves, but with most VC funds, the GP's percentage contribution to a fund is very small and ranges from 1% to 10%. GPs are legally liable for partnership debt.

VC funds are usually established for a 10-year period and "closed end," meaning that investors are restricted in their ability to withdraw their investment during the life of the fund. Investments are usually made by the GP during the early years, typically between the first and fifth year, and expected to return all capital within the 10-year period. GPs of VC firms are given broad discretion to invest on behalf of their LPs, given that promising deals may only arise after the fund has been raised.

VC fund agreements usually stipulate the minimum and maximum investments the fund can make in any one venture. A typical VC fund invests in approximately 10–12 investee companies with individual investments of between 5% and 15% of the individual fund's total investment capital.

VC firms will charge a management fee to cover GPs' salaries and the expenses to source investments, perform due diligence, monitor performance of investee companies, and manage exits. A percentage of each VC fund raised, usually 1%–3%, is "top-sliced" as the management fee and is paid whether or not the fund performs well. Given the high risks of failure with VC investments, without a management fee, VCs would not be incentivized to take on the risks of forming partnerships. However, the management fee can be a source of contention with some LPs. Because it is a flat rate, VCs get more for raising bigger funds and receive payment whether or not they perform.

In addition to a management fee, VCs generate income from "carried interest," which represents the VC's share of fund earnings. Carried interest is a profit share and fully dependent (100%) on fund performance—and is paid only when investee companies experience a liquidity event (i.e., are sold or go public [IPO], which typically occurs 5–10 years from the start of the partnership)—and only after LPs have been paid back all of their investment. VCs typically seek a 20%–30% share of fund profit for carried interest.

Once a liquidity event occurs, return proceeds are returned to each LP rather than reinvested into new opportunities. An important benefit of the LP structure is that the VC fund itself is not a legal entity for tax purposes. This means that any gains and losses pass directly to each LP, and taxes are applied to each investor rather than to the fund. As mentioned earlier, another benefit of the LP structure is limited liability of the fund, meaning that liability from investee firms cannot be passed on to the investor.

Should the GPs take profit from early exits, only to experience later failures that decrease profitability, they are responsible for paying back profits once the partnership comes to an end (and all the investee companies financed by the fund have experienced a *liquidity event*, i.e., an exit). This payback is referred to as a "clawback."

A common criticism of VCs is that the profit share from carried interest is larger than the share of capital that the VC contributes; in other words, VCs have a significant upside potential for a successful fund, while GPs typically contribute only a small proportion of the financing. One study found the GPs contribute less than 2% of total fund financing.[17]

At the same time, GPs face significant challenges in generating returns within the lifetime of a VC fund. They must organize the partnership and the capital contributions of different LPs; source, perform due diligence, and invest in outstanding investment prospects in the first 4–5 years; work alongside entrepreneurs and organized board members, mentors, and so forth; and manage the liquidity event. Many VC funds are not profitable; one U.S. study found that 62% of funds failed to exceed returns available from public markets, after fees and carried interest were paid.[18] We will return to the issue of VC returns later in the book.

VC follows the "portfolio" model, described earlier, which involves investing in a number of different ventures to diversify risk and increase the odds that a proportion of total investments will realize the returns expected. The portfolio approach to investing recognizes that most investments fail or do not generate a positive return. For example, a VC fund is $500 million with a 10-year life. The GP seeks to invest in approximately 5 new deals per year over the first 4 years of the fund, suggesting 20 deals of $25 million each. The fund would need only 3–5 of those deals to be 30–50X multiple returns (on the original investments).

The time-restricted nature of VC funds places considerable pressure on the GP to identify and harvest a high-return investment. Importantly, each potential investment must meet an explicit return rate stipulated by the LPs. Achieving a substantial return for investors is necessary if the VC firm intends to raise a new fund and sustain itself as a business. Leading VC firms tend to be oversubscribed, as investors believe that those who produced high returns in the past will do so in the future.

VCs usually invest in a venture by purchasing convertible preferred stock or employ a variant of convertible preferred stock called participating preferred.[19] In an investment situation characterized by large information asymmetries, preferred securities may be used to force entrepreneurs to signal their confidence in the company's business plan.[20]

> **Preferred versus common stock.** VCs seek preferred stock, compared to common stock, which is typical of founder shares and BA shares. A key difference is that in the event of a liquidation event, the holder of preferred stock receives both the principal amount of the preferred stock and shares of common stock. This can be a contentious issue between BAs and VCs and is further discussed in Chapter 6.

Attracting VC investment typically requires evidence of a large market opportunity in a fast-growing sector. However, VC funds will differ regarding particular criteria that include revenues or market share in a particular time horizon. Two examples of revenue predictions used by VCs as a condition for investment are shown in the following text:

✓ A $100-million to $300-million revenue stream within 5 years, requiring a market potential of $500 million or more and a market share of at least 25%

✓ $60 million to $80 million in revenue in 3–5 years[21]

Although VC retains an elevated status amongst technology-based entrepreneurs seeking investment, few new venture opportunities meet VC

Clarifying Concepts

What Entrepreneurs Should Know About Raising VC

Venture capitalists (VCs) focus on "picking winners"—looking for companies that will earn their investors high returns, usually as capital returns arising from a significant increase in a company's valuation. General partners (GPs) of VC firms are responsible for identifying the winners emerging out of a confluence of new technologies and markets.

VCs are very explicit about the investment return they seek. Each investment is expected to produce a high return that offsets expectant losses from other deals—which characterizes the investment *portfolio* model. VCs are also obsessively detailed in structuring an investment deal, given that they are investing other people's money; the VC fund is time constrained and deals often require substantial follow-on funding.

Being highly cautious in their investment decisions, VCs will undertake a comprehensive due diligence appraisal of the business, where claims in the business plan are verified by domain experts. Any level of uncertainty over the technology, intellectual property (IP), management team, market, financial projections, or expected rate of return can result in rejection.

Entrepreneurs seeking VC also need to find an appropriate match. VCs that are industry specialists and have considerable in-house expertise and experience can add more value beyond the funding. Newer VC firms might not have such expertise and some VCs may rely more on GPs who are "financial technicians." More experienced VC firms are also likely to possess substantial knowledge on deal-making and managing investments and exits, as well as having good networks across the industries in which they invest. Finally, entrepreneurs need to be prepared to give up substantial equity and relinquish control over business decisions in return for VC investment.

investment criteria (see "Clarifying Concepts" in the above text). VCs fund significantly fewer new businesses than BAs, and distinctions between BAs and VCs will be discussed in the next section.

Business Angels

Introduction

The term "angel" investor purportedly comes from the theatre, where wealthy individuals took high risks in funding the production of Broadway shows. The provision of risk capital by wealthy individuals for the support of new ideas and innovations goes back as far as the seventeenth and eighteenth century systems of patronage.[22] By contrast, VC is a more recent form of risk capital and emerged post 1945, after World War II.

Business angels (BAs) have funded many well-known businesses over the years that include Facebook, Apple, Ford Motor Company, Bell Telephone, and many lesser-known ventures. At the same time, we must acknowledge that these success stories don't represent BA investing as it typically happens.[23] BA investment is called risk capital for a reason; there are many more failures than successes.

Who Are BAs?

BAs are defined as high-net-worth individuals who invest in unquoted companies and whose investments are private transactions, which are not subject to any public disclosure. BAs are also referred to as "informal investors," given that these individuals typically do not make up a known population[24] and do not rely on a formal institutional infrastructure to support their activities, unlike the VC market. The definition of BA investor has broadened to include individual private investors who neither have the personal ability (or inclination) to perform the due diligence required for responsible investing nor are in a position to take board seats or help the firms with their management problems.

BAs can be described as a "class" of PE investor that is the principal source of seed and start-up capital that funds initial stages of venture growth. Evidence suggests the significant impact of BAs on the early stage investment market. The BA market in the United States and United Kingdom is estimated at 2–5 more than the institutional VC market (which was $23 billion in 2007[25]) and estimated to provide approximately 80% of seed and start-up capital for high-tech entrepreneurial ventures.[26]

The concept of "smart money" distinguishes BA investment from 3F funding in recognizing that many BA investors provide more than investment and often seek some level of direct involvement in their investee businesses.[27] BA investors can contribute their business experience, particular skills (e.g., finance, accounting, marketing, operations, sales, product development, etc.), and networks and contacts and provide credibility and legitimacy to a new venture.[28] BA investors are also typically local investors, as discussed in "Clarifying Concepts" in the following text.

Clarifying Concepts

Business Angels as Local Investors

Business angel (BA) investors can be distinguished from VC by a greater focus on local investment, with BAs rarely investing outside their locality (i.e. less than 2 hours drive away). This is characteristic of BAs in most countries. BAs rely heavily on trust and perceptions of good character of the entrepreneur and team. BAs typically rely more on personal communications with entrepreneurs rather than contractual terms in protecting their investment compared to VCs, reinforcing their preference to invest locally and be in close proximity to their investee businesses. Some BAs also display a strong sense of social responsibility and community involvement in supporting local entrepreneurs and businesses.

It is unlikely that traditional BA investing will evolve into a substantial source of international "cross border" finance. Investing further afield requires knowledge about foreign market entry requirements, including different consumer tastes, legal and business regulations, and regulations affecting the international movement of capital. Different legal environments will affect investment deals because contracts, once negotiated and agreed upon, must be upheld and enforced by legitimate and competent legal jurisdiction. Bankruptcy laws are also important and can stimulate or constrain demand for external sources of risk capital. In uncertain or underdeveloped legal and regulatory environments, traditional private equity risk capital sources may be absent, but some level of publically supported development capital may be available. An informal and unregulated local market will also be operating at some level in providing risk capital. We discuss "cross-regional" investing in more detail in Chapter 7.

VC by comparison: The vast majority of VC firms invest in their own national markets. A 2013 study by Ernst and Young found that only approximately 20% of VC firms in the United Kingdom, Brazil, India, and Israel invest outside their home countries. Other VC firms—in Germany (92%), France (82%), Canada (69%), and the United States (49%)—invest internationally.[29] Growth in emerging and Asian economies is attracting international VC activity as well as stimulating local VC development, particularly in the case of China.

Types of BAs

Most BA investors have created personal wealth from business themselves but come from a variety of backgrounds and may have different motivations for investing. We consider different types of BA investors below:

- ✓ **Retired business people:** They seek investments that allow them to "keep their hand in business" and to help a new venture to grow with some mentoring and guidance.
- ✓ **Early retirement or made redundant:** They expect to take a more active role.
- ✓ **"Near-professional" investors:** They are primarily profit seeking and tend to invest in industries in which they are familiar. These individuals often stimulate the formation of BA syndicates or networks (discussed later in the chapter).
- ✓ **Entrepreneur angels:** They seek to help build new enterprises. Entrepreneur angels are more likely to:
  - ○ be comfortable with the challenges, issues, and setbacks that the entrepreneur and new venture will face in building the business and reaching profitability;[30]
  - ○ invest based on the personality of the entrepreneur;[31] and
  - ○ invest in ventures characterized by imperfect (i.e., asymmetrical) information but with the potential for high returns, similar to VCs.[32]

Research suggests that BA investors with entrepreneurial expertise outperform those without it, especially in earlier-stage opportunities while BA investors who invest in opportunities where they possess specific industry expertise have lower failure rates.[33]

Different BA investor motivations, represented by investor "types," may influence the level of engagement between entrepreneur and investor, as suggested in Table 2.1.

What this suggests is that the entrepreneur should carefully consider how aligned their expectations, perceptions, and goals are with a potential BA investor. While trade-offs in securing investment should be expected (e.g., investment amount is less than requested, equity stake demanded by the investor is higher than expected, etc.), an entrepreneur should be comfortable

Table 2.1 Business angel motivations: Implications for entrepreneurs

Level of involvement expectations	Implications for entrepreneur
Solely seeking profitable return on investment	Ability to achieve progress milestones and focus on financial outcomes?
Active day-to-day involvement in business and management of business	Willing to relinquish some control and "share" business decisions with investor?
Mentoring of entrepreneur	Comfortable with a high level of regular interaction and advice from investor?
Seeks to offer strong technical and industry sector experience	Willing to adapt, modify, or reposition product to market with investor input?

with the role to be played by the BA investor in the business. As suggested earlier, some BAs are wealthy individuals seeking a profitable return, and their sole contribution to the entrepreneur and new venture will be finance.

An unmotivated and uninspired entrepreneur can increase the business risk for the BA investor by withholding information or misallocating funds (i.e., asymmetrical information and moral hazard issues mentioned earlier). The entrepreneur may also simply abandon the venture despite contractual obligations if the relationship proves stressful, a particularly devastating prospect for any venture that relies primarily on the entrepreneur's vision, skills, capabilities, and knowledge.

Profile of a BA

Juliana Iarossi is a U.S.-based BA who invests through her company, Coalesce Capital LLC (LLC refers to *limited liability company*). She is also an active member of the BA network Atlanta Technology Angels and cofounder of 2X Angel Investor Network, which is focused on supporting women-led companies. Educated as an engineer, Juliana has more than 20 years experience in financial services, working in both commercial and investment banking. She has made five investments in distinctly different businesses that include technology and retail/consumer products (both digital and tangible products). Two of her investments were done as a solo BA and three as part of the BA network.

Juliana's investment philosophy is based on allocating a portion of her household investment portfolio to early-stage companies. Her background in due diligence, funding companies, negotiating transactions, and turnarounds provides her with a greater level of comfort with this type of risk. As she states, "This does not mean that I will be more right than wrong in the outcome…it only means that I will be less shocked at the failures and losses."

Juliana suggests that her experience allows her to identify "red flags," inconsistencies, or unrealistic goals relatively quickly without plowing through detailed business plans and multiyear financial models, which she suggests are generally not useful at the seed stage or early in the development of a new venture.

According to Juliana, entrepreneurs need to gauge early the expectations of potential investors and determine how patient potential investors will be once their money is deployed. She suggests that some investors, not just nascent investors, have unreasonable expectations regarding company valuation, the nature and frequency of interaction with the founder and involvement with the company, and how quickly an exit may come about. "Views from Practice" in the following text provide further insights from Juliana on what the entrepreneur might expect from engaging with a BA.

Views From Practice

An Interview with Business Angel Juliana Iarossi (United States)

What are your key investment criteria? "I generally invest in companies where the capital I contribute is meaningful…where capital is needed to finish product development, run pilots and build the customer acquisition process or where the company can scale up with a relatively small amount of additional angel capital before an institutional round (if that is needed at all).

I invest in business technology and models that I understand and in companies with a service or product that has a clearly defined need and use. I also invest where there may be something else that I can add to the process in terms of contacts or expertise. I stay away from businesses where there is a long regulatory process or that I think has potential of being regulated away. I also have intentionally tried to seek out and support women founders."

Are there particular "deal-breakers" that will compel you *not* to invest?

"Yes, (1) if an entrepreneur is defensive or arrogant when asked questions and challenged on the business model, in other words appears un-coachable or unwilling to respectfully listen and discuss issues and alternatives; (2) if there is not a reasonable justification for valuation of the company; (3) if a founder proposes throwing a lot of capital into an action without looking for a lower cost way to test the waters; or (4) if the entrepreneur has given too much of the company away to earlier investors or if the capitalisation table is just too complex."

Do you invest differently as a solo business angel versus when you invest as a member of a business angel group?

"I generally have significantly more involvement with the founder and company when investing on my own or with a business partner than with a large angel group. When I'm investing as part of a larger angel group, I try to do my own investigation of the line of business and founders, and I certainly make sure that I participate in conference calls with the founders, other angels and due diligence meetings that may be open to potential investors. The angel groups that I am familiar with that have a robust deal flow have developed rather sophisticated and structured screening and due diligence processes in order to keep up with demand and provide quick answers to entrepreneurs as to whether a deal has potential with the group."

The BA Market

The confidential nature of PE investing and variation of BA investors make it difficult to gather data and to accurately measure the BA market. There also remains a level of definitional confusion as to who is a BA and who is not. In emerging and developing countries, BA investing is not yet recognized as a class of PE investor as it has become in most developed economies over the past few decades.

Nevertheless, existing methods provide an approximation of the scale and scope of the BA market and BA investing activity. Table 2.2 presents a picture of BA investment activity across a number of market characteristics, using comparisons between United States (U.S.) and European

Table 2.2 *Business angel (BA) investment activity**

Market characteristics	United States	European Union
No. of individual BAs	268K	250K
No. of BA syndicates/groups	300+	300+
Total BA investment (2012)	US$22.9 billion	US$6 billion
Average deal size (including BA groups and syndicates)	US$342K	€136K (based on 2009/10 data) Range (92K–365K)
Individual BA investment Examples...	US$85K Range (25K–1 million)	€50K Range (€18K–150K)
Investments by sector	Software (23%); healthcare/medical devices (14%); retail (12%); biotech (11%); industrial/energy (7%)	ICT, biotech, health care (50% of total); financial and business services; creative industries

Sources: Sohl, 2013; Centre for Strategy & Evaluations Services, 2012.

ICT = information and communications technology.

data—the two most active markets for BA activity. As shown, the U.S. continues to dominate the BA market in terms of total amount invested, which is approximately four times greater than that estimated in the European Union (EU total from 27 countries). The total number of active BA investors appears similar.

U.S. BA deals also appear to be larger than in other markets. U.S. data for 2012 suggests that approximately 67K entrepreneurial ventures received BA funding, with the average angel deal size of $342K (average individual investment of $85K), average equity received by the investor of 12.7%, and average deal valuation of $2.7 million. This contrasts with the European Union, where the median deal value was €136K (average individual investment of €50K).[34]

Investments from individual BAs tend to be relatively small (e.g., average of £25K in Scotland) but vary significantly (e.g., $25K to $1 million in the U.S.[35]); much larger investments are available from BA syndicates or groups, discussed in the next section. An earlier U.S. study found that ventures on average are 11 months old when receiving their first BA investment, with 70% of ventures not having yet generated revenues.[36]

What types of businesses or sectors do BAs invest in? Table 2.2 identifies that software is most predominant in the U.S. Two further observations should be mentioned. Industrial/energy investing has remained a significant sector for U.S. BAs for the last few years, suggesting a continued appetite for clean tech. Another observation is in retail, which remains a predominant attraction for BA investment.

In the European Union, information and communications technology (ICT), biotech, and health-care sectors dominate BA investments and represent more than 50% of the total number of deals in the visible market in most EU countries. Other sectors include finance and business services, creative industries, environment, and clean technologies with varying weight in the different countries.[37]

Market conditions will affect the supply and demand of BA investment as well as the types of sectors that may be more or less attractive to investors. We discuss market condition effects on raising BA finance at the end of this chapter.

Business Angel Syndicates and Networks

Business Angel syndicates (BASs) and BA networks (BANs) are increasingly commonplace in markets where individual BA investors are highly active. As shown in Table 2.2, there are over 300 BASs and BANs in the United States and a similar number in Europe. A BAS occurs when two or more individual investors come together and take an equity stake in a company. In some cases, a BAS may be created from the efforts of solo BAs who require additional investment to "follow their money," and attract additional investors who join the syndicate. By comparison, a BAN refers to a group or organization that facilitates the matching of entrepreneurs with BAs.

Individual BA investors syndicate their investments or join a BAN for a variety of reasons:

- ✓ Expected higher return from pooling money and investing in larger deals.
- ✓ Greater due diligence in assessing new opportunities from pooled experiences.
- ✓ Deeper pool of investor experiences and skills to support syndicate investments.
- ✓ Ability of new investors to learn from more experienced investors
- ✓ Social camaraderie available by investing with others.
- ✓ More visibility to potential opportunities by concentrating investors in a group or network.

A manager-led BAS—as opposed to investor led—will use executives to manage their investment portfolio that suggests a more "professional" approach to investment management. Whether or not a BAS is investor led or manager led will depend on the needs and preferences of its investors (we discuss BAS investment management further in Chapter 6, pp. 177–78).

BASs and BANs operate in an unregulated market and as such, cannot make recommendations on, or profit from, related investments. Individual BA members must make their own investment decisions and receive profit only from those investments they have made decisions on. BASs and BANs with executive teams charge management fees to cover operating expenses but cannot afford to undertake formal, in-depth due diligence similar to VCs. They instead rely heavily on their members, advisors, and wider networks to engage in due diligence. The level of expertise and experience that can be drawn upon informally will influence the quality and depth of due diligence.

The case of Archangel Informal Investment Ltd. (see "Case Insights" below) identifies a manager-led BAS, where a small executive team sources and screens deals, recruits new investors, coordinates the investment deal process, oversees management of investee companies, and manages the exit process. Executives take on the role of "investment gatekeepers," and entrepreneurs will likely have their business plan initially screened by the executive team rather than by investors. More scrutiny of the business plan may occur, particularly from executive teams acting on behalf of large, successful groups or syndicates. It is important to emphasize that investment decisions remain with investors, despite the active role of executive teams.

The BAS "model" represented by Archangel consists of a tight core of five primary, lead investors who provide a central decision-making function, with an outer ring comprising more passive investors who do not have the time to come to investment presentations. Many BANs operate more like "dinner clubs," where all members are provided with the investment opportunity and the investment develops from there.[38]

For the entrepreneur, syndicated investment may provide more capital (including follow-on financing), deeper knowledge, skills and capabilities to support the new venture, and greater experience in taking ventures to successful exit. The entrepreneur may also benefit from a BAS which specializes in the sector and has developed investment expertise around a narrower set of similar investment opportunities.

BA syndicates and networks appear to favor ventures that already have revenues; one U.S. study found that 63% of investment deals were in companies with revenues, with 56% of the deals in new companies.[39] Entrepreneurs are well advised to familiarize themselves with the syndicate or network, its investment profile and preferences, and executive team members. Extensive information is available on most BAS and BAN websites, including investment criteria, previous and current investments, case study examples, and guidelines for seeking their investment. Preparing and pitching for investment is discussed further in Chapter 4.

Case Insights

Profile of a Business Angel Syndicate

Archangel Informal Investment Ltd., formed in 1992, is one of the oldest, largest, and most successful business angel syndicates (BASs) in Europe. Over £55 million has been investing in 60+ investments, resulting in 8 exits (3 initial public offerings [IPOs]). Approximately £10 million is invested per annum, with average investment around £615K (ranging from £300K to £1million), involving an average of 22 investors and 4 rounds of funding.

An explicit investment philosophy has guided its approach to investing since 1992, when its cofounders identified an opportunity to pool their resources and invest in promising local business ideas. Both cofounders had retired from respective business positions and did not know each other, but were introduced by a mutual friend—a well-known corporate solicitor—whose legal firm supports early-stage investment deals in the United Kingdom.

The presence of trust—of each other and of the intermediary—is identified as a critical element in their decision to undertake initial co-investment activities and form the BAS. The partners first created a "four pillars" philosophy that identified their investment objectives:

- Put something back into the economy
- Support young enterprise

- Have fun
- Make money

The cofounders then established four guiding principles to focus on the *types of investments* they would pursue:

1. To invest in new businesses that would benefit from their combined business experience and would accept their commercial guidance.
2. To find investments offering high returns ("can this company make a million?").
3. To only invest in businesses less than 1.5-hour drive away ("to go fix any problems").
4. To avoid lifestyle businesses but avoid being narrowly focused only on a few sectors.

Archangel remains committed to the original four pillars philosophy and guiding principles, which any new investor joining the syndicate is expected to follow.

Business Angels (BAs) Versus VCs

This section considers the similarities and differences between BAs and VCs, beginning with suggested similarities. Return on investment is the primary motivation for VC and BA investors. Experienced BA investors will follow an investment portfolio approach similar to VCs, where a number of investments are made to diversify the risk of investing in only one or a few companies. Larger BASs and BANs may also be more selective in sourcing on high-return investments and have more sophisticated due diligence processes.

Fundamental stages of the investment process are also generally similar between VCs and BAs, as shown in the following text (and discussed in detail in Chapters 4 and 5):

✓ Deal origination, where promising investments are discovered
✓ Deal screening, where an overabundance of opportunities are reduced

✓ Deal evaluation, where opportunities are assessed and due diligence performed

✓ Deal structuring, where investor and entrepreneur clarify and negotiate deal terms

✓ Deal agreement[40]

Some BA groups form funds, known as **"sidecar" funds**, which are used to complement regular investment activities.[41] Sidecar funds invest in deals that have been screened by the group or syndicate, but the source of funds may include nongroup members and incur management fees, as discussed in "Clarifying Concepts" in the following text.

More mature and highly experienced BA groups share some similarities with small VC funds, in their use of sidecar funds and professional executive managers. However, the LP structure and associated regulations are key factors distinguishing VC from BA markets.

Clarifying Concepts

Sidecar Funds

Sidecar funds are committed sources of capital that invest (i.e., "ride") alongside regular investments of some business angel (BA) groups. Although they are used primarily to raise more capital to invest in more new deals, they have different purposes. For some groups, increasing the number of new investments with a sidecar fund allows individual investors to diversity their investment portfolio by investing smaller amounts into more companies. Some sidecar funds are only used for investments that meet specific pre-established criteria, such as initial public offering (IPO)-only deals or deals involving a certain size and configuration of investors.

Some sidecar funds, such as Band of Angels Venture Fund (U.S.), source their funds from outside their group, to include pension funds, corporations, and university endowments. Other groups, such as Tech Coast Angels (U.S.), restrict fund membership to BA investors only. Some BA groups charge management fees on their sidecar funds to cover the costs of due diligence and deal structuring.

Distinctions

The VC market is more highly regulated and more formalized than the BA market. A key distinction is the LP structure, whereby investors (LPs) provide a vast majority of VC fund investment but have no say in investment decisions. VCs have a fiduciary obligation to maximize investor returns and GPs are under pressure to allocate funds in the early years of a fund, requiring a high volume of potential deals to be sourced and assessed. The need for time-sensitive high returns results in a formally structured and comprehensive due diligence and investment management approach.

VCs have a dual identity as both principals and agents that may be inherently conflicting. As agents to their investors (LPs), VCs have short-term pressures to obtain results with a profitable exit from their investment but also face longer-term pressures to build their reputations to raise future funds.[42] By contrast, BAs are their own principals, investing their own money and under no constrained time pressure to exit.

VC investments are common in industries that have high levels of *information asymmetry* that characterize "disruptive innovation," defined as a radical alternative to existing products or services available (discussed in Chapter 3). Such investments carry high risks but potentially very high returns and generally require significant levels of financing that only a VC fund can provide. This also requires more in-depth, comprehensive, and expensive due diligence compared with BAs.

BAs, by comparison, follow a more informal investment approach; they invest their personal wealth, are responsible for their own investment decisions, and manage their investments as they see fit. This gives BAs the ability to be much more selective in who they fund and what investment criteria they adopt to inform their investment decisions. BA investors may also bring more variety to the strategies in how they invest and build companies, relative to formal VC.[43] In the absence of a time-constrained fund, BAs are less pressured to force an exit.

While VCs are very explicit on investment returns, there is more variation with BAs, given the different risk–return profiles of each BA investor. For example, a VC is more likely to stipulate a 10X return on an investment in 5 years, with the company achieving 25% market share and US$100–300 million in revenue.[44] BAs also seek investments capable of achieving a strong return, but there is a wide range in the expected return on investment.

BASs do not typically charge the entrepreneur an arrangement fee for the initial investment or require the entrepreneur to pay due diligence costs, as with VCs. The use of extensive legal agreements in completing an investment deal will also be less than with VC deals. With more formal BASs, the entrepreneur may be required to pay an annual fee to cover the costs of ongoing investment monitoring.

While many VCs specialize in financing promising technology firms across different sectors, few invest in the early stages. Some VC firms do support nascent ventures through specialized seed funds, but only a small proportion of VC directly supports the development of new technology (as distinct from other activities of new firms such as management, production, and marketing). "Research Notes" in the following text explains why VCs generally avoid early-stage ventures.

Research Notes

Why Venture Capitalists Avoid Early-Stage Investments

Venture capitalists (VCs) tend to avoid early-stage ventures for a number of reasons. One reason is that the *structure* of VC funds does not accommodate the nature of early-stage investing. VC costs to appraise, to perform due diligence, and to monitor an investment are high—and tend to be fixed, regardless of the size of investment. This favors larger deals—and the trend to larger VC deal sizes has also shifted investment to favor ventures in later stages of development (refer to Figure 2.3). Another reason is the difficulty in forecasting an investment return for early-stage ventures that often possess technological uncertainties, inexperienced management, and time-to-market risks. Although there is a limited number of VC "seed" funds that specialize in high-potential start-ups, VC returns from early-stage investing have generally been poor.

VCs prefer businesses that have begun to develop a track record and can generate significant growth with a large injection of investment and have subsequently contracted their expertise and competencies away from early-stage investing. A Bank of England study found that less than 5% of VC funding is used for start-up and early-stage finance, compared with 20% in expansion capital and as much as 75% in managed buyouts or managed buy-ins (MBO, MBI).

In addition to VC funds becoming much larger in recent years, with VC investments in the United States typically $5 million or more, the life of some VC funds have also become longer than the traditional 10 years, with funds extending to 12 to 15 years. These trends have affected the supply of VC for early-stage ventures and for those businesses seeking smaller amounts of growth capital and have stimulated the demand from this market for alternative private equity sources, namely, business angels.

Sources: Mulcahy, Weeks, and Bradley, 2012; Pierrakis and Mason, 2008; Bank of England, 2001.

Differences in the *investment process* between solo BA investors and VCs tend to be greater than between BASs and VCs. As noted earlier, larger BASs or groups may employ an executive team who manages some of the investment process on behalf of investors and coordinates the investor network, drawing upon investors to mentor, advise, undertake due diligence, and takes seats on the boards of investee companies. Table 2.3 summarizes some key distinctions between BAs and VCs.

The case of Par Equity (see "Case Insights" in the following text) offers further distinctions between the VC and BA investment process. Based in Edinburgh (UK), Par Equity provides VC finance through Par Innovation Fund, which focuses on in-revenue and innovative companies, while Par Syndicate invests as a BAS in high-growth potential, innovative companies that may be in-revenue or prerevenue. Par Equity completed 25 deals in 2012, with 5 being new deals and 20 being follow-on funding deals. Paul Atkinson, founding partner, suggests that Par Equity tries to apply BA thinking to their VC fund investment. They realize that people are investing their own money and will attempt to do everything possible to ensure that their investee businesses don't fail.

Table 2.3 Investment characteristics of business angels and venture capitalists

Characteristics/ criteria	Business angels (BAs)	Venture capitalists (VCs)
Source of investment funds	Personal money, family wealth	Includes private and institutional investors, for example, pension funds
Motivation to invest	Varied: make healthy ROI; personal involvement in business; support local start-up community; tax relief	Maximize investor return
Stage of venture	Start-up, early or late stage of venture growth	Late stage of venture growth; some VCs have seed funds
Geographic focus	Local (>2 hrs from home); cross regional for some groups	Nation-wide; some more regionally focused
Types of business	Varies by investor, sectoral experience, and interests	Large, fast-growing markets; build scale in business
Return criteria	Varies by investor; 20%–30%; not always predetermined	Minimum 10X return; 40%–50% IRR
Level of involvement in business	Personal and participatory	Managed investment function on behalf of passive investors
Average investment	High variation; $25K to $1 million; $100K to $4 million for larger BA groups	$250K–$30 million for single VC; 500K–$100 million for syndicated investment
Investment horizon	Longer: 5+ years; often won't force an exit	Shorter: 3–5 years; exit driven
Investment deal process	Shorter, standard legal agreements	Longer, extensive due diligence, and contractual arrangements
Investment structure	Common stock	Convertible preferred stock
Exit strategy	Trade sale, IPO, dividends	IPO or trade sale

IPO = initial public offering; IRR = internal rate of return; ROI = return on interest.

Case Insights

A *Hybrid* Private Equity Firm: *Par Equity*

Par Equity originated as a regulated (i.e., venture capital [VC]) investment manager and started raising capital for Par Innovation Fund, to make discretionary decisions with other people's money as well as that of the founding partners. At the instigation of its early investor base,

Par's founding partners made the decision to form the Par Syndicate. Although VC funds allow "investment scalability" with the ability to raise institutional money and to invest in larger deals, high investment returns are possible within both models.

The Par Syndicate, as a business angel syndicate (BAS), operates on the basis that each investor makes up his or her own mind about each investment opportunity that Par evaluates. Par's role in respect of the Par Syndicate is to filter hundreds of possible opportunities down to around twenty a year which the Par Syndicate will consider and, from these twenty or so, approximately five may result in an investment being made. Each BA must decide how much or how little work they wish to do in evaluating each opportunity and, if they wish to invest, how much they will put in.

Par facilitates a formal due diligence process, broadly comparable to that which a VC would undertake, but does not provide a valuation or recommendation to the BAs. Typically, a new BAS will build a portfolio of investments whose follow-on funding requirements and oversight requirements will become more onerous, with the result that new deals can tail off unless there is a continuing growth in the BAS's membership. Investment exits are critical to the long-term survival of such syndicates, as exits provide evidence of track record and also cash for reinvestment. The highest priority is therefore given to investee companies to get value from existing investments. BAS networks may need to be "refreshed," as some BAs are not able to follow on invest or have maximized the funds that they will invest. Some investors will wait for returns before further investing.

Initial Public Offering (IPO)

The biggest investment returns for VCs and BAs are from an IPO, described as the sale or distribution of stock to the public market for the first time. An IPO allows a business to raise money at a competitive price and also provides an exit option and liquidity event for investors, allowing them to cash out and invest in other opportunities. An IPO exit requires exceptionally high projected revenue levels and market capitalization. Successful IPOs are characterized by experienced management teams, solid operational and financial administration, professional advisors, and audited accounts (usually over the last 3 years).

A key disadvantage of an IPO is the high transaction costs that include legal and underwriting fees and investment banking and accounting costs. When new funds are raised through the IPO, the venture will be required to pay approximately 5% of the funds raised in commission, in addition to advisor fees. An IPO may be an unprofitable strategy when raising smaller amounts of money.[45]

The entrepreneur and management team considering an IPO should be aware that once the venture becomes a public company, all aspects of the business are examined and reported. The board of directors and shareholders play a major role in how the business is operated, with attention focused on share price and valuation. Formal reporting, achievement of short-term financial targets, and adherence to business controls and processes will be closely monitored and controlled, beyond what was likely experienced under previous VC or BA contractual arrangements.[46] The IPO as an exit strategy is discussed further in Chapter 6.

Market Effects on Raising PE Investment

Access to PE risk capital will be influenced by external market conditions as well as by the investment returns and level of profitability being achieved by PE investors. The VC industry is known to be highly cyclical, with periodic changes in supply and demand conditions.[47] "Research Notes" in the following text suggest lessons from different market conditions.

Research Notes

Lessons From Boom and Bust Markets

The ability of entrepreneurs to raise private equity investment following the dot-com boom and bust (1997–2001) was made difficult by a subsequent hardening of financial return criteria after investors experienced significant losses. Balance sheets were overleveraged as investors were drawn to supposedly novel web-based business models that did not have sustainable revenue-generating characteristics or distinctive features from competitors. Between the fourth quarters of 2000 and 2001 alone, total venture capital (VC) funds raised dropped by more than 80%. Sun Microsystems cofounder Bill Joy reflected on the dot-com period in 2001, stating, "A couple of years ago, even the bad ideas were getting capital. Now we have gone too far in the opposite direction, shutting down investment in good ideas."*

Similarly, the genomics bubble and bust that followed shortly after the dot-com boom and bust identified the challenges of investing in complex, science-based technologies where product development was expensive and lengthy and where market profitability was highly uncertain. Research suggests that the impact of VC investment on innovation is some 15% lower during boom periods compared to normal industry periods, with this difference suggested to be the result of VCs diluting their support by taking on too many companies in booming markets.

The more recent global credit crisis of 2008 saw a contraction of bank debt financing that affected access to growth capital for business angel-backed companies. The need to inject additional capital into companies that would otherwise have raised debt financing reduced the level of equity capital available from these investors to fund new business opportunities.

Sources: *Branscomb and Auerswald, 2002:16; Lerner, 2002; Gregson, Mann, and Harrison, 2013.

Changing market conditions will also affect investment deal terms that are available for the entrepreneur. For example, risk–return criteria of investors will be affected by uncertain or volatile market conditions, where interest rates, inflation, or credit conditions are in flux. Valuation of the new venture may be reduced, or deal terms may include restrictions on follow-on funding.

The reverse may be true under strong market conditions, where higher prices being obtained for exits in certain sectors may increase investor competition for promising opportunities and increase valuations. Factors affecting valuations when negotiating an investment deal are further discussed in Chapter 4.

In theory, the supply of investable opportunities should also drive the demand for PE investment. Few regions can emulate the levels of entrepreneurial venturing and financing—VC and BA—occurring in a region such as Silicon Valley, with its dense, interconnected entrepreneurial ecosystem of recycled entrepreneurs, entrepreneurs-turned-investors, service providers, world-class technology-based institutions, and sociocultural ethos which favors risk-taking and tolerates a high level of business failure.

Although it would be expected that higher BA investment activity is to be found where there is a higher level of entrepreneurial activity, this is not always the case. For example, in many EU countries, strong tax incentives have been used to stimulate high-net-worth individuals to invest in new ventures (Appendix A describes the UK's Enterprise Investment Scheme, where between 30% and 50% of income tax relief is available on investments per tax year). In the United States, there is no federal tax incentive program—although some states have instituted income tax credits—and tax incentives do not appear to be as significant a factor in stimulating BA activity as in the United Kingdom.

Public coinvestment policies, which match public funds with BA investment on the same investment deal terms, have also increased the level of syndicate investment activity as well as the size of investments. Such policies have allowed small-country markets, such as Scotland—with a low business birth rate, moderate level of entrepreneurial activity, and strong public science base—to develop one of the most active BA markets in Europe. Average Scottish BA investment deal sizes (with coinvestment) are higher than either the U.K. or EU deal averages.

One question is the extent to which policies to stimulate BA investment translate into exits that in turn stimulate entrepreneurial venturing and financing. Another question relates to whether or not the absence of any noticeable VC activity or coinvestment deals between BAs and VCs limits the ability of local ventures to finance their transition from early growth to high growth, as shown in Figure 2.3 in the following text, or to scale quickly with VC finance and bypass BA investment.

Summary

Entrepreneurial finance has been described in terms of a "funding escalator" that begins with small amounts of private (and public) financing to start the new venture and progresses to larger amounts of investment

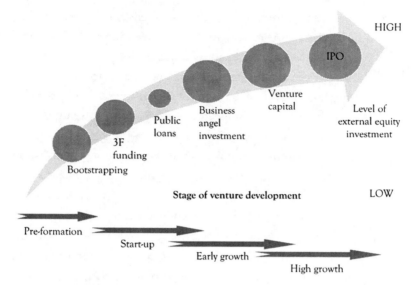

HIGH

IPO

Venture
capital

Business
angel
investment

Public
loans

Level of
external equity
investment

3F
funding

Bootstrapping

Stage of venture development   LOW

Pre-formation

Start-up

Early growth

High growth

Figure 2.3 Entrepreneurial finance: Funding escalator

capital required for growth, potentially leading to raising investment in the public market (i.e., IPO), as shown in Figure 2.3.[48]

Figure 2.3 positions BA investment between 3F funding and VC in financing start-up and early-growth ventures. Most BA investments occur early in the life cycle of a new venture, suggested in Figure 2.3 and fill a financing gap between smaller levels of 3F funding and larger VC funds. Given the wide distribution of BA investors and their tendency to invest locally, BA investors also fill regional gaps in the provision of early-stage finance.[49]

Figure 2.3 suggests that entrepreneurs may turn to BA investors after exhausting 3F funding and turn to VC when BA investment can no longer finance high-growth that may require significant investment only available from VCs. While such funding escalation does occur, this "linear" association between progressive sources of finance and stages of venture development, as suggested in Figure 2.3, can't be generally applied to explain entrepreneurial finance for a number of reasons:

✓ The majority of new ventures created each year "self-finance" using 3F sources without the need to raise PE investment.

- ✓ Early-stage ventures with high growth potential may attract formal VC, bypassing BA investment, for example, due to the successful piloting of an exceptionally novel product.
- ✓ BA-supported ventures may be constrained from progressing to VC funding, not by lack of demand for higher investment but by BA shareholders whose common stock has less claim to venture assets and earnings than VC-preferred stock (discussed more in Chapter 5).
- ✓ Early-stage ventures are not a homogeneous group and display high variability in how they progress through development stages and access finance. For example, some start-ups may experience rapid growth, supported by VC seed investment while others may take significantly longer in the early growth stage—for example, in biotechnology, where an innovation requires clinical trials and further refinement before launching into the market.

Although **debt financing** has not been discussed here, it is a vital source of future funding for new ventures. A track record of business activity and buildup of assets in the business will provide a level of collateral from which to access debt finance. The concept of "relationship lending"— traditionally considered an advantage of the "local bank"—suggests that over time, lenders (often the local bank manager) acquire information, data, perspective, and a personal relationship with the entrepreneur/ founders that reduces asymmetrical information problems.[50] In one sense, 3F funding from family members is a form of relationship lending, with love and unconditional support often the primary factors inspiring the release of funding to the entrepreneur.

Relationship lending is also a relevant concept with business angle investment—typically more so with solo angels than with BA syndicates or networks. A strong relationship between investor and entrepreneur may positively influence initial investment decisions as well as decisions to provide follow-on financing and is discussed further in Chapters 4 through 6.

PE investors are, in one sense, market speculators who anticipate and profit from their proper selection of investments today that will have higher value in future market conditions. Studies of investment returns consistently identify the higher-return performance of portfolio investors over those who invest larger amounts in a smaller selection of companies. The high uncertainty and volatility in "picking winners" applies to both VC and to BA investors.

Entrepreneurs should also recognize that patterns of investment behavior exist in the market that will influence what sectors are preferred by investors at any particular time. The VC industry in particular demonstrates "lead follower" behavior, as demonstrated during the dot-com period, where VC firms follow others into a market that looks promising. Yet, many of the significant VC investment returns have come from market opportunities that weren't identified.

The decision to raise external financing is a significant step for any entrepreneur. A common insight from experienced investors is that the entrepreneur often doesn't appreciate what they are buying into when they take other people's money. For example, the entrepreneur's longer-term prospects in accepting PE investment will be in the context of an investment exit, with most investors expecting the business to be sold in order to recover their investment. "Clarifying Concepts" in the following text considers some implications of accepting PE investment for the entrepreneur.

Clarifying Concepts

Implications of Accepting Private Equity

The entrepreneur seeking private equity (PE) investment must be willing to give up equity in his/her venture and be able to meet the conditions and obligations set out in a formal investment deal agreement (discussed in Chapter 5). Key implications of taking on PE investment include:

- ✓ Reduction of percentage ownership of the business:
  - ○ That is, dilution in existing shareholders' equity.
  - ○ Further dilution if additional rounds of capital injection are required.
- ✓ Potential restrictions on management decision-making, such as management remuneration, issue of shares, taking on or extending debt provision, and so forth.

✓ Requirement to implement more formal accounting, finance, governance, regulatory, compliance, and reporting practices, and associated record keeping.

✓ Creation of formal board of directors. All venture capitalists (VCs), most business angel syndicates (BASs), and some solo BA investors will require at least one seat on the board.

✓ Expectation of achieving pre-established business performance targets (or milestones):
  ○ Failure to achieve targets may result in termination of management contracts and changes to team, loss of voting rights, or venture being sold or liquidated.

✓ Projected exit strategy and associated time frame (e.g., trade sale, buyback, or initial public offering [IPO]).

We now turn to a discussion of what makes an "investable" business opportunity more likely to attract the interests of BA investors in Chapter 3.

CHAPTER 3

What Makes a Compelling Business Angel Investment Opportunity?

Understand your first customer; it may be your Investor.

This chapter considers the question: What makes a compelling business opportunity for a business angel (BA) investor? Given the diversity of BA investors and their investment criteria, there is no standard, validated set of business characteristics that if met, will assure an investment offer. However, investable businesses share some common characteristics that we discuss in this chapter.

We first consider different types of markets that provide opportunities for entrepreneurial venturing, including understood, new, and service-based markets. Opportunities arising from different types of innovation and technologies are also discussed. Across these markets, we assess where investable opportunities can be identified.

The chapter then suggests guidelines for building an investable business case—which discusses the business model, competitive advantages, business planning, and approaches for crafting a business plan (BP). The chapter concludes with a discussion of common pitfalls in business planning.

Markets for Investable Opportunities

Introduction

An investable business case begins with an attractive market opportunity, which can be found across different markets and in different sectors. Figure 3.1 suggests three broad categories of potential markets: understood markets, new markets, and markets for services, with each offering

Figure 3.1 Markets for entrepreneurial venturing

different challenges and opportunities for entrepreneurial venturing and
for ventures seeking to raise external investment.

Understood Markets

Understood markets are those where existing businesses compete within
well-defined industry boundaries and whose products and services are
known and familiar to customers. There is typically a dominant business
model that determines how business is done and profits are made (business
models are discussed further on p. 72). The competitive conditions facing
the new market entrant can be understood by examining how existing businesses compete with each other for customers, market share, and so forth.

New opportunities in understood markets arise from providing new
solutions to old problems and offering better versions of existing products
or better execution in providing products to customers or both—or to other
businesses (e.g., the business-to-business [B2B] market). New solutions
require offering a significant-enough level of differentiation that avoids
price competition with existing firms. While the strategy of benchmarking
competitors is common in understood markets, assessing opportunity with
existing competition may not reveal opportunities for significant differentiation, leading to incremental changes that favor existing firms.

Some understood markets are mature and highly competitive, characterized by ongoing efforts by existing firms to replace competitor products
with "better, cheaper, faster" models. A new venture entering such a market faces competitive disadvantages across a number of dimensions compared to the dominant business model, as suggested in "Case Insights" in
the following text.

Case Insights

Understood Market Opportunities: Small Household Appliances

The small household appliance market (e.g., toasters, kettles, coffee machines) is populated by large, established multinational players in addition to local players. Investors would be seeking a proposition that clarifies how to gain advantage in a market characterized by:

- ✓ Brand recognition (disadvantage or advantage if existing brands are weak?)
- ✓ Established distribution channels to customer (disadvantage?)
- ✓ Strong price-based competition (disadvantage?)
- ✓ Constant volumes and lowering prices (disadvantage?)
- ✓ Growing demand for innovative products in certain niche markets (advantage?)
- ✓ Growing demand from customers for after-sales services, for example, guarantees, 24/7 assistance, web-based engagement, and so forth (advantage?)

The competitive nature of this market would focus the investor's attention on how the entrepreneur will overcome disadvantages and leverage potential advantages noted above. The business case for the entrepreneur might emphasize:

- ✓ Identified market niche reflecting a changing demographic favoring new designs, functionality, cost, use of web-based advertising, and social media.
- ✓ Design and new product development (NPD) capabilities superior to existing players.
- ✓ Hip new brand (that may be "contrary" to existing, mature, well-known brands).
- ✓ In-house capabilities to innovate and rapid time-to-market capabilities.
- ✓ Entrepreneurial team with high-level experience in sector.
- ✓ Potential for growth into other markets with competencies developed in this market.

Referring to the example in the preceding text, a new offering of a well-designed, multifunctional set of appliances, launched as a hip new brand, may appeal to younger consumers with restrictive kitchen space whose distinctive needs and tastes represent a sizable market. A new entrant would need to establish enough competitive advantages, for example, superior market knowledge, operational capabilities in appliances, new innovation design, and so forth, that together can overcome competitor efforts to imitate or emulate.

"Resegmenting" an Understood Market

Within understood markets, there are often smaller "segments" of customers/users who share more narrowly defined needs, desires, or aspirations. Entrepreneurs attempting to resegment an understood market should attempt to create arguments that existing firms can't win. This can be done by demonstrating a superior understanding of the resegmented customers and their needs and offering a new value proposition for the segment that makes it difficult for existing firms to make similar claims. This can be done across different understood markets.

One example that highlights successful market resegmentation is that of Southwest Airlines, cofounded by entrepreneurs Herb Kelleher and Rollin King in 1971 after conceptualizing the idea on a cocktail napkin. Southwest is now the world's largest low-cost air carrier. We consider key features of their resegmentation strategy in Table 3.1 on the next page.

The short-haul, low-cost model established by Southwest Airlines has been emulated by subsequent entrepreneurs in other countries: for example, Westjet (Canada), Easy Jet (UK), and Ryan Air (Ireland). A common feature of these low-cost entrants is their success in offering a low-cost value proposition made possible by operational efficiencies that full-service, long-haul air carriers find difficult to emulate.

New Markets

New markets refer to technologies, products, and services that offer entirely new value propositions for customers. New markets are often associated with the concept of innovation. "Incremental" innovation, common in

Table 3.1 Resegmenting a market: Southwest Airlines

Value proposition	Operational activities
Low fares; one-way fares	Highly trained front-line staff; use of humor and fun on flights via cabin crew; no seat assignment; drinks/snacks only
High-frequency flight options	Operational efficiencies to reduce costs: reduced flight turnaround (less than 20 minutes on ground); one plane to reduce maintenance/operational costs (e.g. Boeing 737); 30% fewer employees per aircraft
Direct flights; point to point (no "hub and spoke") Uncongested airports	Short-haul flights only; careful selection of cities based on fit with offering; no code shares; independent baggage handling; 85% penetration of local markets
Flight safety and arrival–departure operations not to be compromised	Operational excellence, dependency, and consistency of on-time flights stressed; highly trained staff

understood markets, refers to an extension of previous knowledge and the incorporation of new improvements into existing products, processes, or services. "Disruptive" innovation refers to new knowledge that can significantly change the dimensions of performance previously available to customers or end users.

Joseph Schumpeter, the economist who highlighted innovation as the basis for economic growth, suggests five types of innovation that arise from new ideas, as shown in Table 3.2.[1]

Different innovations arising from new ideas can challenge the market positions of existing businesses. Schumpeter calls this "creative destruction," whereby successful new products, services, and processes replace existing ones, causing the erosion, demise, or in some cases, death of existing companies. The constant churn of new ideas, the entry of new innovations, and the birth and death of businesses is an accepted ethos of a capitalist market and the infinite source of entrepreneurial opportunity.

Different market drivers generate the new and different types of innovations as depicted in Table 3.2. Market drivers include new scientific breakthroughs and technological advancements, changing legislation, demographic change, shifting consumer values and tastes, market disruptions or shifts, and so forth. Such drivers may create new market needs that offer new opportunities for entrepreneurs, as described in "Case Insights" in the following text.

Table 3.2 Types of innovation

Type of innovation	Description	Examples
New good or service	One in which users are not yet familiar or new level of quality of a good or service	MP3 player, cellular phone, digital camera, microwave oven
Process innovation	New method of production or new way of handling a commodity commercially	Lean production, computer-aided design, software
New market	Entirely new market; for example a market in which users are not yet familiar with a new product, service or process	Foreign market entry, re-positioning of product for new customer category
New source of raw material	Or half-manufactured good	Silicon, plastics, steel, nanoparticle, stem cell
New organizational form	New business models, organizational structure, and so forth	Lean start-up, self-organization (e.g., Wikipedia), collaborative organization (e.g., Proctor & Gamble)

Case Insights

Regulatory Drivers for a New Service

A new regulation in Alberta, Canada, requires oil and gas companies to reduce gas emissions arising from drilled wells. An engineer-entrepreneur perceives an opportunity to build a business case for a new emissions control venture and seeks external investment. Some suggestions for building an investable business include offering the following: superior understanding of regulatory requirements for customers; best-in-class technology for detecting, monitoring, and reporting emissions (including systems optimization and quantifiable services); and a management team that includes people with strong and credible emission backgrounds (given the importance of strong personal relationships in this sector).

New opportunities may arise from integrating different innovative ideas and concepts to create a value proposition previously unseen or unanticipated by customers. Henry Ford created a new category of "value proposition" for a large market by introducing a series of innovations. These included process innovation with the mass assembly line; product innovation, with the Model T offering low cost but high functionality, for example, easy to operate, to maintain, and handle on rough roads; and a new organizational form, which controlled the entire company value chain, from sourcing raw materials, for example, steel, glass, tires, and other car components, to selling to and servicing the customer. Ford also challenged conventional wisdom that company fortunes rely on listening to the customer. As Henry Ford stated, "If I had asked people what they wanted, they would have said faster horses."

Novel technologies and business concepts are often associated with emerging and untried markets. The "Blue Ocean Strategy" refers to markets and industries not in existence, where an opportunity exists to create demand conditions that can lead to high levels of growth for the firm.[2] The entrepreneur or existing firm may bring to the market a very different value proposition than previously available to users. In doing so, such a strategy may bypass competing directly with others in an understood market.

The Nintendo Wii is one example, where a novel technology (a motion control stick that integrates movements of a player directly into a video game, for example, tennis, golf, water skiing, sword fights, etc.) opened up an untapped market of nongamer consumers. The Wii's ease of use and broad array of entertaining game options appealed across demographics to include family members of all ages. The Wii was also less expensive; having no DVD or hard disk but possessing the innovative motion control stick that interfaces across different games. This contrasted with much more expensive, more sophisticated consoles available in the existing games market.

In defining and exploring an uncontested market space, the entrepreneur must establish that a latent customer need is not being well served, as suggested in the Wii example. The Wii offered a completely different value proposition from the two leaders in the "understood" gaming console market, Microsoft's Xbox and Sony's PS3. The Wii also defied conventional management theory, which suggests that a firm should compete on either differentiation or cost leadership but not both.[3]

The case of FanDuel, described in "Case Insights" in the following text, identifies how repositioning a value proposition, rather than a radical new one, offers opportunity for a new market entrant.

Case Insights

Uncontested Markets for New Ventures

FanDuel is a daily fantasy sports games venture targeting the U.S. market. It was co-founded by five entrepreneurs in 2009 and has raised approximately $18 million from business angel and venture capital investors in the United Kingdom and United States. The venture has annual revenues of $12 million and has 52 staff across their New York and Edinburgh offices.

FanDuel does not have a radically different value proposition, as suggested by the Blue Ocean concept. However, it has identified an uncontested market space by compressing traditional seasons-long fantasy sports leagues (i.e., pick your players and compete with other teams) into daily games, allowing users to complete games quickly and receive more immediate prize money (FanDuel paid out $50 million in daily prizes in 2012). FanDuel's annual growth rate of 250% and over 60% market share suggests that start-ups that identify an unmet need can quickly dominate an uncontested market.

Emerging markets, in areas such as renewable and clean energy, "big data," bio-informatics, and others, may offer high-return opportunities compared to understood markets but carry high risks. In Chapter 2, we suggested that venture capital (VC) investment (and larger business angel syndicates [BASs] and networks) is common in businesses that offer a radical alternative to existing products or services and require significant investment capital.

However, the lack of customer experience, familiarity, and judgment of a novel value proposition increases its market acceptance risk. Creating consumer awareness to stimulate demand in a new market will require superior market knowledge, in addition to an economically viable business model.

New markets also require the entrepreneur's attention to market timing issues. Entering a market too early, for example, may require financial reserves to cover expenses until market demand becomes sufficient to cover costs. Entering a market too late may forego any potential first-mover advantages to establish market share, reputation, and brand name although first-mover advantages should not simply be assumed (see "Research Notes" in the following text). New and growing markets will attract new competitors, particularly if barriers to enter the market are low. Investors will seek assurances that a new venture can sustain its differentiation and competitive advantages.

Research Notes

First-Mover Advantages in New Markets

The benefits of first-mover advantages are often highlighted in business plans and presented to investors. Suggested benefits include a monopoly in the absence of competitors; higher profit margins; ability to shape customer preferences to favor the first mover; strong brand positioning; difficulties for market followers in imitating innovative products (e.g., Apple iPad); advantages to extend product lines, and so forth.

However, evidence suggests that in markets started by a novel product, the first to market (i.e., the pioneer) is often the first to fail. Breakthrough innovations may be "costly, crude, and unreliable" when they first appear in the market, providing an opportunity for early followers to leapfrog pioneers*—particularly in new markets that undergo significant product improvements in their early stages. High levels of technological and market uncertainties may result in slow acceptance by potential users, and early followers may use pioneers' experiences to learn about consumer tastes, potential size of the market, and new designs and manufacturing techniques.

While first movers have low survival rates in new product markets, findings suggest that those who survive can reap the widely acknowledged benefits. Early followers appear to have advantages in markets where product improvements from the first mover are more likely or where market adoption is initially low.

Sources: Min et al., 2006; Agarwal and Bayus, 2002; Christensen et al., 1998; *Olleros, 1986:11; Carpenter et al., 1989.

New markets are often associated with novel technologies, but commercial and investment risks associated with new technologies are well documented. One study found that of 1,091 inventions, only 75 reached the market (less than 7%), with only 6 of these inventions earning high returns (i.e., above 1,400%) and 45 losing money.[4]

Investors are confronted with more than the usual asymmetrical information problems in assessing novel technologies. Investors typically "benchmark" a new technology with similar or related technologies to verify technical and business risk, but this may not be possible for a novel technology or for a market that doesn't exist. Further, the evaluation and due diligence may require specialist domain knowledge or experience that is scarce. Most investors who cannot validate these risks will not invest.

New ventures in emerging or rapidly moving industries may engage in collaborative practices to reduce risks as well as to enhance competencies, such as entering partnerships, alliances, joint ventures, and intellectual property (IP) agreements and exchanges (referred to as "open innovation") with other businesses.[5] Collaboration success is likely to involve finding another company with a similar vested interest in the same customer.

However, dependence on third parties for technology development, licensing of required IP, and so forth, may be viewed skeptically by investors, given the difficulties in monitoring third-party performance or ensuring distributed economic value. If the entrepreneur has a licensing agreement to use a technology, what happens if the distribution rights are retracted by the owner of the license (i.e., licensor)? Investors may also want to see that their investment is developing internal knowledge competencies that increase the market value of the venture and consequently the value of their investment.

Some BASs and VCs may look more favorably at distributed competencies and a more open innovation business model that characterizes complex, knowledge-intensive markets, such as biopharmaceuticals. Larger BASs (and VCs) who specialize in such markets usually have extensive investor and advisor networks from which to support and finance these types of ventures.

Services

Service-based markets differ from product markets by characteristics that include:

- ✓ intangibility: Customers can feel and see results of services but may differ in their perceptions of service quality, performance, and so forth;
- ✓ simultaneity: There is a lag difference between the production and consumption of services versus goods, with many services consumed soon after their production;
- ✓ services are difficult to store, resulting in simultaneity of services already noted;
- ✓ proximity to customers: Many services need to be close to customers, making them potentially less competitive and less global than goods.

Traditional service-based opportunities pose two interrelated risks for investors: low barriers to entry (resulting in high levels of imitation) and difficulties in scaling the business. For example, many service-based "lifestyle" ventures are created with the entrepreneurs providing their own services (e.g., consultancy, skilled trade, personalized service, etc.) to a small group of customers. Start-up costs are typically low and are often covered through 3F (founder, family, and friends) funding.

Scaling up a traditional service business may require high levels of training, mentoring, and recruitment, in addition to establishing cost-effective, repeatable routines to service more customers if the business is to grow. This assumes that market demand in the segment serviced is sufficient to support business growth.

Experienced investors suggest that traditional service markets are unlikely to offer large returns for investors (e.g., 10X return on original investment), but can provide healthy 3X returns.[6] Services are all about people, although so are technology companies. However, with a technology venture, the investor can leverage on the technology in excess of bodies deployed. With traditional services, scalability is often defined by the number of people deployed.

However, service markets have undergone significant change in the last few decades. Services now dominate the gross domestic product (GDP) of most western economies, accounting for approximately 75% of the global economy and remain the fastest-growing sector.

One reason for the domination of services in the global economy is the Internet and rise of web-based services. For example, online sales have now surpassed traditional high-street sales in a number of countries (e.g., UK), also suggesting a significant change in consumer purchasing habits and attitudes toward online commerce.

Web-based service markets have very different characteristics when compared with traditional service-based markets:

- ✓ Due to the ubiquitous nature of the Internet, barriers to entry for web-based businesses are very low and the potential reach is very large.
- ✓ Market segmentation allows for more focused target marketing and advertising and low-cost transaction pricing.
- ✓ Start-ups can complete more equally with established firms on the same "high street."
- ✓ Core competencies include appropriate technologies, speed, agility, creativity, and partnerships, making traditional productivity–cost–revenue economics less applicable and relevant.

Online software development has been one particular high-growth market. Low capital costs of development, access to open-source software, the ability to test the market without needing to develop a fully fledged product, and access to a global customer base—comprising multiple market segments—make this a fertile space for entrepreneurs. Despite low overheads and the high potential for scalability, investors would want to understand the revenue-generating capability and sustainability of the business model.

Another reason for the domination of services is that many companies have redefined existing products in ways that shift the financial model away from selling a good to selling a service. This has occurred through reassessing customer needs and problems and formulating new product service solutions, as suggested by the example in the following text.

Service by the hour: The iconic engine manufacturer Rolls Royce now charges service fees based on "uptime," which is the actual time that the engines are operating on flying aircraft. This allows airline customers to pay as their own revenues are generated from their passenger ticket and freight/cargo sales rather than purchasing the engines up-front. Rolls Royce is essentially selling "time" rather than engines and has reframed their business to offer a "power-by-the-hour" service.

New service opportunities are identified in the provision of different complementary services to products, such as education, all-in-one services, and interactive experiences that reinforce the core business. Increasingly, traditional physical products, traditional services, and manual processes are being transformed into digitalized products and processes. The significant growth in mobile devices is driving much of this innovation.

Software-as-a-service (SaaS) marketplaces have emerged and continue to provide new venturing opportunities, following the successes of Amazon and eBay. Ventures such as Salesforce.com and others have leveraged existing service creation capabilities and available web services to expand offerings of hosted business applications.

The names of web-based ventures attracting VC investment are well known, which include Facebook, Twitter, Skype, Flickr, Google, Youtube, and so forth. The ability to globally scale web-based ventures and gain rapid acceptance with limited advertising or promotion has made this market attractive to VCs. The "value is in the traffic" has summed up a previously accepted notion that capturing sales from even a small percentage of high-volume traffic to a website will reap high revenues (e.g., monetized conversion).

However, investors have learned the hard way that valuing new web-based ventures based on the number of users, site traffic, high-featured web pages, or comprehensive web content does not equate to sustainable revenues or superior profits.

High failure rates, low entry barriers, high uncertainty over sustainable revenue, and a certain level of unfamiliarity by many existing BA investors regarding web-based business models will offer challenges to the entrepreneur in securing BA investment. At the same time, a new generation of successfully exiting Internet entrepreneurs are reinvesting in this market—as BA investors and VCs.

Building an *Investable* Business Case

Building an investable business case requires more than positioning the entrepreneurial opportunity into an attractive market. It requires an appropriate business model.

The business model canvas, developed by Alexander Osterwalder and Yves Pigneur, provides a simple but effective approach to developing a business model. Table 3.3 describes nine building blocks of the business model canvas and related questions that generate "hypotheses" to be tested to validate the business model.

Table 3.3 Business model canvas[7]

Building block	Hypothesis-generating questions
Customer segment (CS)	Who is the business customer? What are their wants and needs? What are they willing to pay for?
Value proposition (VP)	What compelling things does the new venture provide to customer? What needs are satisfied? For example, convenience, risk or cost reduction, performance, newness, design, brand/status, and so forth.
Channels to market (CM)	How is the value proposition sold and delivered? Will venture directly control the channel (sales force, web sales) or use partner channels (e.g., wholesale distribution, use of partner-owned websites, etc.)?
Customer relations (CR)	How will the business interact with customers? What relationship does the customer expect? How important are CRs to the VP? How will CRs be integrated into the VP and how much will it cost?
Revenue streams	What are customers willing to pay for receiving the VP? What do they currently pay (identifying competitive offerings)? How will the business receive revenue?
Key resources	What assets must be in place to make the business model work? For example, intellectual (IP, partnerships), human (know-how, specialized skills), physical (location, logistics, CM), financial (cash, lines of credit, etc.).
Key activities	What key things does the business do to deliver on the VP? For example, new knowledge (product, service) design, creation delivery, repeatable set of processes that generates a scalable VP for each CS.
Key partnerships	What activities and expertise are outsourced? How to reduce time to market, reduce costs, and enhance reputation using partners? How to optimize partnerships to extend capabilities and access customers?
Cost structure	What are the key cost components and cost drivers of the business? For example, fixed versus variable costs, economies of scale (cost advantages as output expands) and economics of scope (e.g., use of same marketing or distribution channels to support multiple products).

While existing firms execute a business model, new ventures are looking for one. A business model explains the logic and describes the rationale of how a venture creates, delivers, and captures value. Many entrepreneurs who seek external investment fail to present a clear business model; instead, they spend considerable time explaining their product or service without validating the level of demand or interest by prospective customers essential for business value creation. This may lead the investor to ask: Is the entrepreneur simply an opportunity identifier?

The business model canvas, shown in Table 3.3, provides a balanced approach to building the business case, which begins with establishing the distinctive value proposition that will serve an identified customer segment. "Clarifying Concepts" in the following text suggests some questions for crafting a compelling value proposition.

Clarifying Concepts

Crafting a Compelling *Value Proposition*

The value proposition is what compels the customer to buy and should satisfy specific needs, wants, or desires for a defined customer segment. The questions below provide further guidance for the entrepreneur in crafting a value proposition:

- ✓ Can you demonstrate superior understanding of the targeted customer and market?
- ✓ What problem is the business solving?
- ✓ Is the product or service needed desperately by a particular set of customers?
  - ○ What is driving buyer motivation?
    - What evidence suggests the customer wants a better solution?
    - What degree of compliance (cost or penalty) results from <u>not</u> buying?
  - ○ How do you quantify or qualify the level of improvement the customer will realize from the use of your product/service

(e.g., at least a 25% improvement on one or more dimensions of the offering)?

  o Where do you have the strongest value proposition for the customer?

✓ Has strong market acceptance been demonstrated? If not, how will it be?

  o How will you articulate this value proposition to your customer?

  o Have you identified your "real customer," that is, the one making the purchasing decision? If the entrepreneur is selling into a big company, who has to say yes?

✓ Is this a fast-growing market segment?

  o Is there high competition in your targeted market?

  o If there is intense competition, what are the claims of the product/service to suggest it will drive sales and/or take away sales from competitors?

✓ How will you protect your VP from imitation by competitors?

If market interest is favorable and early sales occur, then the focus is on sales and marketing to scale the business. If there is no customer interest, then the start-up can "pivot" by changing one or more of the hypotheses generated through the business model canvas. This may include revisiting the customer problem and engaging in creative problem-solving, as suggested in "Case Insights" in the following text.

Case Insights

Creative Lessons From IDEO

As one of the world's leading creative consultancies, IDEO uses different scenarios to test products, initially suspending creativity barriers to brainstorm different new ideas that could potentially be applied to solve a customer problem. IDEO emphasizes the need to apply curiosity and empathy when working with people or businesses whose problems you are trying to solve. Generating deep knowledge of customers and the market allows IDEO to recognize patterns and synthesize information from which the most promising solutions begin to emerge. Breakthrough products are the result of rigorous analysis meeting creative imagination.

The concept of the "lean start-up" suggests validating customer interest through product testing and usage and creating a "minimal viable product" that can generate customer feedback and interest. This approach suggests undertaking market experimentation and customer development before embarking on elaborate business planning or creating a formal BP.[8]

Market segmentation means selecting a particular group of customers to target within a larger market. Deselecting a market is as important as selecting a market. Grouping people according to demographic similarities, such as income, age, gender, geographical location, ethnicity, and so forth, is commonly used to "segment" a market. However, this simplistic approach may fail to identify common needs, wants, or desires across such groupings that may more closely match the venture's value proposition.

Investors will expect that the customer segment chosen is not only a good match for the value proposition, but has strong revenue-generating capabilities, allowing the venture to secure early cash flow. Investors will also be keen to understand how value-creating activities of the business model will be sustained over time to build equity value in the business. This identifies the importance of sustainable competitive advantage.

Competitive Advantage

An investable business should demonstrate a sustainable competitive advantage. Competitive advantage refers to the particular attributes, assets, and capabilities of the venture that will outperform competitors and be difficult for others to imitate or copy.

A resource-based view (RBV) suggests that competitive advantage is based on a particular set of valuable resources and capabilities that the venture controls and that are assembled in a particularly unique way.

Ideally, these resources should be inimitable, non-substitutable, and rare—making them difficult to copy. These may include

- ✓ specialized knowledge that is in limited supply;
- ✓ highly innovative knowledge that cannot be reverse engineered;
- ✓ technological advantage gained through long product lead times:
  - ○ for example, solution to a tough problem that is difficult to imitate;
- ✓ a restricted or contracted source of supply;
- ✓ ownership of or contracted distribution channel;
- ✓ intellectual property (IP).

Some businesses are difficult to copy arising from the strategic deployment of resources and capabilities through the business model, such as operating system lock-in (e.g., Microsoft); high switching costs for costumers or users (e.g., binding customer contracts, as used by many mobile service providers); a network effect that requires generating a high level of users (e.g., eBay); or the use of integrated capabilities, such as combining distinctive marketing and sales and customer service with a customized product (e.g., Dell computers in its early days).

Partnerships can strengthen an early-stage business model and allow the business to scale operations. Partnerships may allow the new venture to leverage its limited set of assets as it builds market credibility, grows its sales, and generates revenues to expand its capabilities.

The entrepreneur should clearly articulate these competitive advantages to investors that highlight strengths of the business model, particular resources, and operational capabilities. For example, if entering an understood market, what is it about the business model that will make it difficult for big players in the market to imitate or to adjust their own business models to compete with the new business?

A large competitor will naturally undercut price if they can produce a similar product or service. Is the product or service "best in class"? If not, on what grounds will the business compete? Does the business have a competitive edge that is long lasting?

The entrepreneur should also be aware that sustaining barriers to entry can also be overstated. For example, during times of rapid technological innovation, new innovations have been known to "leapfrog" existing technologies. Competitors with access to substantial investment can also catch up quicker than originally predicted or forecasted in the business plan (BP). As mentioned earlier, reliance on a third-party IP license might also not guarantee a barrier to entry if distribution rights can be retracted or if nonexclusive licenses are made available to competitors.

Competitive advantages will gradually get competed away as others imitate or capabilities of the business mature. Entrepreneurs who present a vision for sustainable innovation and have capabilities to develop follow-on products and services will strengthen their case with investors.

Intellectual Property

IP is identified as an important source of competitive advantage and refers to creative work, which can be treated as an asset or physical property. These knowledge assets can be sold (or licensed) independent of those people who generated the knowledge. Some IP is protected by rights (IPRs) that give the IPR holder exclusive rights over the use of the creation for a certain period of time. IPRs fall into four main areas; copyright, trademarks, design rights, and patents.

The proprietary protection available from IPRs is not automatically granted (other than copyright, which is an automatic international right) but requires the entrepreneur to file a claim. In the case of patents, three key criteria must be fulfilled and are noted in the following text:

1. Novelty: not previously disclosed publicly
2. Usefulness: capable of industrial application (U.S. criteria—includes some software)
3. Inventive step: at least one; an advance that would not be immediately obvious to someone "skilled in the art" of the field of invention

The key competitive advantage of IPRs is the legal protection to exclude others from imitating the knowledge captured by the IPR. Figure 3.2 shows four examples of IP applications that can provide competitive advantage to a new venture. The first example would be a patent that protects a single technology. If it is a novel technology and the patent claim covers a distinctive inventive step valued by the market and difficult for competitors to imitate, then competitive advantage is gained.

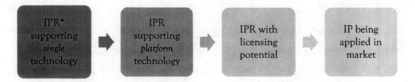

Figure 3.2 Market applications for intellectual property rights
*Patent, Registered trademark.
IP = intellectual property; IPR = intellectual property rights.

It should be mentioned that single patents are seldom valued in isolation. Rather, they are valued with "enabling know-how" (e.g., unpatented technology and IP) that often reside in people associated with the business. The importance of this "tacit knowledge" for IP generation is often undervalued, but a business based on sustaining technological leadership, for example, may be dependent on the tacit knowledge of its founder or development team. Investors will be keen to ensure that the founder or development team remains with the venture and may use different incentives such as stock options.

IPRs that support a platform technology may provide a more significant source of competitive advantage than a single patent. A platform technology is often a key concept or idea, which may not itself be patented but may be surrounded by patents or a combination of IP, such as trade secrets, a registered trademark, and patents. Some platform technologies may have multiple applications that can be deployed in different markets, such as engineering solutions or manufacturing technologies.

A third application is licensing a patent to other parties. Licensing can provide an additional source of revenue for a business in the form of royalties—which are meant to provide fair value to the patent owner (licensor) over the life of a license agreement. Licensing may also provide strategic advantages, whereby the venture "cross licenses" with another firm, with both parties gaining competitive advantage from accessing each other's IP.

The fourth application refers to IP deployed in the market, where its contribution to business success is more transparent. For example, if the market fails to accept the innovation at the level expected, or if a competitor delivers a superior product, then the IP deployed may not be a source of competitive advantage. IP "in use" is a strong indicator of its practical rather than potential value. Some IP will not be deployed without IPR protection, given high risk of imitation, with future value predicted using comparative market transactions, market and customer forecasts, and expert opinions.

The possession of IP and IPRs strengthens the case for investment in sectors such as medical devices or bioscience, where patents will be expected to protect the innovation from high imitation risk and as a basis for future IP development. Patents provide a signal of tangible and tradable value to potential follow-on investors and to the market of potential acquirers of the business (discussed more in Chapter 6).

However, issues over definitive IP ownership rights or reliance on licensing IP from third parties may inhibit the venture's ability to exploit the IP. Investors will seek assurances that the IP is "clean," referring to clear ownership of the IP by the business. IP protection may also be overrated in some circumstances, as described in "Research Notes" in the following text.

Research Notes

Intellectual Property Rights (IPRs) and Competitive Advantage

Although IPRs may safeguard an invention from competitors, they do not guarantee business success and can be an expensive asset. For example, while a patent gives the patent holder the right to exclude others from using the protected invention for an extended time (15 or 20 years), the ability to generate profits is reliant on developing a marketable product that can generate sales. In sectors such as software, competitive advantage is gained more by IP "in use," with short product life cycles and lower development costs reducing the need for lengthy (and costly) protection.

Studies on venture capital (VC) suggest that although "proprietary" technology is important, IP protection doesn't make much of a difference as a unique differentiator for significant VC investment returns. What is more important is the stage of product development and the barrier that is created by the product. Ideally, the product for a VC investor is in beta testing or shipping, if not already being sold in the market. Moreover, the technology and related complementary knowledge should be hard to execute and imitate.

Sources: Powers and McDougall, 2005; Roberts and Bailery, 2004.

Business Planning

Business planning for the new venture involves a continuous questioning and refinement of the business model and related competitive advantages; although a regimented, analytical approach to business planning doesn't suit most start-up ventures. It is suggested that under the "fluid" conditions experienced by the entrepreneur, an ability to "roll with the punches" (i.e. accept and adapt to market conditions) is more important than careful planning.[9]

At the same time, validating the various hypotheses of the business model is necessary to establish a business case that will attract investor interest. For example, in an understood market, what level of differentiation, competitive advantage, and pricing strategy is required to move customers away from existing offerings? When introducing a novel product in an emerging market, what level of market and customer verification is required to validate the business model and refine the product? Are there "first-mover" advantages and how long are they likely to be sustained?

Different characteristics of new ventures make them high-risk investments—which the entrepreneur will need to address in the BP:

✓ Market demand for product or service is uncertain if no sales have been generated.

✓ Limited market signals exist to verify a new venture's market potential, making forecasts of future revenues and profits uncertain and speculative.

✓ New products under development remain subject to technical *and* market risks.

✓ Smallness and limited market presence make new ventures highly susceptible to changes in market conditions, for example, small delays in product release or in achieving revenue milestones may cause failure.

✓ Early-stage technology-based ventures may have a high cash burn rate but need time to reach a critical size and achieve financial self-sustainability.

✓ Venture may have limited access to further BA finance if delays are encountered or business operations become costly and inefficient.

Business Plans

Much debate exists over the merits of the BP and whether or not the entrepreneur should dedicate considerable time and effort in formulating one.[10] The BP is a formal document that articulates the key areas of the business opportunity. Many entrepreneurs engage in some form of business planning but subsequently launch their ventures without creating a formal BP.

Here are some common criticisms of the BP with reflections in response to these criticisms:

✓ *Plan is obsolete before it goes to the printer.*[11] The BP is a work in progress that is constantly refined as new information becomes available (e.g., hypotheses of the business model are tested and verified).

✓ *Formulating a BP can be time-consuming and expensive.* Time-consuming yes, but there could be a high cost if the entrepreneur fails to raise investment because the BP has not been well developed or thought through. Deploying a third party to assist in developing a more profession BP could be expensive but appropriate when raising larger investments from more sophisticated BA investors.

✓ *Investors are skeptical of the financials in a BP, so detail is not necessary.* In fact, investors will very much assess the financials and particularly the assumptions, logic, and economics behind the pricing model, revenues, costs, and numbers. Poorly presented or incomplete financials can trigger investor doubt and uncertainty that the entrepreneur understands basic finance or can manage financial transactions.

✓ *The BP rarely survives first contact with customers.* Yes, similar to the business model—as a new venture engages with customers, refinement is necessary.

However, the BP remains an essential requirement for the entrepreneur seeking to raise private equity investment. The BP provides the investor with a standardized document from which to assess the risk–return profile of the venture and to compare with other BPs that might be under consideration at the same time. The entrepreneur/team needs to present a concise, well-crafted, and informative BP that compels the investor to support their BP over others. The BP should encapsulate key features of the business model canvas identified in Table 3.2.

A new venture BP is a plan about an uncertain future—where limited historical sales and market-related transactions are available to forecast the future. While this may relieve the new venture of overly biased views of the future based on past performance, the trade-off is that forecasts, predictions, or assumptions in new venture BPs may be viewed with much skepticism by investors. Perceived risk intensifies with novel value propositions, where no comparative products, competitors, or markets exist.

The BP should address some key areas of uncertainty that characterize a new business opportunity. Figure 3.3 suggests four common areas of investor uncertainty.

Different investor groups may request that the entrepreneur follow a particular BP template or may provide guidelines to the entrepreneur for formulating the BP. A traditional, comprehensive BP template is presented in Appendix B, which identifies 13 distinctive sections for developing a BP.

Market uncertainty	Value proposition uncertainty	Sales and channel to market uncertainty	Management team uncertainty
• Generate market study and competitor analysis • Verification of customer need and demand • Identifiable customer segment for first sales	• Value to market verification (who will pay?) • Product verification (beta testing, etc.) • How will customers, suppliers, partners influence value capture?	• Architecture of revenues and costs • How much to charge; how will customers pay? • How to reach and sell to customer and manage customer relations	• Can team convert the business concept to sales and profits? • Does team possess required sills, capabilities and experiences? • Can team manage operations effectively?

Figure 3.3 Addressing uncertainty in the business plan

Below are some suggested guidelines in formulating a BP that aligns more with the business model canvas discussed earlier and addresses the common areas of investor uncertainty suggested in Figure 3.3.

Executive Summary

The executive summary is the most important section of a BP and should fulfill two functions: (1) stimulate interest and compel the investor to read the business plan and (2) present a clear and recognizable investment opportunity. A strong executive summary would answer the following questions:

- ✓ What does the business do or plan to do?
- ✓ What is the product/service (in nontechnical terms), why is there a need for it, and how big is that need?
- ✓ Who are the customers for the product/service?
- ✓ What are the advantages of the business (e.g., advantages over larger, more reputable, or better-financed competitors)?
- ✓ What is the business model? How will the business make money, when will it become cash flow-positive, and what are the growth aspirations?
- ✓ Who will make this happen?
- ✓ What investment is being requested and what will it be used for?

Market

This section offers a concise assessment of the industry, sector, and competitive environment facing the new venture. Insights on market entry into understood, resegmented, new, and service-based markets discussed earlier could also be drawn out. Key information to discuss may include

- ✓ concentration (or fragmentation) of competitors;
- ✓ dominant and emerging business models;
- ✓ critical success factors and core competencies of market leaders;
- ✓ pricing dynamics, revenue streams, and typical cost drivers;
- ✓ dependencies on particular resources, suppliers, customers, or channels;

✓ strategies deployed (partnerships, alliances, networks, etc.);

✓ relevant regulations;

✓ existing and emerging relevant technologies.

This section should present a well-defined, identifiable customer segment that the business intends to target—or is currently targeting. If the entrepreneur has worked through the business model canvas (Table 3.1), then engagement with prospective customers has verified market demand and customer acceptance (assuming a "presales" venture). Without any hypothesis testing or customer validation, the pricing model, along with sales and profit forecasts, remains predictive and may be viewed with justified caution by investors.

Investors will be attracted to a venture that seeks to lead, set the standards, and establish a strong base in a defined market segment. This market should also allow the business to significantly differentiate the product or service from competitors—and this differentiation should be difficult to imitate or neutralize. Demonstrating high penetration of customers and sales, and dominating a market segment, will more likely attract follow-on funding to scale the business as this would verify the business model.

In some cases, the BP may benefit from input from third-party expertise to assess market trends and segments; which may include benchmarking competitors and surveying prospective customers. Independent market research firms with deep industry experience may provide valuable insights in how to position a new value proposition.

Within this section of the BP, investor uncertainty over market acceptance of the product/service can be reduced if the entrepreneur can validate the prospective customers' willingness to purchase. A product/service already being sold in the market is the most compelling evidence of customer acceptance.

UK-based entrepreneur Martin Avison (see Chapter 4, pp. 107–108), who has successfully raised BA finance from multiple investors, suggests that "*evidencing* sales" will substantially reduce the risk to investors. Existing sales suggests that there is a product/service that works; that somebody wishes to buy at a price they are prepared to pay; and that there is an entrepreneur/team with skills to deliver. Martin suggests that evidencing sales should be in the first line of the executive summary to get "noticed above the noise." In the absence of actual sales, we suggest other evidence for the investor that includes

- ✓ letters of intent to purchase or verifiable acknowledgements of intention to purchase. Can the entrepreneur secure from a prospective customer a letter or statement that they are willing to purchase the product/service if offered at a particular price (which provides an attractive margin for the venture)?
- ✓ advanced orders for the product or service. Even if they are nonbinding, they provide compelling evidence of customer acceptance;
- ✓ if selling to a larger company, securing contractual guarantees for sales and an account payable agreement that ensures timely cash flow to the new business.

Value Proposition: Product/Service

This section should clearly describe the value proposition of related products and services. Guidelines on crafting a compelling value proposition were earlier presented (pp. 73–74). The entrepreneur should avoid presenting highly detailed product specifications or scientific jargon, If the investor is interested, he/she will perform further (formal) due diligence and require more detailed technological specifications.

If the business is reliant on sensitive proprietary technology or knowhow, the suggestion is not to fully disclose this information in the BP. The entrepreneur can release further information following an expression of interest by the investor and after the investor has signed a nondisclosure agreement (NDA; discussed further in Chapter 4, p. 113).

IP ownership, secured commitments of key knowledge creators, and arrangements with third parties should also be clarified. As mentioned in Chapter 2, early-stage ventures emerging from a university or research institution can pose additional risks that should be acknowledged and dealt with in the BP; rather than left with investors to ponder and likely raise their concerns (see "Research Notes," p. 14).

Investors may ask if benefits from the product or service can be quantified (even if it is not fully developed). If such benefits cannot be quantified, how will the venture claim or qualify any level of improvement that the customer will realize? How will this affect pricing of the product/ service? An investor may rightly ask: Is the proof-of-concept (POC) project pushing for technical perfection—and unintentionally avoiding business validation?

How can the entrepreneur reduce investor uncertainty if the venture is still undergoing POC? Perhaps most important is validating the business concept and value proposition that will be derived from POC (see "Clarifying Concepts" in the following text).

Clarifying Concepts

Proof of Concept to Business Validation

Even if a technology is highly novel, investors are unlikely to fund what they perceive to be an "extended" proof-of-concept business. Proof of concept (POC), also known as proof of principle, refers to the process of demonstrating a model of a potential commercial product, process, or service that is derived from completion of a well-defined technological challenge. The critical juncture between invention and a validated business case is bounded at the earliest stage with first, an awareness, then a verification of a commercial concept. Based on the resultant invention, product specifications appropriate to an identified market are demonstrated and production processes are reduced to practice and defined, allowing estimates of product cost, required production quality and quantity, and so forth.

The juncture at which a business case may be validated might begin to attract levels of capital sufficient to permit initial production and marketing. However, who is identifying an appropriate market or making the decision to protect intellectual property (often at great expense if patenting is involved)? Some business angel investors (and venture capitalists) have successful experience in exploiting scientific and technological advances, but usually when these advances are embodied in new products and services—whose specifications and costs align with well-defined market opportunities.

Business validation requires sufficient function, low-enough cost, high-enough quality, and sufficient market appeal that will allow the product to survive competition in the marketplace. Only the most advanced POC projects, often involving commercial partners, would generate this information. The "lean start-up" concept suggests generating a "minimal viable product" that can generate customer feedback and interest. The entrepreneur that presents a developed prototype— that has completed beta testing and demonstrated high acceptance and satisfaction with users representing an attractive target market—has made great strides in reducing business validation risk. A successful market-tested prototype will also give the entrepreneur (and investors) further confidence in selling the future product.

Sources: Branscomb and Auerswald, 2002; Ries, 2011.

Sales and Channel to Market

This section of the BP should clarify how the value proposition will be translated to sales and what channels to market will be required to deliver the VP to the customer segment. Investors want to be assured that products/services that form the basis of the VP can be sold at a price that produces a satisfactory profit for the venture and return on their investment.

The entrepreneur should describe the "architecture of revenues" and pricing strategy that will be derived from delivering the value proposition. Suggested questions include

- ✓ will revenues be generated via outright sale, renting, charging by transaction, advertising and subscription models, licensing, giving away product, and selling after-sale support and services?
- ✓ how big is the profit margin on each revenue stream?
  - ○ For example, if the product is better, why is it not more expensive rather than cheaper? Is there high net value for the services? If so, is the profit margin reflecting this high net value?
- ✓ how will revenues be apportioned among others contributing to the value proposition (e.g., channel partners, licensors of IP to the business, outsourced manufacturing, etc.)?
  - ○ Will the business be squeezed between suppliers and the customer?

✓ what is the turnover rate on sales?
  ○ Do sales follow a particular cycle? If so, how long are the business cycles? When is the purchasing decision cycle? When do customers pay?
✓ how many customers need to be converted to sales?
✓ how much are customers expected to spend?

The BP should make clear the logic and justification for pricing decisions. For example, will the value proposition offer a level of customer benefit that allows for premium pricing? Does the pricing model match the realities of the market segment? One example of a pricing model is discussed in "Clarifying Concepts" in the following text.

Clarifying Concepts
Pay-Per-Click Pricing Model

The "pay-per-click" pricing model (or "pay-per-shot") refers to revenues generated on each small transaction of the venture's proprietary product or service. One example from the United Kingdom is a medical imaging company, which provides the imaging machine for a low cost (or for free) to medical practitioners who then charge a fee per image from each patient. The company generates a gross margin (GM) on each shot (e.g., practitioner is charged $20, who charges patient $40 = $20 GM).

This pricing model is preferred to selling an expensive machine in a limited market (e.g., finite number of hospitals able to afford the machine)—and where follow-on sales (i.e., new versions of the machine) are likely to be infrequent, given the robust nature of the machine and effectiveness of the solution it provides.

Underpricing products or services in an early-stage business can lead to profit decay. Indeed, profit decay can occur in any business when the business cycle deteriorates—and all businesses in any particular sector suffer. However, if a business cycle is strong and profits deteriorate, then the business may have lost its competitive advantage in that market.

All markets have different abilities to pay. Will payment from the customer come from an existing budget; a new budget; or disposable income? If the sale is going to hit a company's bottom line, the "pain" must be real. In other words, a new sale will hurt their revenues, so the consequences of not deploying a new solution should exceed the costs of the new sale. For example, what is the cost or penalty for the customer in not purchasing the product or service, as suggested in "Case Insights" in the following text?

Case Insights

Verifying Customer Cost Savings

A new sensor technology with higher sensitivity to potentially hazardous gas emissions will enhance employee safety when working around drilling sites. The entrepreneur owning the sensor could present the business case to drilling firms that identifies the potential consequences of not using a new solution if employee safety is compromised. This might include calculating bottom-line consequences of nonadherence or associated penalties, in the case of new regulatory requirements, or potential liability claims that could arise from failure to adopt an available new emissions technology should an accident occur.

The entrepreneur also needs to validate *who* will pay; in other words, who controls the purchase decision or writes the purchase order? For example, large companies typically follow a formal procurement process, which includes request for tenders, guidelines of potential suppliers, and related cost and timeline restrictions. Procurement from an unknown start-up with limited market recognition may be perceived as too risky, particular if the product or technology is essential to the company (e.g., information technology (IT) or new accounts system).

So, although the entrepreneur may receive favorable feedback from someone in the company, who may be the end user of the product, there might be a low probability for a sale if this user does not influence the final purchasing decision.

Investors will want to understand how the venture will grow the customer segment. Delivering a single product or service to an initial set of customers is likely to be achievable for most new ventures, but does the venture have capabilities to extend distribution to reach more customers and scale the business? The entrepreneur should describe how customer "leads" will be generated and how difficult or expensive it is to secure leads. For example, will it be through social media, traditional advertising, websites, personal networks, tradeshows, and so forth? What are the costs of acquiring customers (CAC)? We discuss CAC in "Clarifying Concepts" in the following text.

Clarifying Concepts

Costs of Acquiring a Customer (CAC)

A common cause of new venture failure is not being able to acquire customers at a low-enough cost to make a profit on sales. Entrepreneurs may be familiar with the phrase "A good product does its own marketing," but what is required to complete a *sale*? Some products are easily understood, some may offer a "trial period," where product claims can be tested by customers. Other products require dedicated sales support, given their complexity, or require on-site installation or set-up. CAC can be significantly different, depending on the product or service and business model.

Reducing CAC with a software-as-a-service (SaaS) product, for example, might involve

- ✓ streamlining the customer sign-up process;
- ✓ creating an effective landing page (or different landing pages for different customer segments);
- ✓ offering a "how-to" or demo video that explains the product and its features and preempts typical product and sales-related questions;
- ✓ offering a comparison matrix that highlights advantages over competitors, supported by customer testimonials or recommendations from "opinion leaders" in that market;

✓ using "inside" sales people, based at one location, that reduces the need for a "field" sales force and would also leverage web-based and mobile communication channels.

In some business plans, CAC is either not made explicit—but is hidden somewhere in the financials—or is absent in forecasting cost of sales. A common problem is underestimating how difficult it can be to move customers away from their existing customer preferences and purchasing habits, even though the value proposition and ability to solve a significant customer problem appears to be validated through the new venture's market research efforts. Even if the new product is better and priced cheaper, it may not be enough to dislocate a customer from a familiar, established competitor.

Investors will seek to understand how the value proposition will be delivered to customers. Will the entrepreneur create and directly control the channel to market (e.g., develop a sales force, web sales, etc.) or use partner channels (e.g., wholesale distribution, use of partner-owned websites, etc.)?

Owning the customer base and channel to market allows a venture to control how it sells and manages its customer segment and provides a certain level of distribution power—which may be attractive to a potential acquirer of the business later on. Controlling distribution channels will address one of the key uncertainties within a BP (Figure 3.3) and may contribute to a higher valuation when raising investment.

However, many early-stage ventures will find creating their own channel, such as building a field sales force, cost prohibitive. Sales volumes need to be estimated with a payback period and compared with costs and benefits of indirect sales via others' channels. Some BPs present plans to sell products and services through different sales channels—which can increase operational complexities in addition to costs.

The decision on channels to market will be affected by the type(s) of product/service to be sold. For example, if the business has introduced a novel product that has generated strong sales, and has capabilities to develop a suite of complementary products to sell using the same channel, then controlling the channel will be important. However, developing a new channel model may be more realistic later in the business lifecycle as the financials confirm the need for channel ownership.

The decision on channels will also be affected by the availability of existing channels. For example, are there potential partners controlling existing channels that can reach the intended customer segment, allowing for immediate sales generation? If so, are they willing to partner? What percentage of sales or margin on sales will they demand? How will this affect the venture's pricing model? Many resellers won't commit to selling others' products until they see clear customer demand.

Partnering with an existing distribution channel or original equipment manufacturer (OEM) may allow the new venture to generate sales and gain market acceptance more quickly—and may significantly reduce the cost of building a new channel. Partnering may also overcome customer uncertainty over purchasing from a new market entrant. One option is to partner with an OEM who sells a new venture's core product or service—that may be cobranded with the OEM. More customized versions or complementary product or services can then be offered above the core offerings to customers of the OEM.

However, partnering with a reputable OEM may result in a sizable percentage loss of margin. The entrepreneur should pay close attention to contractual risks when relying on channel partners or suppliers and others to deliver the value proposition. Well-written contracts with partners, suppliers, and customers are all components of good risk management practice.

Investors will also be interested in the type and style of relationship to be developed with the customer segment; for example, how value will be created and differentiated and customer loyalty built with the new business. The entrepreneur should consider the following questions. How important is the customer relationship (CR) to the value proposition? Does the business need to "own" the CR? What relationship does this customer segment expect with you, and is this a differentiator for the business? How much will owning and managing the CR cost, and how is this incorporated into the pricing model?

For example, will the venture attempt to "purchase the customer" through the use of free giveaways, such as phones or software (i.e., the *"freemium"* model, whereby products/services are free but the customer eventually pays for the premium service)?

Management: Entrepreneur and Team

This section of the BP should convince the investor that the entrepreneur or founding team will be able to execute the BP and deliver on critical targets.[12] Ideally, the entrepreneur should possess capabilities and experiences that are well aligned to the value-building requirements of the venture and has done this before.

Evidence suggests that VCs prefer backing entrepreneurs who are capable of taking the business through to a successful exit.[13] Such entrepreneurs have the potential to make the transition from entrepreneur to CEO and the capabilities to assemble, lead, and motivate a high-performance team.

However, there may be few experienced entrepreneurs who have raised investment or experienced an investment exit cycle—outside of regions with high start-up and exit rates such as Silicon Valley, Route 128 (Boston, MA), or Cambridge, United Kingdom.

Most BA investors will attempt to determine quickly if they feel they could work with the entrepreneur. The entrepreneur must not only appear capable but trustworthy. For some BA investors, the entrepreneur must be perceived as "coachable"; this means he/she will be willing to take on and accept advice from the investor. In this regard, the entrepreneur needs to be somewhat flexible, adaptable, and willing to modify or deviate from original plans if evidence suggests that change is required.

Some BA investors may be reluctant to invest in a "one-person" start-up, particularly if it is founded on a new technology. A founding team can offer more capabilities, knowledge, and collective energy to build a new business. It has been shown that entrepreneurs working with a new venture team are more likely and willing to reexamine their assumptions, revise their plans, and set a new course of action than those who have been working alone.

However, BA investors will differ in how they perceive the risk of investing in the solo entrepreneur. As discussed in Chapter 2, some BA investors may seek a more active role alongside the entrepreneur, which leverages their business experiences and networks. Others may seek to mentor (and invest in) the entrepreneur who they perceive to be capable of building the business, with the expectation that additional team members are recruited later on. For BA syndicates or networks that may not have the resources to perform extensive due diligence on every investment opportunity, a strong management team can make a difference in an investment decision.

In presenting a founding team, the BP should convey a strong match and fit between the experiences, skills, traits, and capabilities of the team and the opportunity. Previous individual achievement is known to be a good predictor of future achievement—and many BPs will highlight individual achievement in the CVs and accompanying reference letters of team members. However, the investor may ask: Is this a cohesive team of collective talents or a group of individual achievers with little team experience?

Previous business success of team members highlighted in the BP will likely increase investor confidence that success can be duplicated. Entrepreneurs and teams who have raised or attempted to raise BA or VC funding also carry forward valuable experience to offer in attempting to raise new investment.

An ideal founding team would possess deep industry knowledge and experiences regarding venture start-ups and growing and taking a company to exit. Such a team would present a clear analysis of the potential market and provide a credible business model and strategy to tackle this market. Industry experience has also been shown to improve the accuracy and reduce the bias of entrepreneur expectations.[14]

The entrepreneur should acknowledgement in the BP (and when pitching for investment) that skill or capability deficiencies may need to be filled in the management team. Some entrepreneurs may strengthen their team with experience from an advisory board, board of directors, and external consultants before raising investment. This may also identify for the investor the extent of the entrepreneur's networks or relationship-building capabilities that will benefit the business.

Entrepreneurs seeking larger investment to support high-growth aspirations will be expected to develop a more complete management team whose capabilities cover major business functions. Such a team has been described in terms of the "Starting Five" and include

1. visionary leader;
2. technology/product champion;
3. sales and marketing champion;
4. operations champion;
5. financial champion.

VCs may intervene to strengthen an incomplete management team but will not compromise on their other investment criteria, which include the need to demonstrate a large market opportunity, sustainable, defendable product advantages, and so forth.

Financials

The financials section is usually the most overly optimistic section of a BP as the prospect of securing sizable investment provides a large incentive for entrepreneurs to overforecast. Entrepreneurs of VC-backed ventures have been shown to be generally overoptimistic in revenue and profit forecasts, although this has been shown to decrease over time as a result of entrepreneurial learning and VC monitoring.[15]

The financial section of a BP should present a credible, evidence-based picture of achievable financial goals. Making a credible business case should already have been established by the time the investor begins to read the financials. Here, the business case is articulated in financial numbers. Although inexperienced BA investors may be less scrutinizing of financial statements and projections, BA syndicates and groups (and all VCs) will spend a great deal of time reviewing them.

Financial projections are not facts but rather are informed predictions of the future, based on the best-available information, up-to-date industry data and comparables, and experiences of the entrepreneur and others formulating the BP. The financial "model" should align with the business model and reasonably represent the future business activities of the venture. Investors will appreciate that the financials are an informed prediction but will want to clearly understand the key assumptions on which financial forecasts are based.

The financials should be prepared according to generally accepted accounting principles (GAAP) and presented in a conventional format, which allows for easy analysis (Appendix C outlines the three essential financial documents for the BP: income statement, cash flow statement, and balance sheet). In some cases, entrepreneurs may benefit from having their financial projections verified by a third-party financial advisor, accountant, or professional investor. The intention is to avoid presenting investors with financials that increase rather than reduce uncertainty about the business. Typically, a BP should provide 5-year financial forecasts.

The financial section should cover some of the questions suggested below. We mentioned earlier that investors should be able to understand the assumptions, logic, and economics behind presented financial numbers:

- ✓ How realistic overall are the sales, revenue, cash flow, and profit targets?
  - ○ What makes these targets likely to be achieved?
  - ○ What concerns do these figures raise?
- ✓ Are customer conversion figures and sales forecasts realistic? Do they suggest an insightful, well-researched (i.e., validated) understanding of the target market?
- ✓ How has the entrepreneur validated product/service prices and expected costs of goods sold?
  - ○ Are prices validated through existing sales; based relative to existing competitors; supported by marketing survey data; verified through a staged pilot launch, and so forth?
  - ○ Are the fixed and variable costs at each anticipated level of output realistic?
- ✓ Is there a need to frequently "renew" the products? How will the venture sustain itself if further R&D or product development is required?
- ✓ How profitable is this business model? How long will it take to see profitability?
- ✓ Does the financial forecast accommodate a range of different business conditions that verifies the robustness of the business model (e.g., worst case, most likely, best case conditions)?

Financial uncertainty for the investor is reduced if the venture is already revenue generating and can demonstrate good cash flow management. A high proportion of new ventures fail because of poor cash flow management. Given the usual timing difference between accounts receivable and accounts payable, the entrepreneur must ensure that sales cycles are understood and that good relationships are developed with decision-makers for purchase decisions and those responsible for paying invoices to the business.

The financial section, along with the other sections of the BP, should suggest to the investor that the entrepreneur/team is capable of adhering to budgets and targeted timescales. The length of time to achieve **break-even** (BE), for example, where sales revenues equal costs, is a critical milestone for the entrepreneur and for those investing in the entrepreneur's business. The ability to demonstrate effective financial management of the business will also be critical in securing follow-on rounds of investment.

In addition to the standard historical financial statements and five-year financial forecasts, the **capital structure** of the venture should be included. This identifies to a potential investor the funds that have been paid into the company to date by founders, other investors, or lenders. Investors will want to see a comprehensive listing of the company ownership to understand who is making claims of ownership on the company.

Within the financials section, the entrepreneur may wish to include an **operational plan** that describes key activities, how they will be managed and monitored, and related costs. Team operational responsibilities may have been noted in the previous section on management team. This might include setting up the business, establishing IT, support systems, infrastructure, human resources and recruitment, performance management, financial control, and manufacturing and warehousing (if required). Traditional business plans may offer a stand-alone section on operations.

A typical operational plan would cover the primary functions of the business, including marketing (market size and growth, customer profile, competition, promotion, and advertising); sales (targets, prospects, actions); R&D (product development, testing, launch, etc.); and human resources (recruitment, training, remuneration, etc.).

Investors are attracted to businesses capable of scaling revenues in the initial market segment and growing into other markets. A scalable business will require a sophisticated level of operational planning and control that is not necessary—and usually not yet planned out—when sales volumes or outputs are small.

Scaling customer transactions, for example, may require redesigning operations, closer attention to process controls and cost management, and potentially upgrading physical facilities and changing location. Logistics may need to be better integrated and quality controlled across a more complex and extended value chain that includes purchasing, human resources, marketing, administrative, and IT infrastructure.

Common Pitfalls in BPs

Table 3.4 identifies some common pitfalls of business plans, organized around key areas of uncertainty for the investor: the market, value proposition, channels to market, and financial forecasts.

Table 3.4 Common pitfalls in business plans

Market	Value propositon	Channel to market (CM)	Financial forecasts
"There are no competitors for this product/service" If there is no competition, there may be no customers.	Unsolved but small problem being addressed; that is, not a significant investment opportunity, but suitable lifestyle business?	Access to customer difficult. CM not available unless business builds it; channel occupied by competitor(s).	Assumptions upon which financials are based are not clear or realistic (given market conditions).
Good identification of opportunity, but assessment of customer segment is weak.	More than one business model; business trying to solve too many pain points.	Market entry strategy unrealistic, not novel to stimulate interest in product/service.	Sales growth shows growth in margins (unlikely if market highly competitive and price sensitive).
Using a "percentage of market capture" forecast, for example, "We only need 1% of this $200million market."	Product too immersed in "deep science"; pathway to market product unclear; that is, is this a tech. solution or business solution?	No clear "scale-up" strategy required for business growth.	Working capital will grow proportionally to growth in sales (must account for credit terms to customers and suppliers).

In some cases, the entrepreneur can make refinements, for example, by providing more evidence on the competitive environment, strengthening the management team, or strengthening the financial model.

However, some pitfalls, such as a solution to a small problem, undefined customers, or weak channel options might not be easily correctable and, as such, are unlikely to attract BA investors. For example, although a value proposition might be well developed for a customer segment, is the segment simply too small to generate a healthy return on investment? The probability of a healthy return from a $250–500 million market is greater than from a $15–20 million market. A smaller market is unlikely to attract interest from a BA syndicate, but may interest a solo BA depending on the initial investment requirement.

Another common pitfall in business planning is assuming market conditions that do not actually exist. This issue of "flawed logic" can be seen in the example of Napster, an online music-sharing venture that came into the market with great fanfare but assumed that it would not be held accountable for copyright violations on MP3 files that its users swapped, shared, and downloaded. Napster was eventually shut down by a U.S. court order over its copyright violations.

Flawed logic can also be seen in the case of web-based ventures that establish customer channels and "value capture" capabilities without a strong value-creating proposition for the customer. This was particularly evident during the dot-com boom around 1997–2001 (see Chapter 2, pp. 52–53). Pets.com, for example, had a compelling website and targeted potential pet owners but could not convince customers that buying bulk dog food online was convenient. Similarly, funerals.com developed its web presence and market channel but overlooked the fact that, when grieved, people prefer face-to-face contact when choosing such a highly emotive and personal service.

Financial forecasts are usually the most difficult and uncertain part of business planning for the entrepreneur, particularly for a prerevenue venture. As mentioned earlier, investors will closely scrutinize the assumptions, logic, and economics behind the numbers. For example, forecasts that suggest sales growth significantly outstripping industry growth forecasts over the next 3 years or that suggest high growth in a stagnant or low growth economy will raise concerns. Sales that grow disproportionately in relation to costs, as shown on the balance sheet, will also be questioned.

Many high-growth new ventures don't show predictable revenues and present a clear picture of sustained operations until year 2 or 3. The initial few years may be required to establish baseline operations, with scaling and expansion in later years. For ventures in sectors with longer product development cycles, such as bioscience, projections need to realistically position when products will be introduced into the market and revenues streams established.

For most investors, financial forecasts should demonstrate that the business is scalable; can achieve cash flow-positive shortly after investment (or hit key product development milestones); and can generate high and sustainable growth. The investor should see a clear path to profitability and be able to visualize a profitable exit for their investment when examining the financials of a good business plan.

Finally, the investor will consider whether or not future investment will be required for this business. If future growth relies on additional product lines being developed, for example, one question will be how this is to be financed. Many investors will pass on investing in a venture that may require large investments from other parties and where their percentage of equity ownership is likely to be reduced (i.e., diluted).

Summary

The three categories of markets discussed in the chapter—understood, new, and service-based markets—pose different challenges in developing an investable business. In understood markets, a distinctive value proposition must be positioned, priced, and distributed in relation to competitors. Is the opportunity based on taking away customers from competitors or growing new business from existing segments?

New markets may offer high rewards for the new entrant but such a strategy may be overreliant on future forecasts and predictions of customer demand. Estimating the level of investment required to transform a novel innovation into a sales-generating product can be highly uncertain. First-to-market advantages for the pioneering venture may be identified by the entrepreneur, but are they sustainable? Nonobvious competition may appear in the form of "fast followers" who benefit from the market validation efforts of the pioneer but have a superior value proposition that has been informed by lessons from the first-to-market entrant.

The rise of service-based markets, stimulated by new product-service offerings and the World Wide Web, has attracted significant private equity investment but has also seen high volatility regarding investment returns. Traditional service-based markets are more likely to attract investors who are experienced in service markets and who might expect moderate but less risky returns from a low-volume business.

Profiling the "ideal" or typical investable business is not possible, given such variation in BA investment criteria. However, a common characteristic is the potential to build significant business value for shareholders. In this chapter, a number of critical requirements for building an investable business case were suggested, including

- ✓ scalable business model with a value proposition based on sustainable competitive advantages;
- ✓ clearly identifiable and reachable customer segment with a compelling need;
- ✓ sound pricing model and strong recurring revenue-generating capabilities;
- ✓ channels for scaling sales and related business operations that can support a growth strategy;
- ✓ a management team with the skills and experience to execute a growth strategy and is willing to work with and take advice from the investor;
- ✓ a route to exit and options for a financial or strategic sale within 3–7 years (discussed more in Chapter 6).

An investable business will have developed just enough to allow a particular BA investor to estimate or calculate an attractive return on investment and to believe that the entrepreneur and team can effectively execute the business plan. The entrepreneur, on the other hand, is challenged to find the right BA investor whose profile is most suitable to the investable opportunity, including adding value to the business and supporting the entrepreneur and team.

Timing will also be a crucial factor in bringing a new venture to the market. For example, the notion of a technology or concept "years ahead of its time" presents a significant challenge to achieve commercial viability and to raise investment. The passage of time will see a new venture further develop and may also see changes in market conditions—where previous assumptions or calculations may no longer apply. This can change the investable profile of the venture in attracting follow-on investment and also affect the options available for a successful investment exit.

We now turn to the investment process and examine what is required to progress through to an investment deal agreement in Chapter 4.

CHAPTER 4

Understanding the Business Angel Investment Process

An investor makes money out of the company, not the process.

This chapter examines the investment process and the different stages that a business opportunity will progress through to a final investment deal agreement. The chapter suggests guidelines for choosing an appropriate investor, preparing to raise investment, presenting the opportunity to investors, and also considers some distinctions between business angels (BAs) and venture capitalists (VCs) in the investment deal process. Factors affecting the decision to invest are also considered. The investment deal agreement, including deal negotiation, is discussed in more detail in Chapter 5.

The Investment Process

BA and VC investors share a similar "staged" investment process, as shown in Figure 4.1.[1] The five stages include deal origination, where promising investments are discovered; deal screening, where an overabundance of opportunities are reduced; deal evaluation, where opportunities are critically assessed; deal structure, where the investor and entrepreneur clarify terms; and finally deal negotiation and agreement.

The purpose of this staged process is to eliminate, at the earliest possible time, those investment opportunities which fail to meet the criteria established by the investor. Each successive stage involves higher levels of expenditure of the investor's time and investigation expense. Further expenses may arise if the investor engages professional services, although

Figure 4.1 Investment stages

most BA investors use their networks to investigate potential investment opportunities, often on a quid-pro-quo basis with other investors.

Although the investment stages are similar, BA investors and VCs will differ in the specific processes by which they evaluate new ventures. VCs will perform more extensive due diligence at the deal evaluation stage and deal negotiation, and deal agreement processes will typically be more structured and formal than with BAs. We now explore the first four stages of the investment process in the following text and consider the fifth stage, deal negotiation and agreement, more extensively in the next chapter.

Deal Origination

Deal origination refers to how investors come into contact with investment opportunities and how entrepreneurs find investors. Many BAs will only deal with referrals and not look at unsolicited business plans. Most don't have to actively search for investment opportunities as they typically receive large numbers of business plans to review. BA investors will use their networks for referrals that may include other investors, service providers (consultants, banks, accountants, lawyers, etc.), existing investment portfolio companies, advisory board members, corporations, and research institutes.

The entrepreneur should secure a third-party introduction rather than attempt to cold call. BA investing is a "people assessment business," and a referral from someone known to the investor offers credibility for the entrepreneur. It also reduces uncertainty for the investor, particularly if the introduction is from a trusted friend or colleague who knows something about the entrepreneur's business. This may also generate a level of obligation to the trusted party by the investor to undertake a review of the business plan.

Risk capital investment communities are typically small and well connected. In regions where BA syndicates and networks are active, there may be considerable coinvestment amongst BAs. This means that investment opportunities become known quickly. The entrepreneur should avoid approaching too many investors at the same time. In regions with only a few active BAs or where BA activity is just emerging, entrepreneurs may need to be more proactive and engage investors directly. The initial approach should be with an executive summary. "Views from Practice" in the following text provide insights on BA and VC deal sourcing, screening, and evaluation.

Views From Practice

Deal Sourcing, Screening, and Evaluation: Par Equity

Par Equity, which offers both VC and BA finance (see "Case Insights" in Chapter 2, pp. 50–51), finds most of its more promising investments through its investor network. This network provides Par with an initial, informal screening filter, with introductions to opportunities from people they know and trust and who understand Par's investment criteria. Par invests in approximately *2 in 100* business plans that they receive. Par prefers to invest in various kinds of technology companies irrespective of where they fit within the sector. However, Par requires defensible intellectual property (IP), a differentiated approach, clear routes to market, and an international scope.

Presented opportunities must pass through three formal screening gates. Par will first assess if someone in its investor network understands the business; if not, it will pass on the opportunity. If it decides to go ahead, Par will meet the entrepreneur/team to discuss the business. If it remains interested following the meeting, then Par will engage further. If it is a business angel (BA) deal, the opportunity will be offered to the Par Syndicate, who make their own decisions whether to invest or not. One of the problems with informal BA investment, according to Par's Founding Partner Paul Atkinson, is that the business might not be examined in detail. More formal due diligence processes are applied by VCs and can be applied by larger BA syndicates, although the latter typically have a less systematic approach.

With a VC deal, Par's investment decision is made by its four found-ing partners who constitute the investment committee. This process entails a review of the business plan, prospects for an investment reali-zation, expected investment return, IP, contractual issues, quality of the management team, and so forth. The unanimous approval of the investment committee is required, and particular attention is paid to the prospects of meeting or beating the minimum expected return threshold. Par attempts to form an early view on the key commer-cial issues, so that the confirmatory due diligence, which is generally where much of the external costs (lawyers and other professionals) are incurred, will only be undertaken at a stage where both parties are broadly confident that the investment will progress, in the absence of unpleasant surprises.

Preparing to Raise BA Investment

Finding the right investor is a critical search and decision process for the entrepreneur but is typically not well planned or thought out. Investors reflect a wide range of different experiences, skills, networks, motivations for investing, financial means, character traits, and personalities. While there is no "ideal" investor, some will be more appropriate and value adding for the entrepreneur and the venture than others. Entrepreneurs should familiarize themselves with those investors who typically invest in similar ventures. Many business plans are rejected outright because the opportunity does not fit with the investor's criteria, which is often made clear on their website or homepage. Few BA investors have the specialist knowledge to evaluate the technical merits of a range of diverse business sectors. BAs prefer to look for investments in industries they know some-thing about or where they have previously made their money.

Evidence from VC studies suggest that specialist investors achieve greater performance than generalists, and surviving ventures initially financed by specialists are more likely to achieve a higher rate of growth.[2] This suggests that new ventures with novel business models or complex technologies will gain more value from investors with related indus-try experience or deep domain knowledge and ideally, experience with ventures at a similar stage of development.

A specialist investor may overcome adverse selection problems that could arise from the entrepreneur's use of information asymmetries to protect the innovation, such as scientific jargon, trade secrets, IP rights (IPRs), and other methods to avoid premature disclosure of ideas and potential imitation. A nonspecialist investor is likely to avoid investing in such opportunities.

Experienced BA investors are more likely to understand the potential of an investment and comprehend what is required to make the investment successful.[3] Experienced BA investors may also be more focused on investment returns, preferring to invest in new ventures with strong growth potential and clear routes to profitability.

BAs will vary not only in their capacity to contribute beyond providing investment but will also differ in the extent to which they desire to be involved in the new venture, as discussed in Chapter 2. Finding the right investor with the right level of involvement could be critical to a sole entrepreneur or a small, inexperienced management team. Solo BAs may be more keen to invest in an ambitious entrepreneur who they can mentor and offer more hands-on support.

Solo BAs may only invest in a few companies, while more experienced BAs may have multiple investments and also invest as part of a BA syndicate or network. "Views from Practice" in the following text offers comparative insights on raising investment from solo BAs and BA syndicates from Martin Avison, a UK-based serial entrepreneur.

Views From Practice

Raising BA Investment: An Entrepreneur's Perspective

Entrepreneur Martin Avison has raised over £3 million in business angel (BA) investment for early-stage technology and service-based ventures. Martin describes raising investment as an "imperfect process," as experienced business people and investors don't always agree on what is a good business idea. This can result in entrepreneurs receiving mixed and sometimes contrasting opinions and suggestions.

Martin has secured financing from both individual BAs and BA syndicates. He suggests advantages and disadvantages of each source below, based on his experiences:

- ✓ Individual BAs are harder to find; they tend to invest smaller amounts of money; they are less likely to have experience of assisting in an exit; and they may struggle to finance further rounds of investment (in countries like the UK, they also cannot access public coinvestment funding as can a BA syndicate).
- ✓ Individual BAs in general are more responsive to business's needs; more rigorous over the due diligence (which Martin regards as a good thing); they often have sector experience; they are usually "willing to roll their shirt sleeves up and get stuck-in"; and the entrepreneur has a direct line of access to the investment decision-maker, allowing for more control and negotiation.
- ✓ BA syndicates are easier to find; offer larger-scale initial and follow-on funding; provide knowledge on exits; offer more extensive industry contacts; and provide a single point of contact for dealing with multiple syndicate investors.
- ✓ BA syndicates tend to negotiate only on the first round of funding and never quite provide funding to get the job done. This requires the entrepreneur to keep coming back for more money. Martin states, "This can have a significant impact on share dilution and can be very un-motivating for the founders… in one company, working on the next round of funding took up 60% of one person's time." With each business going through several rounds of funding, Martin suggests that this may present a significant problem for the business as well as for the BA syndicate.

How important is the personal fit between entrepreneur and investor? Sharing a common vision and strategy to develop and grow the business will be critical. Trust and mutual respect at the outset of an investment is shown to be a contributing factor in successful long-term relationships between entrepreneur and BA investor.[4] The entrepreneur and investor should also understand and agree on the level of involvement that the investor will have in the business.

The entrepreneur may wish to talk with entrepreneurs who have previously received investment from an investor to gain further insights. For example, what type of support did the investor provide? How did he/she react to changes in plans, disappointments, and missed targets? What value was provided on strategic issues, formulating an exit plan, or offering follow-on funding? Would they recommend the investor? Would they recommend you to the investor?

Choosing the right investor has been likened to choosing a marriage partner; you may be together for years, through good times and bad; so choose wisely. As mentioned earlier, to find the right investor, the entrepreneur should build up a network of knowledgeable contacts within the investment community or find a professional advisor who deals with BA investors on a regular basis. Such advisors can be invaluable in recommending particular investors to approach and offering referrals to the investor.

Raising BA investment requires patience and persistence and inevitably takes longer than expected.[5] Most entrepreneurs feel a sense of urgency in raising capital and also expect to close a deal quickly if there is interest on the part of an investor. The investor, on the other hand, is less pressured to close a deal and may be assessing other investment opportunities at the same time. Unless an investment opportunity is significantly unique, novel, and attracting attention from multiple sources, the power and control in the investment process resides with the investor.[6] Although persistence is sometimes required in following up with investors, pressuring an investor to speed up the process is not a recommended approach.

How Much Investment to Raise?

Conventional wisdom has it that the entrepreneur should bootstrap and leverage every strand of nonequity funding source to increase value in the business before raising BA finance. The logic is that raising excess funds prematurely may result in higher capital costs, greater dilution of ownership of the business, and constraints on the business development process itself.

One option is for the entrepreneur to take a small investment round if engaged in proof of concept, often referred to as a seed round. This initial investment would cover beta testing of the prototype (in essence, a public test) and generation of the first product. If a successful product is developed, the next investment round may carry a higher valuation and price that benefits the entrepreneur or founders. Problems or delays would make raising a further investment round less likely or result in a lower price and more expensive investment round for the entrepreneur.

Another option is to determine an initial financing level that will carry the venture through to a cash flow-positive position. A stronger financial position may not require as high a level of follow-on financing, and early investment may remove or significantly reduce business risks and investor uncertainties.

The amount of financing for any particular round is typically the amount of money that will get the venture to the next set of business development milestones. This will make the next investment round easier to secure—or eventually unnecessary. The type of market and sector and stage of the business will influence the timing and financing required to achieve projected milestones.

In some cases, the entrepreneur will benefit from considering the entire financing requirements of the venture across multiple funding rounds rather than considering any particular financing round in isolation. High-growth opportunities may require multiple rounds of financing that allow accelerated growth to secure an attractive market before competitors move in. Engaging with those investors who have the ability to fund multiple investment rounds will be an important consideration. As mentioned earlier, spending time to chase up subsequent rounds or having to engage with new investors can be time consuming and distract the entrepreneur away from building the business.

Deal Screening

The business plan is the standard tool used in deal screening and deal evaluation, which allows investors to consider competing requests for funding. Successful and well-established BAs and syndicates receive an overwhelming number of business plans and funding requests.

As a screening tool, the business plan in one sense, has similar characteristics to the capital budgeting process (CBP) used by large firms—where a standard, comparative process is applied to an "oversubscription" of projects competing for central funds. Those projects that can demonstrate tangible, measurable returns are prioritized over those with less tangible or difficult-to-measure outcomes. Successful projects are those that clearly identify the problem to be solved; offer an effective solution and promise a higher investment return (in comparison to other projects); and can be financed with available funds.

Screening an overabundance of funding requests relies primarily on the executive summary of the business plan. The investor, BA group, or syndicate executive (or VC general partner) will usually have a quick read to assess whether or not the opportunity fits with their investment criteria.

Websites are commonly used by BA groups (and VCs) that allow for the unrestricted submission of business plans by entrepreneurs. For example, Tech Coast Angels, the largest angel organization in the United States, provides guidelines for submitting a business plan online. It also sets out detailed screening criteria that allow entrepreneurs to screen themselves as to whether or not they meet Tech Coast investment criteria (see Appendix D). This provides a convenient way to standardize and manage the submission process and potentially attract a novel opportunity that would otherwise be missed in a formal, referral approach discussed earlier. However, the entrepreneur is still strongly advised to approach investors through third-party referrals where possible.

Only a small percentage of business plans makes it through the deal-screening stage to be formally evaluated. One Canadian study suggests that approximately 70% of potential opportunities are rejected at initial screening.[7] Another study of the largest BA group in the United States (Tech Coast Angels) found that less than 10% of business plans making it past the application stage went on to secure BA investment.[8] This is consistent with other studies, which estimate that the cumulative rejection rate of business plans leading up to deal structuring and negotiation (i.e., over the first three stages as shown in Figure 4.1) is 90%–95%.[9]

A high rejection rate at initial screening is likely to include a higher proportion of unsolicited submissions compared to business plans receiving trusted third-party referrals. Many business plans are rejected during initial screening because they do not fit particular investment criteria or more general criteria of an investable business discussed in Chapter 3. Common reasons for rejection include

- ✓ business located outside of geographical reach of BA investors;
- ✓ stage and type of venture: for example, long prerevenue, product development phase;
- ✓ unattractive sector or market: for example, low margins and high volatility (retail, hotels, restaurants, property); highly competitive or high technical risks or both (e.g., consumer goods, telecom, clean tech, drug development);
- ✓ limited scalability or growth potential: for example, traditional service businesses;
- ✓ weak business model: unclear value proposition; no clear customers; weak customer channels; no "go-to-market" strategy; insufficient profit markets; lack of exit potential;
- ✓ size of initial investment and estimated total funding requirements exceeds capabilities of investor;
- ✓ management team is weak, unconvincing, or has poor reputation;
- ✓ investment is not eligible for tax relief (e.g., UK Enterprise Investment Scheme; see Appendix A).

Deal Evaluation

If the deal-screening process raises investor interest, the investor may request a full business plan or a meeting with the entrepreneur and team members or both before exploring the business plan in more detail. The intention will be to more clearly understand the investment opportunity and raise questions arising from the screening process. The investor may also request contact details of founders, executives, references, and key customers, suppliers, and distributors if available.

The deal evaluation stage may involve "initial due diligence" or limited investigation of the business. Industry and market specialists within the investor's network may be contacted for initial feedback. Network contacts with deep domain experience may be sought, depending on the technology or product and business model. Initial due diligence may also include the following:

- ✓ Market size and competitive landscape analysis
- ✓ Technology and product development plan assessment
- ✓ Site visit to see a demonstration or pilot of existing technology and get to know the business and team better
- ✓ Assessment of value proposition, sales, distribution, and growth strategies
- ✓ Financial model and capital requirement analysis

Some background checks may also be undertaken. Any previous business activities, directorships, and so forth of the entrepreneur and team can now be easily accessed via publically available records and the Internet. All things related to the business are now subject to a close review by the investor and a wider network.

Once contact is initiated between the entrepreneur/team and the investor, the business is being evaluated. Everyone associated with the new venture should be vigilant regarding how they conduct themselves, what they say about their business, and how they engage with the investor or associates of the investor. The entrepreneur and team must be prepared to respond to detailed questions about any aspect of the business.

During initial due diligence, the issue of confidentiality may arise. If the new venture possesses sensitive proprietary knowledge or technology, then it is prudent to ensure that the investor is "put on notice" that full disclosure will require a formal nondisclosure agreement (NDA). "Clarifying Concepts" in the following text offers suggestions for NDA usage.

Clarifying Concepts

Nondisclosure Agreement (NDA)

Entrepreneurs are often uncertain about the NDA—when to use it or how effective it is in protecting proprietary knowledge. Entrepreneurs should not ask the investor to sign an NDA to review the business plan.

Most investors will not sign an NDA at this stage, and such a request may diminish the level of trust between the two parties. Typically, an NDA is used once the business passes initial screening, and the investor produces a term sheet and decides to undertake formal due diligence.

New ventures with sensitive and valuable proprietary assets and intellectual property (IP) should not disclose details until a formal due diligence process is undertaken. Once such knowledge and information is publically disclosed, it is open for anyone else, including competitors, to use. This may also disallow claiming trade secret protection or filing a patent or registered trademark. One suggestion is to tailor the business plan to reveal just enough about proprietary assets to stimulate the investor to undertake formal evaluation of the business.

Following initial due diligence, additional clarification or information may be requested by the investor. This might include an updated financial model or further information on the state of negotiating a distribution channel agreement, and so forth. Some of this activity may deploy professional services firms, research institutions, or specialist market analysis consultancies, but most BAs will attempt to use their networks and contacts.

VCs will typically have a formal authorization process to undertake additional investigation to protect against an initial narrow, biased, or insufficient due diligence process and prior to a formal, comprehensive, and often costly due diligence process. VC deals are, with few exceptions, more detailed and complex than BA investment deals, and discussed further in Chapter 5.

The entrepreneur/team may be asked during this time to present on the business opportunity for 10–30 minutes. In the case of a BA syndicate, this may be to a group of investors and the syndicate executive team. Coaching to prepare for the investment presentation may also be offered by the executive team, along with some guidelines on the objectives of the presentation, make-up of the audience, and what to expect.

Presenting to Investors

Getting through the deal-screening process and being asked to formally present to investors is an achievement in itself for the entrepreneur.

The presentation allows the entrepreneur to showcase the value of the business and to clarify what is being sought from the investor.

Most BAs, syndicates, and groups do not charge the entrepreneur a fee to apply for funding or to present, although some do. The Angel Capital Association (ACA) in the United States recommends that angel groups should charge no more than a few hundred dollars for applications and no more than $500 for presentations and finds that approximately one-third of their membership charges fees.[10]

Once the decision is made to raise external investment, the entrepreneur should be preparing to pitch the business opportunity. The short version of an investor presentation is commonly referred to as an "**elevator pitch**," a hypothetical scenario where the entrepreneur bumps into an investor in an elevator and has only one or two minutes to pitch an idea before the investor reaches his/her floor. The objective is securing a response from the investor along the lines of "That's interesting, I want to hear more." "Entrepreneurs are always pitching" is a common piece of advice, whether it is for investment, partners, resources, or customers.

Much variation exists in what entrepreneurs include in a presentation to investors. An effective presentation requires adequate preparation time, and a common mistake by entrepreneurs is attempting to compress their entire business plan into a verbal presentation. Figure 4.2 suggests nine essential themes upon which to organize an investor presentation.

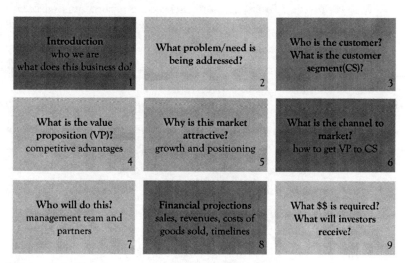

Figure 4.2 Key themes of an investor presentation

Below are content suggestions for each of the nine themes shown in Figure 4.2:

1. A clear, concise introduction of entrepreneur and team. Company logo or slogan should be presented clearly. Try to explain what the business does in only a few sentences. The objective is to capture audience attention immediately.

2. What problem is being solved? What makes this a critical or important problem?

3. Who are the customers who need a solution? What are their distinctive characteristics? Why will they purchase from you? How much and when?

4. Describe the value proposition. How does it fulfill customer needs?
   ✓ Why is this solution superior to the competition?
   ✓ Avoid being too technical and focusing solely on the technology or product.
   ✓ How will competitive advantage be sustained and protected?

5. What makes this an attractive market? Where will the VP be positioned within the competitive mix? How will the chosen market segment convert to sales?

6. How will sales be achieved through the channel to customers? Will new channels be created or will partner channels be used?

7. Who is the team? Briefly identify their accomplishments and previous experiences relevant for the business. Who are the advisors and board members (if established)? Why will this team achieve the milestones, deliver the strategy, and work hard for a return on investment? What new personnel need to be recruited?

8. Financial forecasts must be well aligned with the business case presented up to this point. Sales, cost of goods sold, revenues, profit margins, and time to profitability (or break-even point) need to be concise. There must be a clear but credible path to a profitability "story" emerging from the financials.

9. How much investment is required? How will it be used? What is on offer to investors?
   ✓ Potential exit options (acknowledging that there may be others)

✓ Entrepreneur and team should be prepared for a discussion on equity stake (which we discuss in more detail later)

The entrepreneur should also be prepared to revise or modify a planned, full-length, and formal presentation as investors may have less time than expected, are late for the presentation, decide not to use PowerPoint, and so forth. Being able to deliver a brief yet compelling presentation will come through practiced pitching, available through business plan competitions and "dry runs" with advisors. This will allow the entrepreneur to more concisely explain the business and focus attention on the key value drivers of the business that investors are keen to understand.

During the presentation, investors are most likely to put themselves into the shoes of the target customer and ask themselves: "Why would I buy this product—and why from this business?" They are likely to consider this question early in the presentation. If they can't understand the value proposition or what type of customer they are supposed to be, then they can't answer this question, and the entrepreneur has a problem.

There are some common presentation pitfalls and related suggestions worth mentioning:

✓ Know the slides well enough that eye contact remains with the audience. Reading slides suggests poor preparation. The audience is also able to read slides faster than the presenter can talk.
✓ Be prepared for investors to interrupt throughout the presentation. The entrepreneur should ideally encourage questions throughout, so that any potential seeds of doubt or uncertainties on the part of the investor are dealt with immediately rather than carried through the presentation.
✓ Avoid placing large amounts of text or figures onto slides. Slide content should be brief (e.g., key points that will be expanded on further by the presenter) and easy to read (e.g., large font and strong contrast with slide background).
✓ Spending time to practice in front of other audiences will only improve both the quality of presentation and the confidence of

presenters. Entering pitching and business plan competitions or presenting to professional advisors is recommended.

✓ Providing a copy of presented slides is a courtesy that allows the investor to take notes alongside the slides and refer back to them following the presentation.

✓ Business cards should be offered to the investor or executive team (if presenting to a syndicate or network) either before or immediately after the presentation.

✓ Clarify with the investor or executive team the timeline for next steps or follow-up if it is not mentioned during the presentation.

The investment presentation exposes the business opportunity to greater scrutiny, allowing the investor to make a more informed investment decision. This includes observing strengths and weaknesses of the entrepreneur and team, for example:

✓ How well do the entrepreneur and team understand this business and how to exploit the opportunity?

✓ How do they respond to questions/criticism and how flexible do they appear in taking on suggestions from the audience?

✓ How do they appear to get along?

Following the presentation, the investor will typically suggest a timeline for notifying the entrepreneur/team on the decision. The investor may also provide some immediate feedback on the presentation. When presenting to a BA syndicate, the executive team and investor board may deliberate immediately following the presentation and make a decision (or in rare cases, request further information). Should they decide to proceed, then deal terms will be discussed and formal due diligence requirements identified. The entrepreneur/team is then notified of the outcome shortly after this deliberation and usually in person.

There are three likely outcomes following a presentation to investors:

1. Further information is requested regarding some aspect of the business, possibly resulting in another presentation.

2. Investor declines to invest. The business has some serious deficiencies or does not meet the investor's criteria. The new venture may be referred to another investor whose criteria better relates to the opportunity or to a business advisor or consulting firm that may be able to assist the venture.

3. Investor agrees to invest, and the process moves on to deal negotiation and deal structuring.

Some entrepreneurs/teams will consider refining the business model or revisiting previous assumptions of the business. However, before the entrepreneur commences refining the business after engagement with one investor, it will be important to reflect on the experience, investor comments, and feedback. The issue may not be with the investment opportunity but rather that particular investor's perception of it. In other words, it simply didn't fit that investor's criteria of an investable business.

"Views from Practice" in the following text provides lessons on raising investment from Nelson Gray, an experienced UK-based entrepreneur and BA investor—who invests as a solo BA and also coinvests as a member of a number of BA syndicates.

Views From Practice

An Interview with Business *Angel Nelson Gray*

What are your key investment criteria? "This has changed over the years and what I would look at now is quite different than what I would have looked before. A few years ago I would have been influenced by the classic notion of the "horse and jockey" [the entrepreneur as jockey and the business as the horse] and focus on the entrepreneur's ability, the business model, etc.

I now look at the investment opportunity—which is different than the business opportunity—and ask: is this an investment opportunity that I and my friends, other business angels, can fund—and fund to a successful exit? So, despite how good the entrepreneur is or the opportunity looks, if it requires £20 Million in funding before a successful exit, I would pass on the opportunity at the outset. I don't have £20 Million as a Business Angel to invest. As an early investor, I would also be subject to a heavy dilution by venture capitalists coming in over the top of me.

My question now is: can I provide enough money to create something that we can then pass on to the next level and I can get an exit? If it passes that, then I want to look at the entrepreneur. I don't look at the entrepreneur and ask: i.e., have they done it before, what's their track record in creating money; because none of them have. My question is rather: do I like this person? Is this someone I will enjoy working with? Is this person "coachable"? We won't see here in Scotland an entrepreneur that has done it five times before, like you would see in a place like Silicon Valley."

What are the common pitfalls you see with entrepreneurs *pitching* to you for investment?
"Number one is that the focus is still entirely on the technology—a clever formula, or piece of hardware—and they tell me that people ought to buy this. But they have no idea as to who will buy it, for how much or how they will get it to the customer. If you look at my last two investments, you would struggle in the business plan or the pitch to find any discussion about technology or IP—it's all about what has been done to validate the market. This includes talking to the end user through focus groups, even though they won't be selling to the end user—they'll be selling to the distribution channel. There's a significant difference between end users and buyers; that the person who is going to pay may not be the end user."

The Investment Decision

The personal nature of BA financing decisions, and differences in their investment criteria, make it difficult to fully explain or predict how BAs make their investment decisions. Some factors are directly associated with the business opportunity, as presented in the business plan or pitched by the entrepreneur. Investor decisions at the initial screening stage tend to be most influenced by: (1) characteristics of the entrepreneur and team and (2) the market potential of the opportunity.[11] Product/service and financial factors appear to be less significant.

Investor decisions on opportunities already passing initial screening appear to be influenced by different factors. A study of a large Canadian BA network, with 85 investors, examined 173 proposals that were not rejected at first screening but failed to be funded.[12] The reasons for rejection are shown in the following text, descending from the most important to the least important:

✓ Product and business model issues (39%)
✓ Market strategy weaknesses (30%)
✓ Financial considerations (13%)
✓ Quality of management team (10%)

A well-balanced business plan is suggested from the earlier findings, as some factors less significant during initial screening are significant in later decisions where opportunities are rejected. This supports previous research that suggests that the criteria that BAs use to accept or reject an opportunity change as the decision-making process evolves.[13]

Interestingly, financial factors appear less influential in investor decisions, suggesting that investors may not place much credence in business plan financials. Experienced BA investors will perform their own financial calculations of an opportunity, which may include recalculating the financials presented in the business plan.

Investment decisions are also influenced by personal investor criteria as already noted. The entrepreneur may present an "investable business case" that is rejected by one BA but appealing to another. For some investors, the absence of the entrepreneur having "skin in the game" may be a deciding factor not to invest. This refers to an entrepreneur's personal liability in the new venture and how much personal wealth the entrepreneur has sunk into the business that is likely to be lost if the business fails.

The level of related early-stage investing experience may influence the investment decision. Experienced entrepreneurs who have had poor overall investment returns may be more inclined to seek high growth opportunities, which in turn may increase the pressure on the entrepreneur to achieve a high growth rate for the business.

Another deciding factor is acknowledgment that the opportunity will require investment beyond the investor's means, which may dilute the investor's shares when new investment is attracted into the business. The question for the investor becomes: "Can I get to a capital exit point on the resources that I can draw upon locally to fund this business?" This will expose some opportunities or sectors as not viable for that investor.

BA investors will be also influenced by different factors compared to VCs, such as the availability of tax breaks and the wide range of secondary reasons, as discussed in Chapter 2. For example, BA motivations to contribute to the local economy and support local entrepreneurs or to seek hands-on involvement with an exciting new business will not be shared by VCs, who have fiduciary responsibilities to maximize investor returns.

It is suggested that BAs are more concerned with avoiding bad investments than "hitting a home run" (compared to VCs) because of their limited ability to diversify.[14] Portfolio investment follows the assumption that some investments will fail, some will be written off, some may break even, some may generate a reasonable return, and a few will make a sizable return. Benefits of portfolio investment explain why BAs have organized themselves increasingly into syndicates and networks.

Early-stage investors' evaluative processes are also influenced by factors that are subjective, not necessarily obvious, and may not be directly related to their expressed evaluation criteria.[15] Research on investor decision-making processes continues to offer new insights, as discussed in "Research Notes" in the following text.

Research Notes

How Intuition and Empathy May Affect Investors' Decisions

Research suggests that venture capitalists (VCs) are poor at introspecting about how they arrive at investment decisions, despite the information-rich environment in which decisions are made (e.g., arising from extensive due diligence). This raises the question of whether business angels (BAs) are superior in their more personal and intuitive process to VCs.

Early-stage investors are recognized as intuitive decision-makers who often rely on "gut feel" to explain their use of subjective or even unknown evaluation criteria. The investor's intuitive evaluation can be influenced by the level of personal connection with the entrepreneur, team, or opportunity, or both. Investors may empathetically identify with the entrepreneur that relates to the notion of "personal chemistry." However, it remains unclear how the presenting new venture team can modify or manipulate the communication form in which a new venture opportunity is presented—to influence these "personal chemistry"-related assessments.

The content and quality of the entrepreneur's presentation is shown to have a positive relationship with BA investment decisions. Research also identifies the importance of emotionally engaging investors during the presentation, with a superior pitch able to transmit meaning as opposed to merely transmitting information. Verbal images can create visual images in an audience, such as providing a scenario that demonstrates the purchasing experience of the customer. Communicating a business opportunity in the form of a story has been shown to increase investors' levels of empathetic identification with the entrepreneur, as well as their assessments of the entrepreneur/team's level of motivation. This may positively affect the evaluation by BAs of a presented investment opportunity.

Sources: Carpentier and Suret, 2013; Zacharakis and Shepherd, 2007; Smith et al., 2010, Dane and Pratt, 2007; Villanueva, 2012, Clarke, 2008; Gregson, Carr and Harrison, 2013.

Deal Structuring

If initial due diligence satisfies the investor or executive team that this is an investable business, formal discussions will commence with the entrepreneur. This may involve an exploratory meeting where initial deal terms are proposed. During this discussion, the investor and entrepreneur may agree on a valuation or valuation formula, discuss costs and fees, and decide on the equity to be taken by the investor. The investor will then issue a formal offer in the form of a "term sheet" or heads of terms.

The Term Sheet

The term sheet is a document that outlines the proposed financial terms and conditions upon which an investment will be made. The term sheet is an indication that investors are serious about investing although most of the terms are nonbinding on either the entrepreneur or investor at this stage, with the exception of certain confidentiality provisions. Most BA term sheets include some basic confidentiality obligations (especially if investors have not signed a nondisclosure agreement [NDA]; see pp. 113–114).

VCs and some BAs may include an "**exclusivity covenant**" or agreement, where the entrepreneur is contractually bound to deal exclusively with them while formal due diligence is undertaken. Solo BA investors may not require exclusivity covenants that require the entrepreneur curtail investment discussions with other investors although some may include this in their term sheets.

However, up until the term sheet is signed, the entrepreneur is free to engage in discussions with other potential investors. Should the entrepreneur attract attention from a number of interested BA investors, one option may be to encourage them to coinvest rather than playing the investors against each other for a deal.

The term sheet serves as a basis for preparation of legal documentation required to conclude a deal and makes explicit certain rights and obligations for both parties. These include exclusivity rights already noted, an obligation to honor an agreed valuation, secure commitments for financing from additional sources (such as debt financing or coinvestment expected prior to closing the deal), and so forth.

The terms proposed for an early-stage venture are usually less complex than for a more mature, "going-concern" venture, and most BA term sheets will be fairly standard. The term sheet is usually prepared by the BA but, in some cases, can be prepared by the venture. VC terms sheets are typically more extensive and reflect the VC's formal institutional practices and legal and regulatory requirements.

The term sheet can be one to five pages in length and typically covers three central sections: funding, governance, and liquidation. The term sheet will define the timeline and process from the date of signing the term sheet to the closing date as well as the conditions for closing, including due diligence. Entrepreneurs should be familiar with key provisions within a typical term sheet. A sample outline of a term sheet related to "preferred" shares (which we discuss in Chapter 5, p. 146) is presented in Appendix E.

Entrepreneurs are highly advised to seek experienced legal counsel to ensure that the term sheet is understandable and does not contain any clauses that have not been discussed or clarified with the investor. A verbal offer may not be the last position of either investor or entrepreneur—as minor or noncritical aspects of the deal may still be subject to negotiation and movement on either side. We discuss the role of legal counsel when discussing deal agreements in the next chapter.

Due Diligence

Due diligence refers to the assessment and appraisal of the business, its managers, and the business proposal, where the claims in the business plan are further verified. The objective of due diligence is for the investor to gather sufficient information to determine whether or not to enter into formal negotiations with the entrepreneurs and founding team regarding the conditions of a potential investment.

There are typically two stages of due diligence, with the first stage discussed earlier (see "Deal Evaluation," p. 112). This involves an initial prescreening carried out by the investor (or executive team) which focuses on a fit between opportunity and investor criteria, the market, product, value proposition, and financials. During this prescreening, the investor(s) must clearly see an opportunity and believe that it is achievable.

The second stage is "formal" due diligence, which occurs after a term sheet has been signed. The objective is to determine if there are any serious deficiencies or risks in the business not identified during the initial due diligence process. Formal due diligence is also expected to identify anything that may incur additional costs, create delays, or expose the business or investor to actual or potential liabilities not identified in previous information provided by the entrepreneur/team.

For smaller BA deals, product, market, or technology issues may be straightforward, and investors may undertake less extensive due diligence and use their networks or contacts in local or regional professional services firms that reduce their costs.

Formal due diligence typically involves domain experts that will assess the market, technology, or product, strength of IP, potential claims on IP by those outside the venture, existing contracts or agreements, actual or threatened litigation, and financial models and statements. For businesses actively trading, due diligence will also include all agreements with partners or suppliers, remuneration of management team, preexisting and future commitments, obligations or restrictions, and adherence to compliance regulations or quality standards. VC due diligence will be more in-depth and comprehensive on these topics.

Due diligence not only validates information presented in the business plan but also verifies the integrity and honesty of the entrepreneur and team. More thorough background checks may be done on the management team, and the relationships with customers, suppliers, distributors, and partners may be examined.

Many different criteria are used to perform formal due diligence; up to 400 different criteria have been identified in VC due diligence checklists.[16] Some criteria are industry or sector specific. For example, in sectors characterized by strong science, such as biotechnology, the scientific reputation of the founding team is identified as being of higher importance during due diligence compared to other industries.[17]

Formal due diligence can be costly for the investor, although BAs, syndicates, and groups rely heavily on their extensive network of investors, advisors, and others to assist in due diligence. Investors will seek assurances that the venture is acting in good faith during this period. Some investors will also require an exclusivity agreement, as mentioned earlier. VC will typically require that a penalty for breach of exclusivity be written into the term sheet (see "Clarifying Concepts" in the following text).

Clarifying Concepts

Covering Due Diligence Costs

With successfully concluded deal agreements, the entrepreneur is not usually required to reimburse the BA investor for associated costs. If deal negotiation falters and an investment offer is declined, the entrepreneur is usually not required to reimburse the BA investor unless it has been discussed and agreed upon earlier (as included in the term sheet). However, the investee company in a VC deal will usually be required to reimburse the investor for all expenses associated with the deal, specifically, expenses attributed to the due diligence process. With VC deals, if the entrepreneur withdraws from investment negotiation after due diligence costs were incurred by the investor—or if the business has misrepresented itself in the process—then the entrepreneur may be expected to pay the investor for the incurred costs. VC due diligence costs, particular for complex technologies, can be expensive and may be as high as $250K or more. Some VC funds also charge an "advice fee" if they have been involved in structuring a deal with external parties.

Fatal flaws, red flags, or showstoppers, as they have been called, are serious risks or deficiencies revealed in the due diligence process that cause the investor to withdraw from moving forward on closing a deal. In some cases, problems may be overcome by refocusing original strategy, renegotiating agreements or contracts, or adopting additional controls. For experienced BA investors and VCs, delays or additional costs associated with executing the business plan may result in more stringent deal terms and conditions. However, the experienced investor may decide that the risks are too great and decide not to make the investment.

Valuation

Valuation is a common source of disagreement between entrepreneurs and investors. Entrepreneurs are known to display a high degree of exuberance over the value of their businesses. Unreasonable expectations over valuation may negatively affect goodwill developed to that point between the parties and potentially collapse deal negotiation. Both parties may see valuation as the key to their investment return, with different valuations affecting their percentage of equity ownership that in turn influences what they receive when their shares are liquidated for cash following an exit, that is, a trade sale, acquisition, initial public offering (IPO), and so forth.

Value can be understood as a ratio of opportunity over risk—and *how* to estimate the amount of risk present in an investment opportunity is central to the valuation process. The contentious nature of valuation derives from the high level of uncertainty in attempting to value a new business—with little or no cash flow or financial history—based on its future potential. The level of uncertainty and risk are so significant for most new ventures that traditional valuation methods are highly unreliable and ineffective. Indeed, valuation of early-stage ventures remains a highly judgmental process, based on an "opinion of value."

Yet, valuation provides a starting point for negotiation in finalizing an investment deal agreement and is therefore an important element of the investment process. Valuation is also used as part of the formal due diligence process, to assess the credibility of the claims and assertions made by the entrepreneur/team in the business plan.

Although most valuation methods are not appropriate for new ventures, the entrepreneur will benefit from a familiarity with more common methods, as they may arise in discussion with investors. Some of these methods will be applied during valuation for future funding rounds and when preparing for an exit.

There are many valuation methods available for existing businesses with a trading history, with each designed with different purposes in mind. Valuation is seen as more of a science for a business that has a history of revenues, positive cash flow, or earnings. More common valuation methods are discussed in the following text, including discounted cash flow, comparables, venture capital method, asset based, and rule of thumb.

Discounted Cash Flow

Discounted cash flow analysis (DCF) estimates the present value of a future stream of earnings—such as cash flow, income, interest, and so forth—which are generated from assets of the business, such as products, services, IP, and so forth. The future earnings are then discounted back to a net present value (NPV) of those earnings using a discount rate chosen to reflect the risk inherent in that stream of earnings.

For an existing business with customers and sales and a record of financial transactions, the DCF method is relatively straightforward. Historical data can be used to show revenues, margins, and profit trends and predict a future stream of benefits from current assets deployed and future assets that the business may be developing.

For investors relying on DCF to value investment opportunities, the DCF approach calls for the **discount rate** to increase along with uncertainty to adjust for the risk in the investment. The result is that uncertain investments—such as prerevenue businesses—are penalized with very high discount rates that diminish their perceived value, with potentially novel opportunities being rejected. Such missed opportunities are referred to as "false negatives." "Clarifying Concepts" below describes the discount rate.

Clarifying Concepts

The *Discount Rate*

The discount rate is the rate of return an investor would expect from different opportunities that have equal risk and is the rate of return he/she must receive to justify an investment. It is also referred to as hurdle rate, cost of capital, or capitalization rate. The discount rate is applied to the cash flows over the investment period, and the sum of discounted cash flows determines the value of the business in today's terms. In theory, the discount rate matches the specific risk of the potential investment.

Although the discount rate should represent the risks associated with generating the expected earnings of the firm, in early-stage ventures, cash flow and earnings from assets may be negative, and the concept of discounted value has little relevance. In many cases, the entrepreneur will simply abide by the investor's discount rate. The discount rate for a business angel is typically in the range of 30%–40% and a VC fund in the range of 25%–35%. For high-risk, development-stage ventures, the discount rate could be much higher, for example, 50%–70%. Many investors use a combination of different valuation methods, including the rule-of-thumb approach, which provides an approximate value on different verifiable characteristics of the venture, to be discussed on p. 134.

In summary, DCF valuation is not an effective method for early-stage ventures in the absence of earnings, cash flow, and business history. High risks in bringing a new value proposition to the market make estimations of future cash flows highly volatile.

"Comparables" Method

The market *comparables* approach evaluates the expected returns from a potential business by comparing certain value characteristics with other companies. Such characteristics include capital structure, rate of growth, size and timing of cash flows, and risk. VC firms will often examine comparables of existing types of companies using the four-digit standard industrial classification (SIC) code. VCs will also base valuations on comparable deals with which they are familiar.

With most new ventures, the SIC comparable approach is not likely to generate relevant comparable businesses. One difficulty with the comparables approach is gaining access to valuation numbers of privately held businesses in certain sectors. Another difficulty is ensuring that comparable firms are likely to follow similar business or product life cycles and that the market and geography within which they operate are similar. For example, in comparing a software firm, there may not be much existing historical data but there are likely a number of comparable firms. By contrast, a specialist medical device venture may have few comparable firms.

If the venture is more developed and has an extended sales record, one valuation approach is to apply an industry multiplier to gross sales or gross profit. However, one must be cautious in applying such estimation, as industry multipliers typically represent the industry average, making overvaluation or undervaluation of the business more likely. Choosing an appropriate industry multiplier is also important as there can be a large variance in multipliers (e.g., 1, 3, 5, 10, or more) because the valuation reflects business risk and industry standards. Some new sectors will not have industry multipliers available.

More advanced valuation techniques are required in biopharmaceuticals, for example, which have a long life cycle requiring higher initial investment and more funding rounds over a longer time horizon. On an average, drug development takes 12 years to reach the market, involving a highly uncertain approval process, for example, the U.S. Food and Drug Administration (FDA). Generating a risk-adjusted discount rate (by adding a premium to the cost of capital) is one way of incorporating such high risk into an investment decision.

The most frequently used comparables method is **price/earnings ratio** or P/E ratio, where an estimate of the P/E ratio of a similar company is applied to the estimated earnings of the venture. The P/E ratio measures how much the investors are willing to pay for each dollar of a company's earnings. One valuation approach involves multiplying earnings per share (EPS) by a multiple that reflects the growth rate (GR) of the earnings over a project time period. For example:

EPS = $1.   GR = 15% per year   time period = 4 years

Calculation of value per share = 1×1.15^4

Equity value (or market capitalization) = value per share × number of outstanding shares; for example, if 2 million shares are outstanding, then company value = $3.5 million.

This approach assumes that future values have been correctly assessed, and for early-stage companies, such an approach is highly speculative.

VC Method

The VC method of valuation is a variation of the DCF method described earlier, but works backward from the investor's required rate of return, rather than forward from the cash flow forecasts. The advantage of the VC method over DCF method is that valuation is not contingent on predicting highly uncertain future cash flows. It focuses on the investment going in today—in relation to the amount to be invested in the future.

The VC method requires that the investors estimate how much they plan to initially invest and forecasts a future exit value for the business over a planned investment horizon. Table 4.1 presents two examples to demonstrate the VC method. The examples use the same target return rate the investor is seeking (40%) and the same original invested amount ($750K) but change the forecasted exit value and exit time period.

Comparing the two examples in Table 4.1, one can observe the significant difference in the equity required by the investor to realize a 40% target rate at exit, based on the difference in forecasted exit value. The **premoney valuation**—which is what the investor is valuing the company today, prior to investment—is also affected by the forecasted exit value.

Table 4.1 VC valuation example

Investment characteristics	Example A	Example B
Target rate of return investor is seeking:	40%	40%
Initial investment amount:	$750K	$750K
Forecasted exit value for investment and expected time period:	$35 million in 5 years	$20 million in 7 years
Present value of exit value:	discounts of $35 million at 40% over 5 years: $35 million $\div 1.4^5 =$ $6.51 million	discounts of $20 million at 40% over 7 years: $20 million $\div 1.4^7 =$ $1.90 million
"Premoney" value of the venture:	$6.51 million − $750k = $5.76 million	$1.90 million − $750k = $1.15 million
Future value of $750k invested today:	invested at 40% per year over 5 years: $750k $\times 1.4^5 = $4.03 million	invested at 40% per year over 7 years: $750k $\times 1.4^7 = $7.90 million
How much equity does investor require at the time of exit to achieve 40% return?	$4.03 million $\div$ $35 million = <u>11.5%</u>	$7.90 $\div$ $20 million = <u>39.5%</u>

Capitalization tables are used to model ownership percentages for each round of financing. Each round of financing may be structured to allow the investor to purchase a number of shares that yield investment of a specific dollar amount, or alternatively, target a specific ownership percentage, as shown in Table 4.1.

Internal Rate of Return

VCs will usually estimate a future valuation based on a multiple of earnings over an expected investment period to exit and then work backward using an internal rate of return (IRR) that reflects the investment risk. IRR is the discount rate for the investment and equates the present value of the future cash flows with the initial investment. Calculation of IRR requires that the investor determine an ownership stake in the company post investment.

Early-stage ventures may attract a 50%–55% IRR, with more advanced and developed ventures attracting 20% to 40% depending on the predicted risk. However, even this valuation is highly speculative as more funding rounds may occur, with each setting a new valuation at the time of funding.

IRRs will be influenced by the timing of investment cash flows and the length of time an investment is held, so a fund with limited capital invested and returns from early exits or early valuations can generate attractive IRRs in the short term. The true or definitive calculation of IRR is only possible once there is a liquidity event and final valuation is confirmed, or in the case of a VC fund, when the fund is wound up.

Assets Based Valuation

Using this method, the value of the business is determined by the total value of the company's tangible assets. Two common approaches—not appropriate for early-stage valuation but mentioned here—are equity book value, which refers to the total assets of the business minus total liabilities, and liquidation value, which refers to the replacement value of assets in the business. Asset-based valuation is a common method for the sale of insolvent businesses, where assets are sold off in an attempt to pay back creditors.

The major disadvantage of assets-based valuation is that it neglects the value of a venture's earnings potential and growth opportunities from its assets. How to value a business—before additional financial resources are deployed (i.e., premoney)—also calls into question how the key assets of the business, including IP, are valued before they are fully deployed in the market (i.e., prerevenue).

Many new ventures have strong intangible assets in the form of domain knowledge and know-how capabilities, along with some undeveloped assets that may include pilot/prototype technologies and emerging customer contracts. These assets are difficult to value with assets-based approaches or with most other valuation methods. Although methods are available to value intangible assets, such methods are more appropriate for existing firms reliant on intangibles—and those seeking to understand the impact of intangibles on their financial statements.

While patented technologies can be valued based on the NPV of incremental cash flows anticipated from deployment of technology, this approach doesn't capture the value of underlying assets. Patents are based on "enabling know-how" that includes unpatented technology and IP that often reside in people associated with the business. The importance of this "tacit knowledge" for IP generation is often undervalued.

Rule of Thumb

The "**rule-of-thumb**" method is similar to the comparables method, but rather than comparing the venture to one or several "comparable businesses," the venture is compared to an overall market. Various rule of thumb approaches are used; some will be developed by portfolio investors based on their experiences—and may be relevant to specific sectors or particular development stages of a business.

The "Berkus method" suggested by U.S. BA David Berkus, provides a rule-of-thumb approach that recognizes particular early-stage developmental achievements and their incremental contribution to venture valuation.[18] This method, presented in Table 4.2, implies that early-stage valuation—where a product rollout or initial sales have been achieved—can be up to $2.5 million.

The Berkus method is likely to underestimate valuations on innovative ventures with potentially disruptive technologies, and not all investors will sequentially value a new venture in such a way. However, the method focuses entrepreneur and investor attention on the achievement of critical developmental stages of the early-stage venture and their collective contribution to a valuation figure. Once a venture generates sales and market transactions for any period of time, the rule-of-thumb method is no longer as applicable.

Table 4.2 Valuation by venture development stage

Stage of venture development	Add to valuation up to:
Sound idea (basic value, product risks)	$0.5 million
Prototype (reducing technology risk)	$0.5 million
Quality management team (reducing executive risk)	$0.5 million
Strategic relationships (reducing market and competitive risks)	$0.5 million
Product rollout or sales (reducing operations and financial risks)	$0.5 million

Market Effects on Valuation

In Chapter 2, we described how changing market conditions will affect supply and demand conditions in risk capital markets and how investment returns and levels of profitability will affect investor behavior. We now consider how market condition may affect valuation of a venture seeking risk capital.

During strong economic periods, more investors and capital are available, and new investment opportunities are being sought. As more capital and investors are drawn into the market, there is increased competition for deals, which raises deal prices (and in theory at least, favors the entrepreneur). During periods of "hot markets," evidenced by the dot-com boom (see Chapter 2, pp. 52–53), investors accept more risk, allowing lower-quality ventures to receive investment.

However, investments made during periods of high valuation appear to underperform and result in lower returns for shareholders.[19] One explanation is that investment deals are typically "overpriced" in strong markets but suffer lower exit values when the market invariably slows down.[20] Another explanation is that slow markets reduce opportunities for exits, tying up investor capital and reducing the flow of money for reinvestment in new ventures or to fund further investment rounds. Reduced competition for deals and lower capital flows put a downward pressure on valuations. Finally, heavy losses from the failure of lower-quality investments, as seen in boom and bust markets, will harden subsequent deal terms from investors and lower valuations.

Valuations are also noticeably affected by geography and related local supply and demand conditions. For example, the competition for investment in places such as Silicon Valley, Route 128 (Boston), or New York will be greater than in other places in the United States. Valuations in Europe, Asia, and elsewhere are also less. The effect of geography is borne out by VC data; for example, in 2012, when global VC investment declined by 20%, global median premoney valuations dropped by 20% in the United States, almost 40% in China, and nearly 50% in Europe.[21]

Market cycles will also favor certain types of companies or sectors that make them more attractive to investors and influence valuations. For example, high valuations of SaaS (software-as-a-service) companies is associated with their popularity as acquisition targets for large firms such as Google, Facebook, and Yahoo. SaaS companies also enjoy high revenue multiples (e.g., 3–4 times price-to-sales ratio) because of healthy margins and recurring revenue. Service markets appear to provide stronger and less risky growth prospects compared to other technology sectors, but this will eventually change with evolving market conditions and so will valuations.

The above discussion suggests that valuation methods, whether it be comparables, DCF modeling, or use of price-sensitive economic data for forecasting, will be time sensitive and reflect the nature of the market at that time. The entrepreneur should recognize that as the venture develops, the nature of the business, its geographical location, and regional and global market conditions will all have a bearing on valuation.

Summary

In this chapter, an emphasis has been placed on planning and preparation when attempting to raise BA investment. Among the high proportion of business plans rejected by BAs at initial screening are those that simply don't align with the particular investment criteria of the BA. Other business plans do not demonstrate a large market opportunity or present a strong management team, identified as key factors influencing investor decisions during initial screening.

Many entrepreneurs, particular those from technology-based backgrounds, emphasize the features of the technology or product in their business plans—as well as in their presentations to investors. Studies on investor decisions, along with ample anecdotal evidence, find that the product/service itself is not a key factor in investor decisions. It is *expected* that the product or service will work as described by the entrepreneur or that it has more features or benefits than competitors.

Investors want to hear how the entrepreneur will build value into the business, because it is the value of the business—specifically the value of the share of that business owned by the investor—that provides their return on investment. The business plan and any presentation to investors should emphasize that all the key elements of the business—value proposition, channels to customers, management team, financial model, and so forth, are aligned and positioned in an upward trajectory for building business value.

Investors should also be able to clearly see how their contribution—whether it be limited to investment or include specialized knowledge, mentorship, access to their networks, and so forth—will strengthen, accelerate, and improve the upward trajectory of value creation. As mentioned in the book introduction, entrepreneurs accepting BA investment should recognize that venture development may not be an end in itself but rather a means to an exit, usually through a trade sale. This should be part of the discussion in any negotiation between entrepreneur and investor.

Raising private equity investment is challenged by the fact that many entrepreneurs are busy building a business, finalizing the product or service, recruiting new team members, and so forth. Raising capital can also be frustrating and stressful, sometimes undertaken by the entrepreneur as personal funds are stretched, credit cards reach their limits, research grants or seed funding are coming to an end, and so forth.

However, taking the time to perform "due diligence" to find the right investor, securing a trusted third-party introduction, and crafting a compelling business plan and pitching presentation are more likely to increase the odds of passing through the initial deal-screening stage and having the chance to present to investors. Such preparation will also allow the entrepreneur to reflect more on the business and to understand what makes this a compelling opportunity for an investor. Subsequent feedback from investors will also be more valuable and focused on the nature of the business itself, rather than receiving tips on better preparation, and so forth.

Investor due diligence may be facilitated by advisors, solicitors, business support agencies, and others familiar with the local risk capital market. In some jurisdictions, there are specific agencies that facilitate introductions between entrepreneur and BAs. For example, LINC Scotland, which represents most of the BA groups and syndicates in Scotland, acts as a clearing house for information on investment opportunities and investors' requirements.[22]

The entrepreneur passing through the investment process to arrive with a term sheet in front of them deserves much credit. Here, it will be important to ensure that terms and conditions are clearly understood, and experienced, competent legal counsel is strongly encouraged. BA deal agreements will vary across jurisdictions; the requirement of share preferences, discussed in the next chapter, will need to be carefully considered.

In the absence of a ready market for new entrepreneurial ventures, most valuation methods are not applicable. A new venture's assets are often knowledge based, intangible, and highly specific to the venture, and have yet to be fully deployed into the market. Cash flows are difficult to estimate for a venture with a brief or nonexistent operating history and limited accounting and financial information. Estimating an appropriate discount rate is therefore highly uncertain.

Most BAs will use multiple methods to value an early-stage, prerevenue venture, such as rule of thumb. Entrepreneurs who can articulate the key value drivers of their business will be in a strong position to negotiate on valuation, which we discuss further in the next chapter.

CHAPTER 5

Deal Negotiation and the Deal Agreement

The golden rule is: "he who has the gold makes the rules".
—Keith David

Introduction

This chapter examines the deal agreement—identified as the final stage of the investment deal process, as presented earlier in Figure 4.1. Before the deal agreement is finalized, the entrepreneur and investor will usually enter into negotiation over the terms and conditions of the deal.

An investment deal agreement is structured to adhere to the investor's expected return on investment and to mitigate some of the different types of risk exposure common in private equity investing and also related to early-stage ventures. Different provisions in the deal agreement are also designed to reduce potential problems that could compromise preparations for an investment exit in the future.

We begin the chapter with a discussion on deal negotiation, followed by deal pricing and equity stakes. We then look in more detail at key provisions of a deal agreement; consider business angel (BA)—venture capital (VC) deals; and discuss the role of legal intermediation, which is particularly important for the nascent entrepreneur.

Deal Negotiation

Following on from the last chapter, the term sheet is typically reviewed again upon completion of formal due diligence, to ensure that risks have been adequately assessed. If the investor is satisfied, then final approval is given to proceed with the investment, and formal deal negotiation involving legal intermediation will commence and conclude with a signed deal agreement.

The length of time to negotiate an investment deal agreement is typically always longer than predicted or expected by the entrepreneur and may involve a number of negotiation sessions. Unrealistic expectations to close a deal quickly has been shown to negatively affect negotiations with BA investors and may result in less favorable deal terms for the entrepreneur.[1]

As mentioned earlier, investors hold the power in the deal-making process and will usually dictate the terms of the final agreement. The reason for this is straightforward; investors can and will walk away from a deal if the terms and conditions are not suitable to them. Nevertheless, most BA investors realize that deal terms must be fair enough to motivate and incentivize the entrepreneur and founders to work hard and build value in the business.

The lack of objective methods available for valuing an early-stage ventures doesn't offer the investor (or entrepreneur) a clear set of convincing arguments for arriving at a definitive valuation figure. There is also a "distributive" problem during negotiation, where higher valuation or higher equity means lower valuation and lower equity for the other party. Not surprisingly, this makes valuation a potentially contentious issue.

Nevertheless, valuation remains an important feature of deal negotiation, and the entrepreneur should be able to clearly articulate the venture's business model, revenue streams, and assets that highlight the overall value of the business and its future exit potential. Otherwise, investor terms and conditions could override the entrepreneur's perception of value of the venture.

Entrepreneurs are more likely to value their venture based on what they believe it will become. On the other hand, investors are more likely to value a venture at its current value—applying a risk premium or discount rate that will be similar to other early-stage or start-up capital transactions. The rule-of-thumb method discussed earlier is one such example. Entrepreneurs negotiating valuation with experienced early-stage investors are less likely to find room to negotiate on valuation.

If the entrepreneur decides to challenge the investor's valuation estimate, there should be compelling evidence as to why the valuation should be higher. The entrepreneur may be well served to get advice from those experienced in exit transactions, which will include solicitors experienced in working with BA and VC investors and those seeking private equity (PE) investment. Other professionals who understand the sector are likely to offer educated estimates of company value.

Attracting the interest of other investors can introduce competition for a deal and may lead to a higher valuation for the venture. However, risk capital investment communities are typically well networked, and attempting to play one investor off another is not a recommended strategy.

Most entrepreneurs would rather have a higher valuation to limit the equity of the investor if the venture proves very successful. However, entrepreneurs should also be cautious of high valuations. Although they appear attractive at the time of investment, they can place unrealistic expectations on the entrepreneur and venture to perform, for example, a higher valuation typically increases the expectation of high growth, which may potentially increase the risk of failure.

Experienced BA investors may push the initial valuation down to reduce the pressure on growth and make achievement of performance milestones more likely. The downside is that the entrepreneur will give up more equity at the lower valuation. As mentioned earlier, VC data suggests that investments made at high valuation are more likely to experience lower valuation at exit.[2]

Some BA investors will focus more on predicted forecasts and business-building activities proposed by the entrepreneur and stated in the business plan—rather than attempting to "guesstimate" valuations. Investors may seek a guaranteed, minimum return based on available information and projected forecasts. This method is used by experienced BA investors such as Nelson Gray (see Chapter 4, pp. 119–120), where the emphasis is more on building toward the valuation at exit.

Deal Pricing and Equity Stakes

A common question from entrepreneurs is what percentage of equity stake to offer in return for a particular amount of investment. Negotiation on equity stakes is dependent on the results of formal due diligence and valuation, as discussed earlier. It will also depend on whether or not the deal will be priced. A fair valuation and deal price may overcome issues over exact ownership of equity stakes on the part of the entrepreneur.

"Pricing" an investment deal commonly refers to placing a value on the business and establishing a share price and equity stake, depending on the level of investment being injected into the business. The **premoney value** refers to the value prior to the addition of investor capital, while **postmoney value** is calculated as premoney value plus the addition of investor capital. The premoney value and amount invested determine the investor's ownership percentage following the investment.

> **Example:** A venture receives a premoney valuation at $4 million and the agreed investment amount is $1 million, then the percentage ownership for the investor is calculated as:

$$Postmoney\ valuation = premoney\ valuation + amount\ invested$$
$$= \$4\ million + \$1\ million = \$5\ million$$

> Equity percentage owned by investor = amount invested ÷ agreed premoney valuation + amount invested = $1 million/($4 million + $1 million) = 20%

The **price per share** is calculated as the premoney value divided by the number of shares outstanding prior to the transaction. If there are 1.5 million shares outstanding prior to the investment, share price is calculated as:

$$Share\ Price = premoney\ valuation/premoney\ shares$$
$$= \$4\ million/1.5\ million = \$2.66$$

As shown in the preceding text, the share price is easier to calculate with premoney numbers, and percentage of equity ownership is easier to calculate with postmoney numbers. It is also worth noting that the share price is the same before and after the deal.

Experienced BA investors will be aware that pricing an investment deal too low will not motivate the entrepreneur/founders. Allowing entrepreneurs to retain sizable equity ownership will provide a more powerful incentive for them to build value in the business. BA deals can also differ from VC deals because there may be no fixed equity ownership percentage being sought as with VCs; the focus may instead be on the premoney valuation rather than the percentage of ownership (discussed earlier in the VC method, Chapter 4, p. 131).

If the entrepreneur and investor cannot agree on an initial valuation, they may resolve to leave valuation (i.e., the pricing) to the next round of investors, when the business has developed and more objective valuation methods can be applied. Not establishing a premoney valuation has advantages and disadvantages for both investor and entrepreneur and will influence the type of shares given to the investor, which we will discuss in the section on investment structure (p. 146).

Pricing will also be affected by current market conditions. In down markets, for example, more investment deals will tend to be priced, as investors seek to avoid fluctuations in valuation. In jurisdictions such as the United Kingdom, for BA investors to be eligible for tax relief, the share price needs to be determined at the outset. "Views from Practice" in the following text provides further insights on valuation, pricing, and negotiating deal terms for investors and entrepreneurs.

Views From Practice

Valuation, Pricing, Deal Terms, and Negotiating

Business angel Nelson Gray: "The formula for 'pre-revenue' or first round valuation does not include intellectual property, or skill of the management team, or the quality of business model. These things are part of the basic discount rate requirement and need to be good simply to be considered as an investment opportunity. Most BA investment propositions are unique and estimating the risk is a subjective process. Investors will depend more on the due diligence process."

Business angel and venture capitalist Paul Atkinson: "There are few real concrete facts to anchor the pricing decision. We do the financial projections and DCF analysis but they are not very accurate; being a confection of assumptions that can compound together to produce a wide range of possible outcomes. Pre-revenue valuation isn't particularly a value judgement by the investor. It comes down to believing in the management team and giving them enough incentives to do the work. Price is enough to get you going and enough to give the management team incentive to build the business."

Business angel Juliana Iarossi: "Practically speaking, any term can be negotiated…and there can be more than one way to structure a transaction to obtain similar results. The key is to understand the 'hot buttons' or the certain conditions, which if not met, would cause the other party to walk away. Rather than deal structure being dictated by the type of business, what I've seen is more dependent on where the company is developmentally and by angel, group or region. Certain deal terms are more common by investors in certain regions or from certain angel groups. When investors become comfortable with certain terms, they often use those same terms over and over."

Entrepreneur Martin Avison: "As an entrepreneur, you should 'negotiate hard' and try and speak to several investors or syndicates to establish where you can achieve greatest value (not just based on valuation). However, once the deal has been agreed, you need to work hard to build a relationship with your investor, as they are a crucial part of the team."

Deal Agreement

Investment deal agreements are typically drawn up to achieve the following objectives:

- ✓ Entrepreneur/team has appropriate incentives to maximize value of the business.
- ✓ The investor can become more involved in the management of the company if required.
- ✓ The investor is able to maintain control or exercise some level of control, including preserving the ability to liquidate their investment (more related to VCs).[3]

Figure 5.1 shows some common provisions that will be included in a deal agreement. This is not a definitive compilation or typical deal agreement

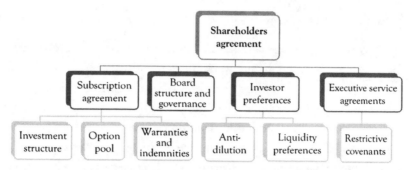

Figure 5.1 *Common provisions of an investment deal agreement*

structure but is presented in this way to highlight some of the more important deal terms and conditions. Some of them will have more or less relevance depending on the legal and regulatory jurisdiction. For example, given tax relief eligibility requirements, securities such as *preferred shares* and *convertible debt* are less common in UK BA deal agreements than in those in the United States. Other terms and conditions will be more relevant to BA investors than VCs and vice versa.

Shareholders' Agreement

The shareholders' agreement sets out the ongoing relationship between the venture and shareholders as agreed in the term sheet. Most investors will be under no illusions that different factors can cause poor performance or failure of a business. However, the legal details contained within the shareholders' agreement are meant to protect investors from unforeseen circumstances that negatively affect their investment and may arise from improper or unsupported decisions by the entrepreneur and management team. Investors will expect that the entrepreneur and team are trustworthy, acting in good faith, and regularly communicating how the business is doing.

The entrepreneur should be clear on what is required to change the shareholders' agreement and the share capital structure in the future. This includes understanding any preemptive rights or preferences demanded by investors or any consent rights over future financing rounds. We now discuss the different provisions shown in Figure 5.1.

Subscription Agreement

A subscription agreement sets out the number and price of shares, funding tranches, option pools, and warranties and indemnities that establish share rights and the conditions precedent to funding. Subscription agreements may also cover future share subscriptions by the investor, founders, and other shareholders and mechanisms to reallocate shares, for example, in the event of over- or underperformance by the venture. We begin with a discussion of the investment structure that describes the types of securities or shares that will be offered.

Investment Structure

BA and VC investors may invest in one of three types of securities as stipulated in the term sheet and summarized in the following text (i.e. common shares, preferred shares, convertible debt). A fourth type, "participating preferred" is less common but included in the discussion for comparison purposes.

Common Shares

Common or ordinary shares are residual value shares of the same class issued to the entrepreneur/founders. Residual value refers to the fact that common shareholders have claim to what remains after other preferred shareholders are paid. Common shares are the basic unit of ownership of a company and allow shareholders to vote on directors and other company events. Common shareholders can also receive dividends.

For the entrepreneur, an investment deal comprising only common stock—rather than preferred stock—produces a simpler capital structure with only one class of stock outstanding. In countries such as the United Kingdom, tax relief is afforded only to investments in common shares, thus making common shares the predominant share security amongst UK BA investors. This is a potential disadvantage for BAs in coinvesting with VCs and will be discussed further in Chapter 6.

Preferred Shares

Preferred stock represents an ownership share in the investee company, similar to common stock, but has a number of particular benefits. Preferred shares pay a consistent, fixed dividend that does not fluctuate and is paid before any dividends to common shareholders are paid. Preferred shareholders have a greater claim on the venture's assets compared to common shareholders in the event of a forced liquidation or bankruptcy.

Preferred shares also contain an antidilution provision meant to protect the preferred shareholder when more shares are issued—such as when raising further funds. The antidilution provision is triggered if the company issues shares below the conversion price, which discourages the company from reducing the share price in future funding rounds. This provides the investor with "downside protection." We discuss the concept of share dilution and antidilution provisions further on p. 157.

One of the drawbacks of investing in preferred stock—for the investor— is lack of voting rights compared to common stock. Preferred shareholders usually do not have a voice in the management of the company; therefore the control of ordinary shareholders (i.e., entrepreneur and founders) remains secure. However, some preferred stock may have blocking rights, which may allow shareholders holding this security to stop a sale of the company, block a board appointment, and so forth. Another drawback is the higher cost per share and limited growth of the dividend.

Preferred shares in essence function primarily as a fixed-income security, whereas common stock can be seen as a form of security for longer-term growth that may not deliver the security of a regular income stream. However, preferred stockholders may miss out on potential gains when common stock appreciates significantly.

Most VCs are unwilling or unable to structure investment agreements without a preferred return. Many experienced BAs in the United States will also demand preferred shares. Importantly, if the entrepreneur offers preferred shares initially, then any future investor will very likely also require preferred shares. If the venture goes through a number of funding rounds, the entrepreneur and founding team may own very little of the business.

Participating Preferred Shares

In comparison to preferred shareholders already described, participating preferred shareholders will be repaid their original investment plus any unpaid dividends upon liquidation, and then share in the remaining assets as if they held common shares. Thus, the participating preferred stockholders receive back their original investment and then receive their share in the remaining proceeds based on ownership percentage (see "Clarifying Concepts" in the following text).

Clarifying Concepts

Participating Preferred Shares

As an example, the entrepreneur raises $4 million of venture capital (VC) investment at a $4 million "premoney" valuation, with equity percentage split 50%—50% post investment. The venture realizes a liquidity event a few years later and is acquired for $20 million. The VC holding *participating preferred* (PP) stock will receive $4 million of participation plus $8 million of common stock [e.g., ($20 million exit + $4 million participation) × 50% = $12 million]. The entrepreneur will receive 50% of the exit price *after* participation is taken out [e.g., 50% × ($20 million − $4 million) = $8 million]. By comparison, if the VC held "convertible preferred stock," the VC and the entrepreneur would each receive 50% of the exit proceeds or $10 million each.

However, if the exit value is lower, for example, $15 million, then the entrepreneur's share of exit proceeds will decrease on a percentage basis [e.g., ($15 million − $4 million) × 50% = $5.5 million] and the investor with PP would receive $9.5 million. The PP provision provides a substantial upside for the investor in the event of a low exit price (essentially at the expense of common shareholders) but once the return-on-investment increases, the PP effect diminishes.

Convertible Debt

Convertible debt refers to financing made initially by debt that will later convert to equity, usually as preferred shares, when the investee company raises its next round of funding. At that time, the debt note "converts" to equity shares at a valuation/price determined by the next investor(s). The conversion of the debt note to equity includes a percentage discount on the subsequent valuation that is negotiated with the entrepreneur (discount typically ranges from 10% to 30%).

Example: An investor agrees to invest $100k and negotiates with the entrepreneur that the risk justifies a 20% discount. On the next round of financing, the next investor values the venture at $1 per share. The $1 per share would be discounted by 20% to $0.80, which results in the $100k converting to 125k shares ($100k/$0.80), providing a 25% return on investment. If the next investor contributes $100k (at $1 per share), he/she would receive 100k shares.

There is an increasing trend by BA groups and syndicates in the United States to use convertible debt, although the overall percentage of BA investment deals structured as convertible debt remains low (e.g., below 15%),[4] In the United Kingdom, convertible debt does not qualify for Enterprise Investment Scheme (EIS) tax relief; therefore, it is not a prominent financing option of UK BA investors. "Clarifying Concepts" in the following text considers implications of convertible debt for the new venture.

Clarifying Concepts

Convertible Debt: Implications for the New Venture

Convertible debt offers some advantages as well as disadvantages for the investee company. One advantage is that the financing does not initially dilute equity, allowing the entrepreneur to retain equity ownership, with the financing carried on the balance sheet as debt. Another advantage is that establishing a premoney valuation is not required until a future financing round. Not "pricing" the new venture allows for a more objective valuation in the future, when the venture is a going concern and offers sales, cash flow, and market-based transactional information.

Convertible debt also allows subsequent investors to avoid investing in a "**down round**" arising from an initial early-stage valuation (i.e. when the premoney valuation drops from one round to the next, for example, if the venture is not meeting performance milestones, the later round is called a "down round.") New investors are likely to prefer to maintain the right to set the initial price and allow the early-stage shareholders to convert to that price with their discount, so long as the discount is considered reasonable and proportionate to the risk taken. However, a higher valuation, while favoring the entrepreneur, can significantly erode the conversion value for the original investor.

For the investor, a properly structured convertible debt note offers the downside protection of debt and upside protection of equity. As with any debt instrument, the investor will receive interest—and the principal can be demanded after a negotiated period. Should the venture perform poorly, the investor is unlikely to convert debt to equity and would instead receive interest over the period and the principal. The equity conversion allows the investor to take advantage of higher returns arising from the conversion, as well as receiving preferred shareholdings, which have priority over founder shares.

In the absence of a price, no voting shares or board seats are given—relieving the investor of management or shareholder-related decisions compared to equity shareholding. Convertible debt also allows an investor to close an investment deal quickly with an entrepreneur as this form of financing typically takes less time and requires less legal fees, documentation, and negotiation.

Larger BA funds in the United States, described as "**super angel funds**," appear to be active users of convertible debt, which allows them to invest across a large number of early-stage ventures with smaller amounts of capital—leveraging the portfolio model. The absence of a required price reduces the need for valuation, extensive due diligence, and negotiation, and the presence of a large fund allows investors to provide more significant financing to those ventures who emerge as the most promising. We discuss super angel funds further in Chapter 7.

The key disadvantage of convertible debt for the original investor (often the BA) is when a high valuation is established by subsequent investors, which may follow from outstanding success of the venture. Although the original investor's funding may have contributed to such success, the investor's discount is now applied to the much higher valuation. This means that the original investor will pay for his/her shares based on a much higher valuation.

Thus, original investors may seek **convertible debt** "with a cap," which establishes a maximum (i.e., premoney) value on which the debt will convert to equity. This protects the original investors against the venture's value increasing too much before the next round. The cap thus protects against dilution as the conversion is based on the overall value of the premoney capital at the subsequent round.

If the investor negotiates a price cap on the debt note that reflects their valuation of the company, this has essentially "priced" the investment. In other words, convertible debt with cap appears similar to a priced round although the cap is not a price as the subsequent round of investment could still come in *below* the cap. If the venture has underperformed and subsequent valuation will be lower than the cap, the entrepreneur would have been better off with a priced equity round.

While it can be argued that a cap attempts to reflect a reasonable estimation of venture value, any investee venture achieving or exceeding performance milestones agreed by original investors would be expected to increase its value since the debt note was agreed. The entrepreneur would be well justified to argue for a higher valuation. In this regard, the valuation cap appears to penalize the entrepreneur for achieving outstanding success, which subsequent investors recognize by setting a significantly higher valuation.

Convertible debt, by its very nature, creates an apparent misalignment in the interests of the entrepreneur versus original investors. A higher valuation favors the entrepreneur, who retains more equity or is able to raise more capital from subsequent investors or both. A lower valuation favors original investors, who will own a greater equity stake at conversion, suggesting that the investors could be less motivated to support or engage in activities that could increase valuation prior to subsequent funding.

The price cap is a trade-off provision in one sense. The investor is assured of a minimum equity stake, no matter how much the valuation exceeds the cap. A valuation that is much higher than the cap indicates that the original investment value has multiplied by funding the entrepreneur. The trade-off is that if the cap is much lower than the valuation—and there are sizable debt notes held by original investors—the investment may be less appealing to new investors—as the next investment round they lead will see original investors converting to preferred shares without contributing new funds.

Option Pools

Investors usually expect that the entrepreneur will reserve a pool of shares for future use to attract high-value appointments to the management team. The entrepreneur should attempt to exclude the reserve pool from valuation as it can affect price per share and the investment value. The entrepreneur may have, or should have, already issued *founder shares* prior to raising equity.

One of the challenges with option pools is determining how much equity to offer to recruit key people. Due diligence on the background, skills, and reputation of a potential new hire is critically important as it may be more difficult to correct a "recruitment error" when the individual becomes a shareholder in the business.

Effective use of the option pool may have a positive effect on business valuation. For example, enticing an experienced, well-respected entrepreneur onto the Board with a small equity stake, who has taken previous ventures to exit, could raise the value of shares.

Funding Tranches

Once the deal agreement documents are finalized and signed, the BA investor will usually issue the first "tranche" payment to the investee venture. Staged payments will be made in the future under the agreement terms but are typically subject to achieving pre-agreed performance milestones. Tranche financing is described further in "Clarifying Concepts" in the following text.

Clarifying Concepts

Tranche Financing

Tranche is a French word that means "slice" or "portion" and is used to describe an investment that is split up into smaller pieces. Many BA syndicates will invest in tranches—which involves agreeing on a designated amount of financing in the deal terms but releasing only a portion of the total amount initially. Additional portions are made available—contingent on the venture achieving certain milestones or preagreed obligations. The tranche requirement, agreed between entrepreneur and investor during deal negotiation, is an incentive for the entrepreneur/team to accomplish pre-agreed business objectives. Tranche financing protects the investor from committing further financing if the business performs poorly or no long appears viable.

The entrepreneur may prefer to structure an investment in rounds rather than in tranches. One reason is that with each round, the probability of venture success goes up, reducing investment risk (and lowering the discount rate). Assuming that venture progress is significant and can be validated, the entrepreneur will push for a higher premoney valuation for the venture in subsequent rounds. Investors in early rounds will attempt to invest in subsequent rounds to maintain similar ownership percentages in a company over time to avoid dilution of their equity ownership.

Unlike tranches, each round is priced independently and involves a new term sheet that will specify characteristics of that investment. Follow-on rounds from BAs are typically larger than a previous funding round (as are the VC series rounds; see p. 154). In representing a greater proportional share of company ownership, the larger round has greater influence. It is critical that the size of each financing round enable the venture to achieve significant milestones to justify selling the next round at a heightened valuation. This is referred to as an "**up round**."

An experienced BA will often identify that a venture will require more than one funding round when examining the venture's original business plan and financial forecasts—and based on their previous experiences. Inexperienced entrepreneurs and investors may assume that the venture only requires a single investment, with the investor committing all his/ her available funds on the initial investment. If investors cannot follow their money, then they are at risk of being diluted (see p. 157 for further discussion on dilution).

When the premoney valuation drops from one round to the next (e.g., if the venture is performing poorly), the later round will be a down round as described earlier. A large drop in premoney value lowers the price per share and makes any large investment by new investors seriously dilutive to existing investors by lowering their ownership percentages. One way to avoid this dilution is for the *existing* investors to contribute *all* the cash needed in a down round.

VC financing is typically offered in "series" rounds, with each round reflecting particular objectives and developmental milestones upon which subsequent rounds are based, as described in Table 5.1. Some VCs will have specialist seed funds, but most VC will enter on a Series "A" round.

We provide a brief summary of VC rounds as shown in Table 5.1. The "seed" round should validate the product, position it into a market, and strengthen the management team. Series "A" should establish the business model and verify a fit between the value proposition and market segment. With the initial market growing in demand for the product/service, the venture should be scaling distribution.

Table 5.1 Summary of VC investment rounds

Round	Description
Seed Round	Provides capital for proof-of-concept (POC), R&D, and prototype development, testing, management team salaries, and so forth. Valuation is based on novelty of the value proposition, strength of intellectual property (IP), and market application. Objectives include developing a strong team, business validation of concept, reduction of technical risks, and preparation for next round of financing.
Series "A" Round	The venture's first institutional financing. Valuation is based on progress made with seed capital, quality of management team, and expansion of sales. Series A investors may take sizable ownership stake of 40%–50%. Objectives are to scale distribution, initiate business development efforts, and attract investor interest in the next financing at an increased valuation.
Series "B" Round	Usually a larger financing round than Series A. Focus is on scaling the business significantly. If it is a web-based business, users are being "monetized." Valuation is based on IP, know-how, and intellectual assets, milestones achieved, comparable company valuations, and use of revenue forecasts. Objectives for this round include operational development, building scale, further product development, revenue traction, and value creation for next round.
Series "C" Round	Later-stage financing designed to provide operating capital to further scale the business, achieve profitability, develop additional products/services, or prepare for liquidation event (e.g. acquisition or IPO). Venture will have predictable revenue and valid company comparables from which valuation can be discounted.

Series "B" will finance scaling the business into additional markets. The business model is validated, new hires include sales people, and new partners (e.g., channel) are secured. Operational efficiencies are preparing venture for rapid expansion. Series "C" is funding used to accelerate growth and expand into international markets, which may include funding growth through acquisitions.

Warranties and Indemnities

Warranties and indemnities are provisions within an investment agreement that seek to transfer the risk of error and concealment (i.e., information asymmetries) to the entrepreneur and management team. Warranties are written statements, which confirm certain key information about the business, while an indemnity is a commitment to reimburse the investor, depending on the circumstances as stated in the agreement.

The entrepreneur as investee will take on personal liability for the accuracy of the warranted information. Common warranties and indemnities include the following:

- ✓ Venture is not involved in litigation.
- ✓ There are no undisclosed contractual arrangements or agreements.
- ✓ Venture owns all its assets and IP.
- ✓ Financial statements, documents, and accounts are accurate.
- ✓ There are no existing conflicting interests.
- ✓ The position of the venture has not changed since last disclosure.

Claims on warranties are usually limited to a particular time period (e.g., within 2 years) of the investment deal, and the amount of claims is usually limited or capped at the amount invested.

Board Structure and Governance

BA investors will usually require some formal representation on an investee's board of directors. Appointed directors can provide entrepreneurs with invaluable experience and business advice and access to their various business networks. With the introduction of an investor as a nonexecutive director to the Board, the entrepreneur and management team will face more accountability for their actions and decisions.

However, when Board seats are allocated to BA investors, the entrepreneur/founders usually retain control of the Board, indicating that Board control is not the primary control mechanism utilized by BAs.[5] We discuss the role of the Board in the postinvestment management of investees in Chapter 6.

In the United States, some BA investors have been known not to take positions on a Board because of potential liability concerns. BAs and VCs may seek "**observation rights**" as part of an investment deal, whereby the investor has the right to observe the business and gain access to all information about the business, without taking an active role in the business. Similarly, "**information rights**" might be requested, which entitles investors to know how the company is performing, and they can request financials, business plans, product, sales, or operational plans, and so forth. These may be requested more frequently than for board meetings, for example, monthly rather than quarterly.

A VC deal will typically stipulate that the investor has the ability to change nonexecutive directors when required. Certain preferences in the shareholder agreement may also specify that a number of activities can only be undertaken with the approval of these preferred shareholders. This can include changes in senior management, remuneration, issuing new shares, obtaining bank financing, declaration of a dividend, and approval of capital expenditure.

VCs may also appoint an industry or domain specialist who understands the market and can monitor and advise on the venture's growth into the market. As the venture approaches an exit option, the VC may replace the industry specialist with a specialist on exits and selling businesses.[6] We discuss the role of governance and "postinvestment" management of the investee venture further in Chapter 6.

Investor Preferences

Different investor preferences are to be found in deal agreements, particularly with U.S. BAs and with VCs. Two more common investor preferences are considered in the following text: antidilution preferences and liquidation preferences.

Antidilution

We mentioned earlier that preferred shareholders benefit from antidilution protection. What this means is that preferred shareholders receive a level of compensation if the investee venture issues stock at a lower price than what the shareholder paid. This compensation gives the right to acquire additional shares so that the average cost of the original investment round is brought down to the share price of the subsequent investment round. Antidilution preferences are not used with common stock, but VCs and many experienced BAs in the United States will demand preferred stock and antidilution provisions. "Clarifying Concepts" in the following text discusses dilution.

Clarifying Concepts

Dilution of Share Value

Dilution is a reduction in a shareholder's relative ownership percentage of a company as a result of the venture issuing more shares. For example, new funding is raised, with the new investor receiving a 10% equity stake in the company. The entrepreneur's 40% of equity is now reduced to 36% (i.e., 90% of 40%). Original shareholders do not give up shares with the arrival of new investors. Rather, more shares are issued, which dilutes the value of existing shares. If there are 100 shares and the new investor receives 10% equity, the venture would have to issue 11 new shares ($11/111 \times 100 = 10\%$).

As mentioned in our discussion of convertible debt, original investors don't want valuations too high in an initial equity round (e.g., priced round) because of the threat of dilution in subsequent rounds. In theory, each time dilution occurs, the venture should be increasing its economic value. However, dilution may occur when a venture is not achieving expected performance milestones and requires more capital to reach these milestones.

If a venture requires more capital, existing shareholders, including founders, are invited to participate in a subsequent funding round but may not have the funds to invest. These investors are subject to being "**crammed down**" and diluted if the subsequent purchase of stock is at a valuation that is close to or less than the initial purchase price— resulting in a reduction in their percentage interests in the venture. The best protection for an investor against a down round is to have adequate funding to follow their investment and avoid the need for new outside investors.

Entrepreneurs seeking smaller amounts of BA investment are more likely to have their total investment requirement covered by the same BA investor; therefore, dilution is less likely. There is evidence to suggest that deals where the BA investor makes follow-on investments generate lower returns; one study found that in ventures where follow-on investments were made, nearly 70% of the exits occurred at a loss.* While it remains unclear what factors contribute to these results, this may suggest that follow-on funding is feeding underperforming ventures.

Source: Wiltbank and Boeker, 2007.

While antidilution provisions guarantee that these investors receive compensation in the event of a down round, they are often accompanied by a key provision termed "**pay to play**" which requires that they participate in the follow-on round. If the investor is not willing to "play," antidilution protection may not be claimed.

The antidilution provision usually takes the form of a **weighted average ratchet**, in which the conversion price of the convertible shares (to common shares) is a function of the number of shares issued and the conversion price of the new issue. The conversion price of the protected financing round is reduced so as to effectively equate the price of the protected issue to that of the new issue.[7] For example, if $100K is invested in preferred shares and the conversion price is $2/share, then the preferred would convert into 50,000 common shares.

In some cases, investors may bind antidilution provisions to venture performance milestones that results in a conversion price adjustment in the event that the venture does not meet certain milestones, for example, product development, revenues, or other business milestones. In this case, the antidilution provisions are triggered automatically if milestones are not met. This would create a large incentive for the entrepreneur and founders to accomplish their investor-influenced milestones.

The existence of antidilution provisions may also incentivize the entrepreneur to issue new rounds of stock at higher valuations because of the implications of antidilution protection to the common shareholders. In some cases, the entrepreneur could decide to pass on taking additional investment at a lower valuation (assuming that the venture has other alternatives to the financing).

While an early-round investor may seek to include an antidilution provision into an investment agreement, it may be the case that the entrepreneur who runs the business efficiently and is achieving pre-agreed milestones will be in a stronger position to control the ability to issue shares without agreeing to protect preferred investors.

Liquidation (or Exit) Preference

Liquidation preference will state how the proceeds from a liquidation event, for example, trade sale, initial public offering (IPO), or dissolution of the company will be distributed. Liquidation preferences will be required with VC deals and some BA deals. In liquidation events, investors will be entitled to their investment and a minimum return ahead of founders. Some liquidation preferences will be also higher than others, such as in an early round of investment where there is not an extremely high price relative to normal valuations.

VCs will often set a liquidation preference (e.g., 1X, 2X, or 3X) meaning that when the venture is liquidated, the VC will get for example, one, two, or three dollars for every dollar invested in preferred stock (plus any dividends owed). After proceeds from liquidation are distributed to preferred shareholders—in accordance with respective liquidity preferences—the remaining proceeds are distributed to common shareholders. A liquidation preference can have a significant effect on returns, even on a relatively small exit, as suggested in the following text.

Example: A BA group invests $1 million for 25% of a venture without a liquidation preference. The venture is sold for $2 million. The BA group would receive $500K (losing 50% of their original investment), and the entrepreneur/common shareholders would receive $1.5 million. If the BA group negotiates a 1X preference in this deal, they would receive $1 million, with the entrepreneur/common shareholders receiving the remaining $1 million. However, if the BA group negotiates a 1X "participating preference" (see p. 148), they would receive $1 million, plus another $250K (25% of the remaining $1 million of common shares). The entrepreneur/common shareholders would receive $750K.

Other preferences are commonly seen in both VC and BA deals. **Drag-along provisions** grant investors the right to compel the founders and other shareholders to vote in favor of the sale, merger, or other "deemed liquidation" of the venture. Typically, drag-along provisions require a majority of preferred shareholders (i.e., 51%) to trigger the provision. From the controlling shareholder's point of view, it allows them to proceed with the sale of the company with as few obstacles as possible.

Some investors will see this provision as an important protection as it allows them to exit their investment and sell the company for a price less than the amount of their liquidation preference. **Tag-along provisions** provide other shareholders with the ability to sell their shares at the same price as the selling shareholders.

The entrepreneur may request a higher threshold of percentage or attempt to require preferred shareholders to convert to common stock to create a majority, which would lower the liquidation preference. The entrepreneur should be aware of the possibility of investors having the unilateral right and power to force through a sale without the entrepreneur or founding team's approval. This is much more likely with VC deals.

Executive Service Agreements

Executive service agreements attempt to bind "key" people to the venture for a period of time and will set out founding team and employees' remuneration and terms of service. It may be the case that some entrepreneurs and management team members accept a deal from an investor whereby the executive salaries are much lower than what they could earn in the private market.

This may become an issue if the deal terms have been unfair, and the founding team has given up a large equity stake in the process. While founders will be expected to accept lower short- and medium-term compensation in anticipation of a sizable return in the longer term, this requires that they hold a reasonable percentage of equity, particularly at lower valuations. Upon subsequent funding rounds, when valuations have risen significantly, it will be expected that original shareholders will have been diluted to a smaller equity stake ... but for a much higher-valued business.

Restrictive Covenants

Restrictive covenants may be included in a deal agreement where the value of the business is based on its intellectual capital (IP) and key individuals. It is designed to provide a contract of employment that retains key IP and people through to a liquidity event, where their loss could seriously jeopardize exit options or negotiations leading up to an exit. Restrictive covenants also reduce the risk of key people attempting to renegotiate contracts of employment when the business is doing well or threatening to leave if the business is doing poorly.

IP deeds are often associated with executive service agreements and restrictive covenants that protect the business from losing key people. IP deeds typically establish that other parties have no rights to any IP, which they develop and which will be assigned to the venture. This provision is particularly important for knowledge-based ventures that rely on intellectual assets and IP as the basis of their competitive advantage.

BA and VC Deal Agreements

Although BAs and VCs share some standard provisions within a deal agreement, VC deals are typically more complex, given the legal liability placed on general partners (GPs) and their fiduciary duty to safeguard the financial assets of their limited partners (LPs). GPs are thus subject to greater liability and potential criticism regarding investments, which influences how deal terms and conditions are drawn up.

Additional provisions in a VC deal agreement and some BA deals may include:

- ✓ **Right of first refusal:** This provision gives other shareholders the right to buy any securities offered for sale by the entrepreneur/founders before being sold to third parties.
- ✓ **Put options:** This establishes that the business will purchase preferred shares back from preferred shareholders at the original purchase price; that may also include interest and accrued and due dividends.
- ✓ *Unlocking provision:* The VC finds an offer for the business acceptable but common shareholders do not. These shareholders must buy out the VC.
- ✓ **Put provision:** This provides the VC with the right to sell the business to the "highest bidder" if an investment exit is not achieved by a pre-agreed date.
- ✓ *Registration and public offering provision:* Similar to the above, except the right to sell the business occurs if an IPO sale has not been achieved after a pre-agreed date.
- ✓ *Voting trust:* Entrepreneur/founders must release certain shares for underperformance, and the VC has the right to take control.

Even when the VC is a minority investor, the investment agreement may provide the VC with the power to intervene to ensure they are able to control progress toward the liquidation event, that is, trade sale or IPO. This may include placing restrictions on actions of the entrepreneur and giving themselves the right to intervene if performance targets are missed. They may release the entrepreneur/founder for poor performance or replace members of the management team. Drawing up these agreements typically requires substantial legal intermediation and costs.

Legal Intermediation

The investment deal process can appear intimidating to an entrepreneur with limited commercial experience although most terms and conditions to be negotiated will be elements of a standard legal investment agreement. Nevertheless, entrepreneurs entering negotiations with investors for the first time require competent legal counsel to assist in understanding what they are "signing up for"—particularly in a deal with an experienced BA investor or VC. Many entrepreneurs underestimate the amount of time it takes to complete an investment deal. Costs are also commonly underestimated; legal fees may range from 5% to 15% of the investment being raised.

Legal intermediation typically involves two sets of lawyers/solicitors who represent the interests of the investor and investee business, respectively. Legal intermediation is inherently biased toward reducing the exposure of risk to the investor. BA investors will enter deal negotiations with an expected outcome because they set the terms and conditions of a deal agreement in almost all cases. They usually act on their own behalf during deal negotiation—even when they have their own legal counsel.[8]

However, entrepreneurs should seek to negotiate an investment deal on their terms as much as possible. This requires adequate preparation and planning. For example, the entrepreneur will be in a stronger negotiating position if key risks and uncertainties have been considered and worked through in business planning (for example, see Figure 3.3, p. 82). Promising prototype results, early signals of market acceptance, and strong initial sales will suggest the potential of the business, but entrepreneurs who display a deep understanding of value drivers—and who present a value-building plan directed toward credible exit options—are likely to strengthen their position with investors.

Entrepreneurs also require *competent* legal counsel. The entrepreneur should undertake due diligence and investigate which legal firms have a track record of successfully advising entrepreneurs seeking BA investment. The entrepreneur should not assume that regular, full-service legal firms or professional services providers have the expertise to properly negotiate and conclude a private equity investment deal. There is ample anecdotal evidence among experienced entrepreneurs, investors, and others verifying the pitfalls of inappropriate or incompetent advice—when interpreting provisions and conditions of a term sheet or negotiating on behalf of an inexperienced venture team seeking investment.

One suggestion is for the entrepreneur to establish a relationship early with a legal firm who is experienced in working with local early-stage companies and risk capital investors. Some of these legal firms will offer reasonable fee rates (or defer fees over a certain period) for promising new ventures, particularly those with the potential to become a future client of the legal firm.

In some cases, legal advisors may provide general advice in the first few meetings that does not incur legal fees, but entrepreneurs are advised to clarify when fees will be applied and how much. "Views from Practice" in the following text presents a solicitor's perspective on preparing the entrepreneur for investment.

Views From Practice

Legal Intermediation of BA Deals

MBM Commercial LLP is a leading UK-based legal firm that works exclusively with early-stage, high-growth technology companies and business angel (BA) investors. Senior Partner Sandy Finlayson was interviewed on his thoughts about BA deals, as presented below.

What is your general advice to entrepreneurs engaging with BA investors? "Entrepreneurs need to think carefully about their business model, but ultimately they must be able to show that they know how to make a profit. Time and time again, there is the issue of the entrepreneur needing to understand that investors require a return on their investment and need to think about options for a liquidity event. Investors want to see a 'need to have' product and to hear all about the potential for profit, not about the finer points of the technology. The technology is usually not the problem. Another key issue is putting together real strong management teams. Of all the deals that I have been involved in, there isn't one case where the scientific founder has led the company to exit."

How do you manage differences over valuation? "Valuation is always an issue and we need to arrive at a solution for both parties. Valuation is much more of an emotive issue than it needs to be. For negotiation, the key is to allow the entrepreneur to understand that they are not giving away equity—what they are doing is selling shares for value—as a result of which they are increasing the size of their balance sheets which may also give them the ability to borrow cash from clearing banks.

Anyone who borrows money from a bank must give that bank security, and if they fail to deliver on their banking covenants, they basically give away that business to the bank. With equity, you are allowing investors to share in a bigger business. Share options provide an incentive for entrepreneurs to deliver value for all owners of the business, but if they don't deliver value, then it doesn't matter, because everyone has lost their money anyways. Entrepreneurs must give the investor a reason to invest and not a reason to walk away. Entrepreneurs also need to choose their investors very, very carefully."

In preparation for investment, the legal firm will typically review the business documents, which authorize the venture to trade and do business, to ensure that it meets the requirements of the investor. This review would normally extend to the shareholder agreement, share option schemes, and other contractual provisions.

The subscription agreement would normally be prepared by the BA investor's solicitors and can be a complex legal document; depending on the types of shares, preferences, particulars of the investee business, tranching and level of investment, and so forth. The entrepreneur's legal firm will review the document, explain the terms and conditions, and work with the investor's legal representative to finalize the agreement.

The entrepreneur/team should be prepared to disclose to the legal team any issues that may affect the decision of the investor and to identify any potential risks in the investee business. The entrepreneur/team would typically be expected to provide warranties and indemnities to the investor. The legal firm can prepare these disclosures and would be expected to advise the entrepreneur on how to deal with these during deal negation. The legal team would also review employment contracts that include executive service agreements, restrictive covenants, "noncompete" clauses, and so forth.

Academic Entrepreneurs and Legal Intermediation

Legal intermediation can be particularly important for academic entre-preneurs seeking risk capital for their university spinouts (USOs); defined as new firms created to commercially exploit knowledge, technology, or research results developed within a university.[9] While some BAs, as early-stage investors, actively seek out and invest in university technologies, there are additional associated risks for investors, which we discussed earlier in Chapter 2 (p. 14).

One of the common risks associated with investing in USOs relates to IP, which is often the core competitive asset of the USO. There are typically three scenarios for IP that can have a bearing on the attrac-tion of the USO as an investment opportunity, which we discuss in the following text:

1. "Assigned" IP means that the university gives up ownership of the IP and it becomes the property of the USO. In theory, the USO is in a better position to attract private equity investment.
2. "Licensed" IP means that the university retains ownership of the IP but grants a right to the USO to use it for certain purposes. Ideally, the license will be exclusive (i.e., only the company can use the IP) and subject to no other restrictions, but this is less common in many jurisdictions. Depending upon the technology in question, the uni-versity may wish to restrict the license by field of use or geographical territory.
3. "Delayed assignation" means that the university will grant a license to the USO with the option for assigning the IP at a later date if and when the USO achieves certain milestones or a certain valuation. This allows the USO and investors to secure future ownership of the IP but also allows the university to reclaim and reuse the IP if the USO fails or is unable to exploit the IP.

Following on from the preceding text, a related factor impacting the value of the IP is the scope and breadth of the IP covered by the license or assig-nation. The IP should have wide-enough claims to allow for its commer-cial application in the market. If the transferred IP is not sufficiently wide enough, then the USO may need to approach the university at a later date to obtain another license—which will be subject to separate commercial terms. The licensing agreement, which sets out the royalties and other payments the USO will be obliged to pay to the university, will also have to be assessed in the context of the projected future value of the IP.

This leads us into another potential risk of investing in a USO. The IP valuation technique typically used by universities (using UK data) is based upon the historical research costs behind the IP.[10] This is a "backward calculation" that accounts for the investment in research costs that is then used to attribute IP value at start-up. Such an approach does not factor in market value or attempt to predict its future value in use. Thus, if research costs have been significant, there may be a premium placed on the value of the IP without any estimation of future costs in making the IP commercially viable. Different university systems may have different valuation techniques.

The historical research cost approach to valuation has a number of implications for academic entrepreneurs and risk capital investors. Investors may be faced with substantial proof-of-concept or "business validation" costs in addition to retaining the university as an equity partner and/or paying licensing royalties.

For the academic founder(s), the requirement of multiple financing rounds to develop a novel product may result in them owning very small stakes in their own ventures upon exit. Research in the United Kingdom found that even starting equity stakes for academic founders (i.e., following an initial equity round), were low, less than 20% compared to over 50% for most independent entrepreneurs.[11]

In addition to IP risks and associated costs of commercial translation and product development, and so forth, there are risks associated with the academic founder(s). A deal agreement would include restrictive covenants to ensure that the founders remained with the business during the critical early phase.

In some cases, such as in drug discovery where development costs and proprietary IP are significant risk factors, academic founders are likely to be asked to sign "noncompete" clauses within the executives service agreement. At the same time, proper incentives are required, and in some cases, it may include the option to return to the university while retaining a small founder equity stake.

This brings us back to the importance of legal intermediation for academic founders. "Research Notes" in the following text considers how legal intermediation is used in deal negotiations between BA investors and academic founders and why IP valuation is a contentious issue between investors, founders, and universities.

Research Notes

Legal Intermediation for University Spinout Ventures

Legal advisors can play a prominent role in negotiating a deal on behalf of university spinouts (USOs). Research suggests that BA investors require more legal service provisions when negotiating with academic entrepreneurs because intellectual property (IP) is often not properly secured or assigned from host universities and because business documents requested from the entrepreneur are incomplete or poorly presented. Poor negotiating tactics are also suggested, for example—when academic entrepreneurs attempt to renegotiate and enhance their equity stake during legal intermediation—beyond those discussed during previous "informal" negotiations (i.e., at term sheet) with investors.

Valuation of IP is identified by BA investors as one of the most contentious issues in deal-making with USOs and host universities. Sole reliance on the value of the IP or patent in negotiations eventually weakens the bargaining position of USOs and universities as investors negotiate on the basis that these parties are not able to apply IP into a commercial application. BA investors will negotiate away from their preferred position on warranties to conclude a deal but are not willing to concede on compulsory transfer agreements or equity stakes. Entrepreneurs will make concessions on a number of issues to secure the USO's future financial position.

Findings suggest that legal advice should be sought by academic entrepreneurs *at term sheet* rather than later, that is, *post term sheet* when investors typically employ legal counsel. Findings suggest the need for third-party coaching of academic entrepreneurs on negotiation tactics, as it appears that poor "investor readiness" of the venture as well as weak negotiation skills of the entrepreneur can compromise deal terms for USOs. Difficulties in dealing with some universities over assignment of IP and equity stakes also reveals that some BAs simply avoid USOs emerging out of these universities.

Sources: Gregson, 2011; Mustar, Wright and Clarysse, 2008; Lockett, Murray and Wright, 2002.

Not surprisingly, research suggests that BA investors possess a stronger bargaining position than academic entrepreneurs in negotiating and concluding an investment deal, even when the entrepreneurs are represented by competent and reputable legal advisors. BA investors appear willing to negotiate away from their preferred position on warranties to secure a deal but are not willing to concede on equity stakes or on "compulsory transfer agreements," described in the following text in "Clarifying Concepts."

Clarifying Concepts

Compulsory Transfer Agreements

Compulsory transfer provisions (CTPs) have been found to be a contentious issue in deal negotiation between academic founders and business angel (BA) investors. In one UK study, the majority of academic founders (71%) found it inequitable to be forced to transfer their shareholdings when they were no longer involved with the USO. BA investors, on the other hand, were generally not willing to compromise on this contract provision. CTPs are usually included in a deal agreement to allow founders to retain shares or percentage of shares after a defined period of time (provided these shares become nonvoting shares). The price of shares being transferred is usually dependent on the length of time the founders have been with company, calculated on a sliding scale or otherwise.

CTPs, in effect, offer a **"good leaver"**—**"bad leaver"** provision. For example, if a founder returned to university after contributing to the business (and was not in breach of their service contract), their period of "sweat equity" would be recognized with an allowance to keep their shares or to sell their shares back to the business, with the sale price reflecting commercial or fair market value. However, if a founder resigned early or breached the service agreement (e.g., for bad behavior, poor performance, etc.), he/she would be required to sell the shares back for par value (i.e., face value or original price paid).

CTPs have particular relevance to deals with USOs, where founders may retain some role with a university after taking an executive position in the business, for example, taking a period of leave from the university, with the option of returning at some future date. Investors will be cautious when dealing with founders who may abandon the business when things become difficult, especially if they have preestablished alternatives in place.

Summary

In this chapter, we suggested that an investment deal agreement is structured to adhere to an investor's expected return on investment. Various provisions and conditions of the agreement are meant not only to reduce the investor's perceived risks associated with that investment, but also to provide adequate incentives for the entrepreneur/founders. Experienced BAs are likely to apply a standard set of deal terms across different investments that will reflect their particular investment criteria. We also emphasized that entrepreneurs need to be realistic on the time horizon required to raise capital from BA investors. The general rule is that it takes longer than expected.

We discussed how discount rates and equity stakes are determined. Generally, the less risk that is perceived for the investment, the lower will be the discount rate, and the greater the potential return perceived by the investor (e.g., exit value), the less equity ownership he/she will demand. In some cases, valuing and "pricing" the deal is postponed and left for subsequent investors, when valuation can be more objectively determined.

Postponing pricing the deal is more common in the United States, where different share preferences reduce the risk of original investors being diluted with subsequent higher valuations. In countries such as the

United Kingdom, tax relief provisions for early-stage BA investors require that deals are priced and that investment securities be in the form of common shares, that is, which carry no preferences.

Valuation of an early-stage or prerevenue venture was identified as a potentially contentious issue in deal negotiation between entrepreneur and investor. Experienced BA investors will emphasize that the only important valuation is the exit valuation, and that focus should be on building value in the business rather than on early valuations. Investments made at high valuation may be more likely to experience lower valuation at exit, as suggested from VC data.

We suggested that entrepreneurs should be cautious about high valuations for a number of reasons. One is that they can place unrealistic expectations to achieve high growth. Another reason is that the valuation method offered by the investor may be more credible and realistic.

As mentioned earlier, entrepreneurs often value the business based on its future potential, while investors are more likely to value the business at its current value—applying a discount rate that reflects the current stage of the business. If exit values could be predicted with more objectivity, then the entrepreneur would have a case for a higher initial valuation.

We discussed the investment structure and different types of shares, identifying the preferences often demanded by VCs and some BAs that will have implications for common shareholdings. The entrepreneur should be aware of the potential impact of different securities on raising additional capital and on exit value. For example, "participating preferred" shares will have a small impact on exit returns, but for a smaller exit, the impact will be more substantial.

Finally, we considered the role of legal intermediation in the investment deal and emphasized the value of experienced legal counsel for entrepreneurs entering investment negotiation for the first time as well as for academic entrepreneurs. We suggested that the weak "investor-ready" status of the new venture and poor negotiations tactics weakened the negotiating position of academic entrepreneurs with BA investors.

The entrepreneur and BA investor require fair and equitable deal terms and conditions that will motivate both parties to work together and build the business. We now turn to the "post investment" phase in Chapter 6 and discuss what typically happens following conclusion of the deal agreement.

CHAPTER 6

Investment Management, Staged Financing, and Exits

The only valuation that really matters is the one at the end.

Introduction

In this chapter, we discuss the "post investment" period that begins with the signing of the deal agreement and concludes with a liquidity event or exit. Upon signing of the agreement, the entrepreneur and investor now share a common purpose of building business value toward a future profitable exit. This shared vision should influence most business decisions—whether they are about customers, recruiting new team members, or forming strategic partnerships—and should be revisited regularly.

A key challenge for the entrepreneur and business angel (BA) investor in the post investment period relates to "aligned incentives." How the venture progresses toward intended outcomes—or deviates from them—will influence the degree to which the entrepreneur and investor interests remain aligned or diverge. If interests diverge, how will this affect further funding, control over business decisions, exit options and strategies, and so forth? We return to this topic later in the chapter when discussing staged financing and exits.

We begin the chapter with a brief discussion of the entrepreneur–investor relationship and then consider how BAs and venture capitalists (VCs) manage their investee ventures and the role played by boards of directors. Next, we discuss staged financing, examine coinvestment between BAs and VCs and some factors that influence venture growth and scalability. We then turn our attention to the investment exit and consider valuation and exit options, which focuses primarily on financial and strategic sales and initial public offerings (IPOs).

Entrepreneur–Investor Relationship

Entrepreneurs who have raised BA finance will each have a different version of their relationship with BA investors. The nature of the investment deal itself—the terms and conditions that establish guidelines on decisions, actions, and behaviors of involved parties—has been shown to influence the subsequent relationship between entrepreneur and investor. Offering fair, simple deal terms and giving autonomy to run the business (by the investor), and making small concessions on equity (by the entrepreneur) can establish trustworthiness and mutual goodwill early in the relationship that can carry through the post investment period.[1]

The level of investor involvement in the business post investment can also affect the relationship with the entrepreneur and should have been discussed during deal negotiation, for example, such as the investor taking a seat on the board of directors as per the shareholders' agreement. Entrepreneurs should be clear on the role that investors will play and their expected level of involvement in day-to-day business activities.

BA investors are known to rely on a "relationship-based approach" to reducing risk that is based on trust and goodwill with the entrepreneur. A positive relationship can allow the entrepreneur to get on with developing the business and reduce the need to closely manage or monitor the entrepreneur/team to mitigate information asymmetry risks.[2]

This relationship-based approach aligns with a "patient investor" approach, which suggests that BAs, more so than VCs, tend to support and follow the wishes of the entrepreneur and founders; tend to allow the venture to solve its problems; and will rarely force an exit.[3] Such characteristics do not apply to all BAs as experienced BAs and larger groups and syndicates may be more active in managing exits and intervening to solve problems on behalf of their investor members.

Entrepreneurs are often attracted to BA groups and syndicates that have a successful track record in taking new ventures to exit. Such investor groups will also typically have more extensive networks of contacts from which to draw Board members, mentors, advisors, and potential customers for the investee venture.

However, managing a large portfolio of investments may also leave less time to provide advice and support for each investee. VC research suggests that when more new ventures with high potential appear—and demand for VC support increases—VCs might be tempted to acquire more firms at the cost of quality.[4] This makes them more similar to banks, which do not offer managerial support but tend to finance a much larger number of firms.

Post Investment Management

Regular monitoring of the "investee" venture is an essential feature of the post investment period—and the amount of time that BA investors will spend in post investment activities can vary widely. One study of German BA investors found that a typical BA averaged 1.34 days per month on each investment, with the most time devoted to their most recent investees, with more active investments involving one day per week.[5]

Performance milestones are typically used to monitor venture progress, with financial milestones being the most common. BA investors will expect that the venture establish financial targets, put in place relevant measurement and reporting systems, and provide explanations for financial performance at each Board meeting. Related documents that will be required for Board meetings may include the following:

✓ Balance sheets and income statements, cash flow projections, debtors, and creditor reports
✓ Sales funnel or pipeline; prospects and potential sales
✓ Tenders and contracts
✓ Actual and planned production
✓ Product development

BA investors will vary in how they monitor and manage their investees; some preferring to monitor more formally through board meetings, while others have more regular reporting practices and requirements. As discussed in Chapter 2, geographic proximity is seen as a substitute for some of the more formal control mechanisms deployed by VCs. Entrepreneurs may also be given communication guidelines, clarifying expectations and responsibilities. This is common with BA syndicates and groups.

BA investor Juliana Iarossi (see Chapter 2, p. 38) takes an informal approach to monitoring her investee ventures in requiring monthly updates on progress. She suggests that milestones, metrics, and dash-boards[6] tend to be a more relevant way to monitor growth during early emergence rather than using monthly financial statements. The problem with financial statements, she suggests, is that they do not provide information on product development, customer pipeline and feedback, talent acquisition, or pricing strategy.

BA investor Nelson Gray (see Chapter 4, p. 119) begins his Board meetings by asking the management team for a report on cash flow, future cash flow projections, and the "time to out-of-cash (OOC)." Time to OOC, also referred to as the "drop-dead date," remains one of the most common causes of new venture failure. Increasing time to OOC requires reducing cash burn or increasing cash through more sales or both, selling of assets, and so forth.

Nelson focuses management attention on sales and cash flow targets for a minimum of 3 months before the OOC date. The reason for this, he suggests, is that it will take a minimum of 3 months to raise the money once the management team has achieved something that can attract potential next-round funders. For the next board meeting, the management team will be expected to achieve something to increase the time to OOC, which includes options to raise new investment. Nelson suggests that this refocusing is continuous with new ventures, as "they never believe that they will run out of money."

While there is a general perception that missed milestones will immediately curtail release of further funding or trigger investors to gain control, evidence suggests that missed milestones are rarely used to effect changes in control in the business.[7] However, if the venture begins to suffer from poor results, performance milestones may be used to stage future financing—where the threat of abandoning the business is made real by a refusal to provide further funding if the milestones are not achieved.

BAs are reluctant to force early changes in management, preferring to assist the entrepreneur in refocusing the business or in recruiting new management team members. However, larger and more experienced BA groups and syndicates—through their executive teams—are more likely to intervene to make changes on behalf of investors. This will depend as well on the terms and conditions of the deal agreement.

Monitoring the investee venture by larger BA syndicates and groups will often occur through the executive team, with more regular support provided by an investor member who will often take a position on the board of directors. "Clarifying Concepts" describes post investment management through a BA syndicate.

Clarifying Concepts

Post Investment Management With a BA Syndicate

The entrepreneur raising finance through a *manager-led* business angel syndicate (BAS) will often engage with an executive team rather than with investors directly. The executive team may screen, perform due diligence, close the deal on behalf of investors, and be actively involved in post investment management and exit strategy. Once investors make their investment decisions, the executive team may sign on behalf of the investors, with copies of the signed agreements sent to the BAS office and to each investor. The investee company may then sign a standing order to set up regular payments (usually quarterly) to cover an investment-monitoring fee. These fees typically range from 1% to 3%.

The BAs may then appoint at least one director to the investee's board of directors, sourced from either core investors or trusted individuals known to the syndicate who can add value to the investment. This director will work with the company to define critical business milestones, and a plan may be developed and agreed upon to address any missing elements from the business, such as the need to make a key appointment for the management team, establish a key channel partner, and so forth. If a board chairman is required, then this position may be filled with a trusted and experienced individual from the BAS network, with the entrepreneur/team's approval. The ability to draw upon a larger network of investors and advisors is one advantage of syndicates and groups over solo BAs.

One UK-based BAS requires the submission of regular company accounts that are examined by a member of the executive team who is a chartered accountant. Investee companies are requested to discuss their performance generally, but especially if the executive team member identifies potential concerns upon review of financial figures.

A report on every syndicate company is generated each month, which includes financial results and overview on company activities, which are discussed at each board meeting.

Venture Capital Post Investment Management

Compared to BAs, VCs take a more detached view in making decisions on their investments. VCs monitor their portfolio firms closely, deploying more formal monitoring methods to overcome information and agency problems. General partners (GPs) may not devote too much time on distressed companies if it compromises other portfolio investments and their ability to source and evaluate new investments.

A series of missed targets (usually sales, profitability, contractual agreements, etc.) or loss of key staff can create pressure on GPs to intervene, which may include changing the management team, finding a buyer for the business, or other actions to realign the business to achieve agreed targets. VCs will usually put in place contractual terms that make clear the consequence of missed financial projections. These may include:

- ✓ Election of more investors on the board of directors.
- ✓ Replacement of the entrepreneur who is often the CEO at the time of initial investment. This may result in reassigning the entrepreneur to another role, allowing the entrepreneur to retain a board seat or outright removal from all venture activities.

If the decision is to replace the entrepreneur/founder, there is uncertainty as to whether the business will be better or worse off. Investments where the original entrepreneur remains with the business may outperform investments where the entrepreneur leaves or is replaced, according to some VC research.

Research note: One VC firm—in examining their investments across different dimensions—found that the one trait of all their successful companies was that the original CEO at initial investment was still the CEO at the sale of the company or initial public offering (IPO).[8] This has influenced their investment criteria—which places more emphasis on whether or not they believe that the existing CEO could bring the company to a successful outcome.

Board of Directors

As discussed in Chapter 5, BA investors may request or require a seat on the board of directors of the investee company. This will depend on their level of investment and equity stake, ability to commit time to being a board member, agreement by the entrepreneur and so forth. Some BA investors may avoid a board seat because of liability concerns related to making board decisions (more common in the U.S.).

The board of directors is charged with managing the venture and its affairs and will initiate the most important decisions, including decisions on liquidation, trade sales, and IPOs. While shareholder approval is required for certain transactions, shareholders typically do not have the power to initiate an exit event.[9]

Most VC-backed ventures allow both the VC and the entrepreneur to choose external directors, with certain "tie-breaking" board seats reserved for directors mutually agreed upon by the VCs and the entrepreneur.[10] The philosophy followed by many VCs is that the entrepreneur should control the business when the business is doing well while the VC should control the business when it is performing poorly.[11]

If VCs seek to take control from the entrepreneur/founders, they may demand majority board control in exchange for additional investment, although this may not be required, as VCs may gain additional board seats with each round of investment. In most cases, this also means that the control shifts from common shareholders to preferred shareholders over successive stages of financing.

As the venture develops, the relationship between the entrepreneur and the board may change. The early-stage venture typically needs advice and direction from the board in moving the business to profit, with the entrepreneur managing a wide range of business development challenges. However, the later-stage venture will need more advice from the board on strategic issues, with the entrepreneur needing to delegate more operational duties to focus on managing growth, partnerships, strategies for exit, and so forth. Option pools may also become important as the entrepreneur continues to strengthen the management team and board of directors.

Staged Financing

BA investors typically do not provide the entrepreneur with all the capital required to implement the business plan in a single financing round. In Chapter 5, we referred to tranche financing as the slicing of an agreed investment into portions that are released as milestones are achieved. Tranches can also be released according to particular time periods, although this is less common.

Staged financing with VCs can occur over a relatively short time period and at shorter intervals, arising from the time-restricted nature of VC funds. We noted earlier that VCs invest in "series" rounds (refer to Table 5.1, p. 154). However, GPs may have different time horizons and investment objectives for a VC fund at the end of its investment period versus for a fund at the beginning of its investment period.

Tranching investment in stages can provide incentives to the entrepreneur to focus on achieving milestones, with the prospect that the venture will fail if further financing is not secured. Typical milestones include product development; sales and cash flow; licensing IP; and the raising of additional sources of funding.

As mentioned earlier, tranche financing gives the investor the right to abandon further support of a venture whose prospects no longer appear promising. This allows investors to avoid "feeding losses" by continuing to invest in a nonproductive business. Subsequent tranches to be released to the entrepreneur must be seen by the investor to be productive investments.

Although VCs are known to refuse to provide further tranche financing to companies when they learn negative information,[12] this is less common with BAs. Once BA investors agree to an investment, there is usually a strong level of commitment to follow through on the investment.

The benefit of tranche financing is that the time, money, and effort required to finance the entire investment will be considerably less than that required for new rounds of financing, which require new due diligence, valuations, new term sheets, and so forth, and potentially new investors. Tranche financing involves a single term sheet and single agreement with the investor, and releasing tranches is relatively straightforward.

One drawback of tranche financing is that the entire investment (including all tranches) may be made on the initial valuation of the new venture, when it is considered high risk. With new rounds of financing, the entrepreneur can argue for an improved valuation based on the milestones accomplished to date, resulting in less equity dilution. In theory, each investment round should validate (or not) continuing investment, and each new round should leverage investment returns for earlier rounds and earlier investors.

However, many entrepreneurs underestimate or do not appreciate the extent to which they may be diluted when raising additional rounds of investment. There is often an argument that the deal price should be higher to offset their dilution. Original investors may be more difficult to deal with in this situation, and tension in the entrepreneur–investor relationship may arise as a result.

The entrepreneur should carefully consider the decision to raise equity as a tranche or round/series in terms of the venture's milestones and financing requirements. In this regard, *timing* of investment will be an importance consideration. For example, a new venture with a number of projected milestones, for example, proof of concept, securing distribution rights, customer contracts, and so forth might be better off raising multiple rounds, particularly if its cost base is relatively modest and it can survive if there is some delay in financing. "Research Notes" in the following text further discusses the topic of stage financing.

In theory, the need for staged equity financing should decline as the venture becomes more established and gains more of a reputation in the market.[13] Ventures that become "going-concern" businesses, with steady revenues and profits, should also be able to access bank debt financing. However, depending on credit conditions in the market, this may not be the case, and subsequent rounds of equity investment may be required.

Research Notes

Does "Staged" Financing Improve Venture Performance?

Research is inconclusive as to whether or not staged financing *improves* venture performance or leads to better returns for equity shareholders. Studies on venture capital (VC) confirm that staging is a powerful instrument for monitoring and control of investee firms, which allows investors to abandon nonperforming businesses.

Staging may have a positive influence on VC investment returns when used at the beginning of the investment relationship, according to some studies. However, research also suggest that ventures in distress receive more frequent rounds of cash injections as investors "gamble for resurrection" in the hope of minimizing their investment losses.

This is referred to as the investor's "*termination dilemma*," whereby a decision to postpone termination may allow the venture time to turn around the business but may also result in more losses for the investor, that is, in throwing further good money after bad. Research suggests that VCs may "window dress" nonperforming ventures in the interim to avoid showing a poorly performing business or potential loss in their portfolio.

What are the potential implications of this research for business angel (BA) investing? It is unlikely that the termination dilemma is as severe as with VCs, in the absence of time-constrained exit requirements and presence of an investor-led decision-making structure. However, executive managers of BA syndicates and groups will influence how distressed ventures are managed and are positioned to investors for further financing consideration.

Sources: Krohmer, Lauterbach and Calanog, 2009; Wang and Zhou, 2004; Gompers, 1996.

BA–VC Coinvestment

The funding escalator concept described in Chapter 2 (refer to Figure 2.3, p. 55) suggests that VCs and BAs may coinvest in ventures, which have progressed sufficiently to meet VC criteria but require new financing that exceeds the funding limits of BA investors. Although we noted the limitations of this model in explaining escalating investment, debate continues over the extent to which BA investment can act as a bridge to VC finance.

Research Note: One Canadian study found that over half (57%) of the ventures receiving BA financing subsequently obtained VC funding.[14] However, U.S. research suggests that the probability of follow-on VC is significantly lower—and that the BA–VC invest-ment relationship is not as strong as suggested.[15]

BA investors raise a number of issues related to coinvestment with VCs. One issue is the special class of shares—with preferential return rates and protections—which is a precondition for most VC investments (discussed in Chapter 5). BAs voice concern that they will get "crammed down" by the VC and may expect a valuation "uplift," which means that their investment will be converted to a higher price prior to the next funding round by the VC. Early-stage investors may argue that not only did they take high risks but that they also assisted the new venture in building business value to achieve the higher valuation.

The VC may counterargue that uplift cannot be justified as the venture may have been initially overvalued. Further, the VC may point to the uncertainty behind the valuation criteria used by the original investor(s). VCs may further suggest that the early-stage investors exposed themselves to such risk by not being able to "follow their money." Such scenarios are not uncommon and can lead to the perception that the process is unfair and that VCs do not adequately reward the "de-risking" efforts of earlier investors.

Another concern for BA investors is the potential loss of control and influence over an exit event (e.g., "drag-along", "tag-along" provisions; see Chapter 5, p. 160). The injection of more sizable VC funds with preferences may allow the VC to control the terms of investment and the timing of an exit. For example, the VC may block an exit event that is calculated to be below the VC's targeted internal rate of return (IRR) but which offers the BA investor a satisfactory exit. Taking VC investment may also increase the time to exit significantly, given the trend toward larger VC deals and toward longer time horizons to close VC funds. U.S. research finds that many VC funds last longer than the typical 10-year fund window and up to 15 years or more.[16]

A further concern, for BA investors in the United Kingdom, for example, is the inability to structure their investment deals in a similar way to VCs and to take preferred shares, if they wish to benefit from the Enterprise Investment Scheme (EIS); the national tax relief option. As mentioned earlier, EIS rules require that the BA investor take "ordinary" shares with no preferential return rights (refer to Appendix A).

Many BAs, who are themselves sophisticated investors, are unwilling to expose themselves to this risk and will therefore not coinvest with VCs.

In the United Kingdom, this has influenced the growth of BA groups and syndicates where securing a larger pool of investment capital allows BA members to deliberately select deals they can fully fund through to exit—without the need for VC investment.

At the same time, there are BA groups and syndicates that actively participate with VCs, particularly where VCs allow BA investors to invest on the same deal terms as the VC. In a few cases, VCs have been known to suspend their demand for preference shares and enter a BA-led deal with purchases of ordinary shares.

From previous discussions, entrepreneurs should recognize that not all capital "is the same." As mentioned earlier, if the entrepreneur offers preferred shares initially, then any future investor will be very likely to also demand preferred shares.

Some BA investors identify knowing when to "take the money off the table," a phrase that refers to an existing shareholder selling privately held shares to an incoming investor. We consider the example below.

> **Example:** A VC agrees to invest in a high-growth venture that has already attracted early-stage BA funding but wants a sizeable equity stage for their larger, incoming investment (i.e., to have more control over the exit). Founders and original investors do not wish to get diluted or see a lower valuation. One solution is for the BAs to "take some money off the table," by selling shares to the VC as part of the investment round. This leaves the VC with more equity ownership, the BA makes money, and the entrepreneur doesn't get diluted (as fewer new shares are issued). In some cases, BAs may be willing to offer VCs some preferences on their stock if the VCs allow them to take money off the table.

Investors may also allow the entrepreneur/founders to sell some of their shares as cash compensation (in the U.S., this does not typically incur payroll or other taxes, and the resulting gains are also taxed at a "long-term" capital gains rate that is lower than the rate for ordinary income).

Investors appear to limit founders to liquidate no more than 15%–20% of their equity to ensure that founders remain committed shareholders in the business. This option is more likely when the investment is performing well and the venture is raising external follow-on financing and unlikely with tranche financing from a single investor.

Venture Growth and Scalability

High growth is a key criterion for an investable business, which typically includes the presence of a large or growing market and high customer demand for the value proposition. The ability of the entrepreneur/team to scale the business and manage costs to support growth is also a key criterion, often assumed by investors after reading through the financials of the business plan.

Yet, many entrepreneurs pursue the objective of high growth for its own sake—without considering the investment exit and, specifically, how growth is building business value. For example, are capabilities being developed in the business that creates significant competitive advantage? What are the implications of gaining market share in a new versus understood market—and will this be sustainable? How profitable is the business model?

Although growth is often associated with more profit, evidence is inconclusive in determining whether or not higher growth means higher profitability. One study of the fastest-growing firms in the United States (i.e., the "Inc. 500") found that extraordinary high growth, measured by *sales* and *number of employees*—was not related to firm profitability.[17] The study found that firm age was a factor, with younger firms experiencing slightly higher profitability rates. What this suggests is that the entrepreneur will benefit from knowing how to accurately assess how growth is impacting profitability.

Growth funding is referred to as "expansion financing" and is used for increasing production capacity, market or product development, sales force or channel expansion, or to provide additional working capital. By definition, it is similar to a VC Series B round (Chapter 5, Table 5.1). "Clarifying Concepts" discusses scale-enhancing assets.

Clarifying Concepts

Scale-Enhancing Assets

A new venture with a small market share in a large market can expand initially with little impact on product price. However, rapid sales growth typically requires or results in a sizable increase in "scale-enhancing" assets. These include physical assets, such as plant, equipment, inventory, infrastructure, and so forth; human resources such as sales people, administrators, and programmers; and new partnerships to strengthen existing channels to customers or to build new channels.

Scaling the business also requires more effective execution of the business model. Standardizing certain processes to take advantage of scale economies will emphasize more routine patterns of business activity. This will require more sophisticated performance measurement and reporting systems because what the business knows and measures about its market and customers will become critical in managing growth and understanding how the business is generating and capturing value.

Expansion finance can also provide a platform for negotiating debt to repay an investor. Many entrepreneurs seek finance at this level to provide a boost to their business so that they can reach a size and profitability where they can convert equity to debt. This "**recapitalization**" enables them to gain larger critical mass. In some cases, it will allow the entrepreneur to gain back the equity passed to the investor as part of a financing deal. Such a strategy may enable the entrepreneur/founders to generate the level of security required to "buy out" the investor(s).

Investment Exits

The investment exit, having influenced the original investment decision, is likely to dominate business development strategy and influence key decisions made by the venture in the postinvestment period. The investment exit can be defined as the process whereby entrepreneurs/founders and investors remove themselves from primary ownership and decision-making structures of the business.[18]

VCs will have different mechanisms to control an exit, which we have covered earlier. These include controlling the investee's board of directors, obtaining specific contractual rights (e.g., liquidation rights), and having the power to abandon further funding to the investee. Controlling the board of directors allows the VCs to initiate an exit, particularly if they need to liquidate an investment because of their own liquidity needs. VCs typically do not obtain board control until in the later stages, when Series B or C rounds have increased shareholdings and preferences to hold a majority position.

The exit allows BA and VC investors to reallocate funds to other new investments. The exit also provides a signal to current and future investors of a BA syndicate/group or VC firm (i.e., limited partners [LPs] and investor members) regarding the quality of the investment group.

The entrepreneur seeking BA financing should be prepared to accept that their venture and shareholdings will be directed toward an exit as a condition of the investment. A trade sale will usually see the business cease to exist as an independent entity, and in many cases, see the entrepreneur and management team also exit the business.

A successful exit is the reward for undertaking risk, creating something of value, and dedicating personal resources and time into the venture. Many entrepreneurs, buoyed by the experience, will seek to do it again. The notion of the "serial entrepreneur" and the recycling of entrepreneurial talent and investment is a critical factor in successful entrepreneurial ecosystems notably Silicon Valley. Other entrepreneurs may retire to pursue individual hobbies or turn to philanthropic and charitable work. "Views from Practice" in the following text provides insights on preparing for an investment exit.

Views From Practice

Preparing for an Investment Exit

Juliana Iarossi (business angel [BA]): "Investing during early emergence of a new venture means that the company will likely change from where it was at funding, so the concept of an exit is a bit tenuous. Similarly, if an emerging venture is doing something that hasn't been done before, there will likely be no well-trodden exit paths to follow. With that said, I still look to see if there are logical and natural strategic partners that would be interested in acquiring the company, including companies seeking to enter into the market, competitors, or companies offering complementary products. It is also important to understand what the company owns, produces or does that is of value to another entity if the overall business is not successful. The route to exit is just one of many factors that needs to be considered during due diligence."

Paul Atkinson (venture capitalist): "Exits are an art and not a science. In an ideal world, you have a queue of would-be purchasers, a company growing fast with no untidy latent diligence issues and a management team who stand to pocket a tidy sum if the deal goes through. In the real world, you have to make the best of what you've got. It's all about little things that can tilt the odds in your favor; although there are some quite big fundamentals as well—trying not to run out of money, for example. As an investor, you try to leave a huge safety margin in terms of what capital will allow the company to get to a point where it should become an attractive target."

Nelson Gray (BA): "I've invested in traditional games companies, but would not invest in others, because of the difficultly in seeing an exit. In one investment, the games developer received money from a publisher for a new game; money flowed back into the developer to create a new version of the game, but there was no desire by anyone to acquire the games developer company. Applications are also a difficult investment. Who is going to buy them?"

Martin Avison (entrepreneur): "There has been a step change in the BA market regarding exits, where exits are now a regular topic at every board meeting. This is perhaps where the interests of management and investors could separate. If the entrepreneur doesn't wish to exit, but investors do, there may be 'drag-along' provisions in the contract, whereby if the majority shareholder wants to sell their share, then the minority are forced to join the deal; on the same terms and providing you have the same class of share. So the definition of the word 'majority' is going to be important. A mutual understanding of exit expectations would be a worthwhile discussion at the due-diligence stage"

Exit Value

Venture value at the time of exit is difficult to forecast. Uncertainty over exit value can lead to unrealistic expectations regarding initial valuations, as we discussed in Chapter 4. However, with the passage of time, much more information and data is available from which to assess a venture's business performance. Sales, growth trends, positioning among competitive products, customer feedback, market and media perceptions of the business, engagement with partners and suppliers, and so forth provide the basis for more objective valuation of the business.

We have discussed previously that all markets have cycles, and exit valuations will be influenced by the changing mood of the market—and the measurements applied by shareholders of the ventures as well as potential acquirers of the business. Private equity (PE) investors who own shares in different businesses (i.e., following the portfolio approach), should expect to see their values fluctuate over time.

BA investors will ideally seek to exit when the market for the investee venture is highly attractive. Having been directly involved in eight exits as an investor, Paul Atkinson of Par Equity suggests that each one has a unique set of circumstances that make identifying an "ideal exit" difficult. With most of the exits, Paul suggests that "timing is everything" and cautions that "If buyers emerge that appear to be buying for over-exuberant reasons; then it is probably time to get out." He suggests that you can't beat the market, but the hype of a business, over-exuberant investors, and so forth do provide signs that the market or sector may be peaking or is at maturity.

Exit value will clearly be influenced by the "actual" value that someone is willing to pay for the venture in the business-for-sale marketplace. Valuation, then, can be highly speculative and very much in the eyes of a potential acquirer. This may explain the wide and sometimes surprisingly erratic prices paid for relatively new start-ups—some that have little or no revenues or prospects for high revenues. This also provides some explanation as to why more successful ventures have wide-ranging fluctuations in the price of their shares.

The above discussion suggests that a business does not become a compelling exit opportunity because it can be acquired at close to its asset value. Neither does it become a sound exit opportunity simply because of a solid financial position, reflected by a healthy price-to-earnings ratio (PE ratio). In some cases, the venture has found a niche market that is highly attractive to other companies, and the venture may even be acquired before it begins to achieve high growth. Thus, exits can occur when there is still further growth to occur in the venture or before the investors had expected to exit the investment.

Given the dynamic nature of markets and exit options, investors are justifiably concerned about how different valuations or exit strategies will positively or negatively impact their expected return on investment. A sale or merger proposal that appears favorable to the entrepreneur but not the investor can raise problems that may affect the governance and control of the venture and preferred route to exit.

At the same time, if investors lose faith in the sector, venture, or entre-preneur/team, they may want to exit the investment. VCs and some BAs could force through a sale at the preference value against the wishes of the entrepreneur/founders. If the entrepreneur has conceded a large number of preferred terms in the deal agreement to attract sophisticated investors, a low exit valuation may leave little for the original founder(s) and common shareholders upon exit.

Exit Options

The vast majority of BA exits occur through a "**trade sale**," where the business is sold to another business, such as a corporation in the same business sector or a related field. BA investors may actively manage a trade sale or rely more on the managing directors to lead a trade sale. "Views from Practice" offers further insights on trade sales.

Views From Practice

Preparing for a Trade Sale

The former CEO of a medical device venture offers his views on what makes a successful trade sale. The venture received investment from a UK-based business angel syndicate and was acquired for $30 million by a global health-care company in 2010.

  ✓ Exiting a business is a strategy; all aspects of engagement with a
    potential buyer should be planned and measured.
  ✓ Most mistakes with a trade sale occur in the first meeting.

- ✓ Quality legal advisors are critically important:
  - ○ Advisors can help overcome cultural differences if it is a foreign trade sale.
- ✓ You must know your buyer and the buyer must know you; most successful exits are made to "friends" of the business, people who already know the business. This requires:
  - ○ Developing multilevel relationships with potential buyers.
  - ○ Managing communication with buyers.
  - ○ Communicating value-changing events in the business.
- ✓ Discussion of the product or service should embody its key competitive advantages; these advantages should look "deliverable" to the acquirer.
- ✓ Intellectual property (IP) should be managed for an exit from day one (i.e., from the very beginning of the business):
  - ○ Freedom to operate (i.e., usage and protection of IP across geographies and sectors) and future IP improvements are key issues.
  - ○ With patents, having a longer-term relationship with the same patent attorneys is highly beneficial.
- ✓ Due diligence will be significant and take longer than planned:
  - ○ Need to know your business inside out, as due diligence will find any deficiencies or secrets.
- ✓ Businesses are often sold in the middle of a funding round:
  - ○ Ultimately, a trade sale will be driven by needs of the acquirer.

We discuss two types of trade sales in this section: financial sales and strategic sales. The time horizon for a trade sale exit will depend on whether it will be a financial sale or a strategic sale and current market conditions, but a commonly accepted time horizon is 6 to 18 months.

Another exit option is an IPO, which is much less common and is discussed later in this chapter. A trade sale has an important advantage over an IPO for BA investors because they will normally be able to sell all of their shares, whereas with an IPO, a sell-off of shares may be interpreted in the market as a negative signal.[19]

For some BA investors, receiving regular dividends from an investment reduces the pressure on an exit. However, most BAs will eventually seek a liquidity event and push the entrepreneur to define an exit strategy that releases their original investment.

A **managed buyout** (MBO) is another exit strategy in which the management team offers to buy out existing shareholders. This may be an option if the venture is performing poorly or if investors have lost interest but is not common with BA investments. Another exit option is a **share buyback** where the founding team or other shareholders buy the investor's shares. This is not a common exit strategy and will place investors and other shareholders at odds, with the former seeking a high valuation at exit and the latter seeking a low valuation. Other exit strategies are also available, such as a "secondary buyout," where another investor purchases the business.

Financial Sale

A financial sale and a strategic sale have become increasing recognized in the BA exit literature as distinctive exit options. Academic practitioners, such as Tom McKaskill[20] (Australia) and Basil Peters[21] (Canada), have championed for some time the need for earlier planning to position the business for either a financial sale or strategic sale and to raise the value of the business leading up to an exit.

Financial sales are based on the future profit-generating potential of the investee business. A business purchased by a private equity (PE) fund—which intends to refocus or reposition the business through management, operational, or financial restructuring to increase profits—will also be a financial sale.

An *investee* venture appropriate for a financial sale will typically be high growth and demonstrate the existence of strong market demand and a market with global potential. A potential buyer/acquirer will also expect that profitability has been demonstrated, although this is not always a requirement.

Financial sales will be common in *understood* and *services* markets—in which there are many companies offering similar products and services. These markets include professional services; distributors; transport and construction; retail and wholesale; agriculture; traditional manufacturing;

and so forth.[22] In an understood market, the existence of a fragmented competitive environment may make growth through acquisition an opportunity for a buyer. For example, the investee business may provide the buyer with additional market power from which to make future acquisitions.

The purchase price for a financial sale will be driven by the current and potential profit of the acquired business itself and influenced by market conditions. We have already discussed the importance of market conditions not only for sectors but also for the market in general. Markets for young, private companies are inefficient, making valuations uncertain and highly variable. Market behavior and the timing of a trade sale in a "hot market" will also influence exit valuations and the pricing of an exit deal.

The purchase price will also be affected by the quality of available information and advice regarding the current market for selling a particular type of business, including access to competent merger and acquisition (M&A) specialists. The negotiation skills and tactics deployed in dealing with potential buyers can also influence the purchase price. Having more than one potential buyer can introduce competitive pressure on the interested parties that may result in an elevated purchase price.

Strategic Sale

Strategic sales are based on a buyer being able to acquire capabilities and assets possessed by the "seller" that the buyer can exploit to their advantage and generate future profits. In comparison to a financial sale, a strategic sale may not require the investee business (i.e., seller) to demonstrate significant sales, distribution channels, or extensive secondary services to support sales. In this regard, a strategic sales exit may offer less risk than a financial sales exit.

A strategic sale is based on the notion of "acquirer value," which represents the value that the acquirer attaches to capabilities and assets of the seller. The important feature of a strategic sale is the perception of the buyer as to how this acquisition will contribute to its competitive advantage and new profitability. For example, new technology ventures in Silicon Valley, even when unsuccessful, are shown to be attractive acquisitions for other companies, who are able to integrate acquired knowledge assets, IP, and product lines into their own businesses.[23]

Strategic sales will be appropriate for *new* and technology-based markets, where differentiating IP, deep domain expertise, and recognized brands are key competitive requirements. These markets include information and communications technology (ICT); R&D sectors; biotechnology; clean technology; designer fashions, and so forth.

There is evidence to suggest that founding a business-to-business (B2B) company will also raise the odds of a successful strategic sale. Although most new ventures sell products or services to individual consumers, approximately 90% of the fastest-growing private companies in the United States sell to businesses.[24] "Case Insights" in the following text highlights how differentiating capabilities of a new venture can attract buyer interest and lead to a strategic sale.

Case Insights

Strategic Acquisitions: *Instagram*

A two-year old company—with no revenues but approximately 35 million users—was acquired by social media giant Facebook in 2012. Instagram received over one million new Android users over a 12-hour period and promptly signed a $1 billion acquisition offer with Facebook the following week. The case offers lessons on strategic exits, described in the following text:

- ✓ The company built a large user community very quickly by offering a simple product with a limited number of options for customers.
- ✓ Processing features for customizing and framing personal pictures were easy to use and hassle-free for a wide range of users.
- ✓ Instagram created a recognized brand name and a distinctive social media stream (i.e., channel to customers).
- ✓ The sharing of customized pictures generated a viral appeal that was complementary to Facebook, whose value proposition relies heavily on the use of pictures and images.

For Facebook, the technical expertise and capabilities demonstrated by Instagram's success would be expensive to copy, build, or develop, or would take Facebook too long to assemble or to create internally. Instagram demonstrated significant technological competence in scaling their user base. Many entrepreneurs assume that their technology can scale with their customer growth—but find that they do not have capabilities to scale—and end up failing. Instagram's future growth could have also posed a potential threat to Facebook, so the acquisition also took out a future competitor.

The case demonstrates that strategic sales are not reliant on the sales or profits of the acquired business but on the value which can be generated from the combined entity. The case also highlights the extreme (and uncommon) investment returns possible by risk capital investors. VC Andreessen Horowitz's $250K seed investment in Instagram resulted in a return to the fund of $78 million.

An appropriate investee venture for a strategic sale is one that allows the buyer to diversify into a new market or respond to competitive pressures with new proprietary products. Ideally, the strategic buyer will generate new revenue streams through the acquired capabilities and assets. For example, the investee business may provide the buyer with novel products/services that can then be sold through the buyer's existing distribution channels.

Preparing for a strategic sale requires searching and identifying potential buyers most able to exploit the capabilities and assets of the investee venture. Entrepreneurs should consider whether or not a strategic buyer can be found within the current operating sphere of their business; whether it be a collaborator, partner, supplier, customer, or competitor.

As suggested in the Instragram case, potential buyers are likely to be attracted to capabilities or products that can be seamlessly integrated into their own business activities. Immediate access to superior technical, design, or marketing capabilities, that would otherwise be costly and time-consuming to develop in-house, may be highly attractive. Large firms will also be on the lookout for opportunities to secure such capabilities while also being able to remove a potential future competitor.

Initial Public Offering (IPO)

An IPO was earlier described as the sale or distribution of stock to the public market for the first time. The IPO is by definition a financing event, and as suggested in Chapter 2 (Figure 2.3, p. 55), it would occur at the later stage of the venture life cycle. IPOs are often referred to as an exit event, and in this section we discuss the IPO as an exit option and consider its characteristics, costs, and benefits.

Entrepreneurs with visions of a future IPO will require a business that can meet the highly demanding criteria of a public stock placement. The business will need to demonstrate an exceptional mix of products/ services, strong market demand, outstanding management, and sustainable competitive advantages. Such a business should demonstrate a growth and profitability trajectory that will support the share price for an extended period post IPO, for example, 5 years.

What are the advantages of "going public"? The main objective of an IPO is to provide a venture with access to public equity markets to raise additional capital. This capital can be used for various purposes, which include funding future growth; creating more stock from which to make acquisitions; improving the company's reputation and market standing; compensating employees; and so forth. There are three main participants in an IPO: the issuing venture, investors, and the investment bank, which underwrites the offering.

IPOs are also used as a major funding source for large R&D projects globally. Research by the U.S. National Bureau of Economic Research (NBER) found that raising capital through an IPO significantly correlates with capital expenditures in R&D—up to 4 years after an IPO.[25] This study also identifies the United States as the largest IPO market, accounting for almost 50% of total proceeds. Another study found that between 1998 and 2007, U.S. firms raised more than $623 billion through 2,905 IPOs, representing an average of more than $215 million of capital raised per IPO.[26] Such evidence suggests that IPOs may play an important role in the United States, maintaining a lead in technology-based innovation compared to Asia or Europe. "Case Insights" offer lessons on preparing for an IPO.

Case Insights

Intitial Public Offering (IPO) as an Exit Strategy

The former Chief Financial Officer of a successful IPO shares some insights on preparing for a public offering. The venture received business angel and venture capital investment and floated on the London Stock Exchange, raising £30 million on a £165-million valuation.

- ✓ The run-up to an IPO should demonstrate strong and consistent operating profit.
- ✓ If the business presents a distinctly different value proposition, then traditional fund managers will have difficultly ascribing a value for the business. This requires additional effort to ensure investment managers that the business can be clearly understood, as standard benchmarking methods of valuation are less valid.
- ✓ Promotion of the offering to potential buyers requires dedicated attention by the company CEO and senior managers.
- ✓ A compelling investment thesis is required that clearly sets out the transaction responsibilities and timelines.
- ✓ A promotional pre-IPO "road show" will suggest an indicative share price range that generates feedback from potential buyers. The company board of directors then typically determines an offer price, which establishes an initial company value and identifies the number of shares to be issued and expected amount of funds to be raised.
- ✓ By listing early in the new year, a company may get more attention from buyers whose diaries are less cluttered than later in the year.
- ✓ Funds raised from an IPO may be used for different purposes that include:
  - ○ Entering new markets for existing products or technologies
  - ○ Leveraging current research and development capabilities to broaden product offerings for existing and new markets
  - ○ Expanding sales and marketing capabilities to recruit new customers and expand market share.

In addition to raising capital, an IPO provides a venue for original shareholders to sell their ownership stake and increase their cash liquidity. Each IPO will differ regarding the exact number of shares that will be offered to the public (for example, Google only offered 7% of its shares to the public in 2004). Most IPOs will also have a "**lockup period**" covering pre-IPO shareholders that prevent them from selling shares for a particular period following the IPO, typically 6 months or less. Attempting to sell shares following poor results of an IPO placement may expose shareholders to insider trading.

Investor shares during the post-IPO period can gradually be registered and sold following the lockup period. With valuations of public companies typically higher than private companies, the liquidation of shares can offer an attractive exit for entrepreneurs and investors.

We now consider the disadvantages of going public. An IPO is an expensive undertaking and will require a significant time commitment from senior managers—that is likely to take away from their duties with the business. An IPO requires highly skilled advisors and underwriters to prepare for a lengthy, comprehensive due diligence process and to give the venture a high level of credibility in the public market. The underwriter's discount is typically 5%–7% of gross proceeds from the IPO. The venture will also incur one-off costs as well as recurring costs as a result of being a public company, which have been shown to average $1 million and $1.5 million, respectively.[27]

Another potential disadvantage is that the private nature of business operations and financial performance of the venture must now be publically disclosed. The market is likely to take a public company as a more serious threat, with the venture now facing more competitive pressures from rivals. The venture may also have to disclose proprietary information as part of an extensive due diligence process, which may expose its competitive advantages and weaken its market position.

There is also the possibility that conflicts may arise between the entrepreneur/founders and new shareholders, as managers of the venture are now responsible for a group of dispersed public shareholders, unlike the more concentrated ownership of a privately held venture. "Research Notes" describes the role of VCs and BAs in the IPO process.

Research Notes

IPOs, BAs, and VCs

With an initial public offering (IPO), venture capitalists (VCs) will use their reputation, and together with the underwriters, attempt to provide assurance to public investors about the quality of the venture—that signals the value of the IPO. It is not uncommon for VCs, particularly young VC firms, to "grandstand," which refers to taking actions that signal their capacities to potential investors. A negative consequence of this is bringing companies public too early, which can lead to "underpricing."

VC firms usually have strong motivations to exit following an IPO: to redeploy their assets elsewhere, to distribute assets to investors, and to establish an exit track record to raise further funds. VCs also need to maintain their reputation with underwriters and signal that they will not abandon a poor performer post IPO. Underwriters may require the retention of larger equity stakes, with associated lockups, from VCs in businesses with poor performance.

Business angels (BAs) appear to have a more significant value-enhancing effect on IPO venture performance than VCs, based on European research. Although both focus on the pre-IPO venture and seek to add value during the post-IPO period, the VC focus shifts to those investors in their funds (i.e., LPs) while the BA focus remains on the venture. For BA-backed ventures considering an IPO, evidence suggests that those led by founder CEOs perform better and have higher survival rates post IPO than firms led by nonfounder CEOs. Ventures led by founder CEOs at the time of an IPO also experience higher price premiums and firm valuations compared to nonfounder CEO-led ventures.

While BAs may be less concerned about their reputation than VCs, IPOs will be important for BA groups and syndicates who want to build their reputation and networks to attract new investors and promising investment opportunities. The case of Archangel described earlier (see Chapter 2, p. 44) provides a relevant example. The BA syndicate has generated three IPOs, which has helped to strengthen its reputation with the investment community and with entrepreneurs and raised its profile at the local political and economic development levels. It has also been influential in stimulating more regional BA syndicate activity and recruiting new BA investors.

Sources: Bruton, Filatotchev, Chahine, and Wright, 2010; He, 2008; Lee and Wahal, 2004; Nelson, 2003; Gregson, Mann and Harrison, 2013.

IPOs are also dependent on market conditions and are more common following a period of exceptionally strong industry stock returns and prior to a downturn in market valuations. Ventures going public during a period of intense IPO activity appear to generate poor "long-run" returns, suggesting that investor "sentiment" affects IPO timing. IPOs that occur in "cold markets" show significantly less signs of underperformance.[28] This suggests that positive sentiment among market participants can lead to overvaluation and induce more ventures to go public. Ironically, when the capital markets are normal, IPOs may be available to the ventures that don't need them.

Although smaller ventures can be successfully listed on the public market, they may not attract the level of institutional investment of larger companies. Information asymmetries, discussed in Chapter 2, are likely to be higher in smaller, younger, and less well-known ventures. Because the offer price at the time of the IPO can be misleading—as it does not account for the actual value of firm assets—this may contribute to underpricing. At the same time, a lower price may catch market attention and compel potential investors to learn more about the venture.

Summary

In this chapter, we identified the influence of fair deal terms and conditions on the entrepreneur–investor relationship that will develop over the post investment period. The quality of this relationship is important, given that BA investors often rely on a "relationship-based approach" to reducing risk—that is based on trust and goodwill with the entrepreneur.

The relationship is likely to influence to what extent the BA investor takes a "patient investor" approach with the entrepreneur. If there is high trust, open communication, and solid progress toward achieving milestones, it is much more likely that BA investors will support the entrepreneur and team and allow them to run the business without overbearing monitoring or intervention. Although BAs invest in higher-risk, early-stage deals, they tend to require or demand fewer controls from the entrepreneur compared to VCs.

The notion of a "fast-fail" business may be more difficult for BA investors than for VCs, given the relationship-based approach and the absence of pressure to exit (as with a VC fund). At the same time, we suggested caution in generalizing that all BAs should be characterized in this way. The boundary between larger, successful BA syndicates and groups and VCs is somewhat "blurred" in terms of investment management processes. There is also evidence to suggest that BAs are becoming "less patient" investors, seeking investments that require less capital and time to achieve a profitable exit. This is characterized by the terminology "strategic exit" and "early exit."

Considerations for the entrepreneur in raising equity financing as a tranche or round/series emphasized the need to consider venture milestones, financing requirements, and current market conditions—including the availability of risk capital. For example, during down markets, the entrepreneur may favor committing to an investor who can follow their money, as finding other investors for subsequent funding rounds may be more difficult. However, the entire investment will be made on the initial valuation, which may be further depressed in a down market. If there is near-term market recovery where valuations rise and the availability of risk capital improves, a promising venture will be committed to receiving tranches on the low initial valuation.

We identified a number of issues that challenge BA–VC coinvestment, including share preferences, potential loss of control, and dilution. While some BAs will avoid investing with VCs, others have become more regular coinvestment partners, where concessions, for example, on preferences, taking money off the table, valuations, and so forth, can facilitate coinvesting.

We suggested that building business value for a profitable investment exit is not just about achieving high growth. Building business value can include financial and strategic value, as suggested in our discussion on exit valuation. We suggested that a financial sale exit is based on assigning a value to the future profit-generating power of the investee, while a strategic sale exit is based on the value of the future profit that could be generated by the buyer exploiting the underlying assets or capabilities of the investee. IPOs, it was suggested, are highly dependent on market conditions and appear particularly important in supporting investments in R&D capabilities.

In the next and final chapter, we will follow up on one of the themes addressed in this chapter; namely, the trend of BA investments toward strategic exits. We will also examine alternative funding sources, such as equity-based crowdfunding, and consider its emergence as an early-stage funding source for entrepreneurs.

CHAPTER 7

Summary and Future Trends

Introduction

This final chapter summarizes some key themes discussed in the book and examines recent trends that are influencing how entrepreneurs form and finance their new ventures. We begin with reflections on what entrepreneurs should consider when raising business angel (BA) investment, followed by what constitutes an investable business for a BA. We then revisit the "lean start-up" concept, discussed in Chapter 3, to consider how this celebrated approach to achieving a product–market fit has advantages as well as drawbacks in formulating an investable business.

The chapter then discusses lessons from the market, including the proliferation of BA syndicates and networks and the influence of public policies and regulations on BA investing. We then look at some trends in entrepreneurial venturing and financing, and discuss three particular trends: "strategic" exits, the rise of "super angels," and "crowdfunding." The chapter concludes with some final thoughts.

Raising BA Investment

This book has focused on BAs, which have become the predominant source of early-stage equity risk capital for entrepreneurial new ventures. BAs invest their own money, make their own investment decisions, and rely on a relationship-based approach to risk reduction, which requires a high level of trust between investor and entrepreneur. BA investments, in comparison to (VC) investments, are typically smaller, take place at an earlier stage in a venture's life cycle and are biased toward ventures located in close physical proximity to the BA investor (i.e., less than 2-hour drive away).

Raising BA investment requires patience, perseverance, and planning on the part of the entrepreneur: patience because the investment deal process is investor driven and typically takes longer than expected; perseverance because the investment process is inherently more about rejection than acceptance; and planning because entrepreneurs can save time and increase the odds of acceptance by aligning their opportunity to the most relevant investor profiles. Entrepreneurs must also plan to raise financing *before* it is needed, rather than when it is needed, given the points mentioned earlier.

One apparent paradox is that planning to raise BA investment occurs in a difficult-to-plan operating environment for the entrepreneur, where flexibility and adaptation are often required to align the business with the right market opportunity. The *time to adapt* can also be critical—in positioning and making necessary modifications in the value proposition. Some new ventures may be too early to raise or receive BA investment, while others will be deficient in meeting BA investment criteria even if they develop as predicted. Some level of planning and understanding of BA criteria can also provide a reality check to entrepreneurs regarding the appropriateness or possibility of BA financing.

The entrepreneur needs to carefully consider the trade-offs in taking on any form of equity risk capital. BA or VC investment can propel a new venture beyond the confines of 3F (founder, family, and friends) funding to achieve high growth and to build up significant value in the business. In some cases, this can result in exceptional returns from a liquidity event for entrepreneur and investor—usually in the form of a trade sale or acquisition by another business.

To gain access to such investment, entrepreneurs will see a reduction in their percentage of ownership of the business and in their autonomy over business decisions. When multiple investment rounds are required, or if VC financing is taken on, there can be a significant reduction in ownership stakes and control over business decisions. The entrepreneur may also be required to exit the business alongside the investor upon a liquidity event, or in some cases, may be required to exit the business earlier as part of management restructuring.

Entrepreneurs need to choose their investors carefully. The right BA investor, with the relevant skills, experiences, and networks, can add value to the business beyond the financing. For example, financing a highly novel, radical, or complex innovation that has the potential to create a market that does not yet exist—or to disrupt an understood market—will benefit from an investor with deep domain expertise and related market knowledge. Such an investor will invest due to his/her superior understanding of the potential value of the innovation but will typically demand a high risk premium.

On the other hand, investors with limited knowledge are less likely to add strategic value or be able to accurately assess management team decisions. In such cases, investors may seek to become more involved in the venture to counter their lack of business knowledge. A high level of interference by investors has been shown to be counterproductive by negatively affecting the quality of managers' decisions.[1] Close monitoring by investors may also be counterproductive if, for example, the entrepreneur/team is constantly required to explain and disclose ongoing activities.

Appropriate "due diligence" in choosing the right investor should extend to understanding the details of the investment deal process and deal agreement. Chapter 5 emphasized the importance of engaging solicitors/lawyers with direct experience in BA and VC deals rather than relying on general legal advisors.

In Chapter 1, we suggested that the "common ground"—between a well-informed entrepreneur and receptive BA investor—is where successful investment deals are more likely to occur. Although a number of factors have been discussed in this book that refers to this common ground, we identify three important ones below.

One factor is that entrepreneurs need to consider business risk from the perspective of the BA investor. An unproven product/service, uncertain market demand, and untested entrepreneur or founding team presents a high-risk proposition for an investor. The business plan, along with pitches and presentations, provide opportunities for the entrepreneur to explain how common sources of early-stage risk will be managed and overcome (e.g., market, technical, value proposition, sales and channel to customers, management team, etc.).

Most BA investors apply a standard set of contractual deal terms across their investments that reflect their particular investment philosophy. However, additional terms and conditions may be applied in cases where the investor perceives a higher level of risk. Individual BA investors, compared to BA syndicates and groups, are more likely to vary in how they perceive risk and make investment decisions. Coinvestment with other BA investors requires consolidation of multiple investor decisions, which is often facilitated by executive teams who typically "apply" more objective, return-focused investment criteria in the deal screening for investors.

Another factor is appropriate incentives and fair equity ownership terms from investors that will encourage entrepreneurs to commit fully to building business value and to managing their behavior in a way that reduces information asymmetries.

A third factor is the presence of trust and open, ongoing communication between entrepreneur and BA investor. High trust and a positive relationship can reduce asymmetrical information problems and provide the entrepreneur with the discretion to get on with building the business and making key decisions.

The Investable Business

In this book, we have suggested that there is no ideal profile of an investable business that will meet the investment criteria of a diverse range of BA investors. In practice, an investable business is one where the BA investor perceives that enough value can be built up by the entrepreneur/team over a reasonable time period to generate above-average investment returns. An investable business includes the value-building capabilities, assets, and potentialities of the venture as well as particular strategies, intentions, and capabilities of the entrepreneur/team.

Business *guru* Peter Drucker made the point some time ago that "there is only one valid definition of business purpose: to create a customer."[2] An investable business must describe how the new venture will deliver value to the customer, receive payment from the customer, and make a profit. This description should be encapsulated in an appropriate business model . BA investors will be keen to see a business model that describes predicable profits and offers scalability in sales. It is suggested that a mediocre technology with a great business model is more valuable than a great technology with a mediocre business model.[3]

The business model canvas discussed in Chapter 3 provides a holistic view of how meaningful and distinctive value can be delivered to a customer segment. Such an approach can highlight key business assumptions while identifying strengths and weaknesses in the proposed business model when compared with existing business models in the market.

This book has suggested that different markets—understood, new, and service based—can all provide investable opportunities for the entrepreneur but present different challenges. In an understood market, investors will expect the entrepreneur to demonstrate an intimate understanding of the market, customers, and competitors. Experienced investors may further expect the entrepreneur to articulate how the venture will respond to changing market and competitive conditions. For example, investors may not be convinced that high sales growth can be maintained in a traditionally cyclical market or that competition will *not* intensify with the arrival of the new business.

Resegmenting an understood market may occur through an innovative *redesign* of the BM—that breaks away from the traditional norms of the dominant business model but does not abandon core features of the service or require entirely new customer purchasing behavior. This was suggested in the example of Southwest Airlines in Chapter 3.

However, a new market may be so strategically distinct from an understood market that existing business models don't apply. Emphasis on the business model may be less relevant in the absence of direct competitors, where a "trial and error" approach to learn about the market, clarify the value proposition, and map out a viable business operation should precede building a profit model. The business model should remain agile when exploring a new market and validating customer perspectives with the proposed value proposition—to ensure that opportunities are not overlooked and that the most appropriate opportunity is selected.

Deep understanding and verification of the customer problem can place a new venture in a strong position to define new solutions, which can also inform the most appropriate customer relationship and channel to reach customers. The entrepreneur can build up a direct relationship with a clearly defined but narrow customer segment and may then focus on finding "multiple ways" of satisfying the needs of this segment.

This approach will be relevant in business-to-customer markets as well as business-to-business markets.

Early in the book, we suggested that for new ventures with science- and technology-based origins, overcoming the gap between opportunity discovery and a marketable product requires concurrent technical and market validation. Otherwise, a completed product is searching for a market application—the so-called "technology push" dilemma. Lack of market demand can become all too clear once the technology makes "first contact" with the market. This is where many academic ventures fail.

The need for business validation at the exploration–exploitation interface requires strong market knowledge to ascertain which specific market segments are most promising. This identifies the importance of bringing relevant market and commercial expertise into the founding team as well as engaging BA investors with related domain experience and networks.

Further, entrepreneur "inventors" are known to have a strong attachment to their creations and inventions. Bringing in people without any emotional attachment can contribute a more objective perspective and reduce the risk of building a product, discovering that the market does not want it or need it—and then putting in much effort and investment to convince people that they *should* want it or need it.

An investable business also requires a sustainable competitive advantage. We discussed in Chapter 3 that new ventures often possess intangible assets, such as specialized know-how, product concepts, and unique capabilities that are not yet fully deployed in the market. Valuation techniques described in Chapter 4 are poor at estimating future value from such assets, which can lead to wide variations between entrepreneur and investor when attempting to agree on a premoney valuation.

Entrepreneurs should be cautious about overexposing proprietary product concepts and intellectual property (IP) to the market before they are commercialized but can be more liberal about exposing core assets once they begin to produce significant commercial value. This allows potential partners, customers, and collaborators to be drawn into the business. Moreover, "value in use" can provide a strong defense for core competitive assets against imitation, as suggested in the software industry, where much software is not IP protected.

One of the most effective ways of managing valuable assets is to embed them in a system of supporting activities designed to create a distinctive value proposition. This refers back to the nature of the business model and how effectively it is deployed. Entrepreneurs need to understand *where* they have a distinctive advantage and to articulate this clearly to investors. In one sense, the entrepreneur is appealing to the investor to provide the necessary investment to get "full-scale deployment" of the venture's valuable assets.

Lean Start-Up

The "lean start-up" concept has captured the imagination of many entrepreneurs and was discussed alongside the business model canvas in Chapter 3. Recall that it claims to provide a more productive way of achieving a "product–market fit." The lean concept relies on testing out concepts on customers and iterating or "pivoting" until customer feedback suggests a good product–market fit.

The lean concept suggests experimenting with a "minimal viable product" (MVP) which is a lean version of what might eventually be released to customers. MVP involves a "build–measure–learn" process that brings customers into product development to validate the product idea before potentially "overinvesting" in final development. Customer-mediated interactivity allows the venture to check whether what is being planned adds value to intended customers and users.

The lean concept also draws on the notion that new ventures can beat larger competitors through rapid product development, where novel products are conceived, developed, prototyped, and introduced into the market with significantly less cost and time than larger established firms.

The lean start-up concept appears most applicable to web-based ventures, where the capital required to create and launch such ventures has fallen dramatically. It has been suggested that the average cost to launch a technology-based start-up is $50,000, compared to up to $1 million a decade ago.[4] With software-as-a-service (SaaS), for example, fewer resources are required to get a product to market. Entrepreneurs are now able to brainstorm and choose a new software-based concept, build the product, launch it, market it, and engage customers with it within weeks or months. The availability of new software technologies allows program-mers and developers to create "mash-ups" that can create a completely new online or mobile-based application.

Lean start-ups can also be "virtual," whereby a small, dedicated found-ing team can develop core functions while outsourcing other functions such as administration, R&D, or marketing. A benefit of such a setup is that a higher proportion of operating costs can be variable, meaning that the start-up can manage (i.e., increase or decrease) its cash flow more easily.

The presence of social media outlets in the form of Facebook, Google, Blogs, and so forth provides large market platforms that allow lean start-ups to promote themselves and make their first sales. In the event that market demand is poor, the value proposition can be revised and modi-fied to trial again. Should the market acceptance remain low, the start-up can be terminated with a limited loss of time and investment on the part of those involved.

Potential Drawbacks of Lean

While there are clear benefits for web-based start-ups with the lean approach, there are also some potential drawbacks in its wider application. One is the assumption that product development cycles can be shortened by the MVP approach. For some technologies, the MVP approach may compromise a promising proof-of-concept project, as the MVP "side pro-ject" may increase the time and costs to complete the full development cycle that is necessary to overcome major technical uncertainties.

Proponents of the lean start-up approach suggest creating a sign-up page that outlines the value proposition and presents its novel capabili-ties and features to prospective customers/users—rather than building the service or finalizing the product prototype. For example, Dropbox, the file-hosting service, entered the market with a video of a beta of its yet-to-be-released product that prompted approximately 70,000 people to sign up for the service on the first day.

Although the MVP approach can establish an early level of cus-tomer acceptance and market knowledge, there is a risk of *overreliance* on feedback from customers or users about new products and services;

particularly those that cannot be fully evaluated or appreciated until they are fully developed and commercialized. Attempting to introduce or sell a late prototype product as an early product may compromise a new venture's reputation in the market. Changing a pricing policy or sales strategy may also be difficult once they are exposed to the market.

From an investor perspective, delegating product development decisions based primarily on existing customer feedback and iterations may result in generating *incremental* rather than novel or more radical product solutions.

A lean start-up may also be more difficult for investors to value or price, particularly if the development pathway is iterative, overly reliant on a narrow set of customer feedback parameters, and has bypassed or rerouted through commonly accepted technology or product development phases. Such lean start-ups are more likely to raise investment from those with deep domain experience, including those who have successfully exited a lean start-up business and are now investors themselves.

Lessons From the Market

Lessons from past markets offer further insights on building an investable business and raising equity risk capital. One lesson from the *dot-com* "boom and bust" (1997–2001), discussed in Chapter 2, is that anticipating change in consumer behavior as the basis of a business opportunity can be a risky prediction. The inconvenience of switching and the uncertainty about the structure and services associated with the new product—rather than the actual product—require that a new product and the overall value proposition for the customer be better than the existing one by a large factor.

In their rush to gain market presence with new websites promoting access to different products and services, many dot-com entrepreneurs incurred excessive development costs in trying to lead industry change. Many also failed to understand the weaknesses in their own business models. Undifferentiated value propositions, technical glitches in scaling web traffic, inadequate systems to fulfill delivery on customer orders, and unrealistic revenue and profit models were common causes of dot-com failures.

The dot-com boom and bust also identifies how private equity investors, VCs, and BAs alike can adopt a "herd mentality" to investing. Many investors were lured by a vision of financing industry change and assumed that these dot-com ventures would stimulate a rapid evolution in consumer purchasing preferences. Investors suspended usual due diligence processes and financial criteria to back charismatic entrepreneurs with novel websites, untried business models, and promises of unlimited market and sales growth predicted through the World Wide Web.

The dot-com boom and bust also represents a "dividing point" for the VC industry that continues to have repercussions today. Following the dot-com bust, VCs turned away from early-stage investing, preferring to invest in companies generating revenue and focusing less on product development, prerevenue businesses. This has contributed to the rise of BAs in the early-stage equity risk capital market, as discussed in Chapter 2.

This dividing point can be highlighted with data on investment returns. In 1999, the average VC fund earned a 10-year internal rate of return (IRR) of 83.4% but by September 2012, the average VC IRR was 6.1%; below the Standard & Poor 500[5] which has earned an 8% average return over the preceding decade.[6] While some commentary suggests that recent VC returns have returned closer to "normal" levels seen prior to the dot-com period, there is much debate on the critical state of the VC industry, particularly in the United States. This debate is beyond the scope of this book.

Comparative investment return data on BA investment is not readily available and is less reliable, given the challenges of BA transaction reporting (discussed in Chapter 2), but more recent U.S. data suggests that BA investor returns (using IRR) are between 18% and 38%.[7] What this suggests is that average BA investment returns are superior to VC returns.

Evolving Risk Capital Markets

In this book, we highlighted the growth in numbers of high-net-worth individuals becoming BAs and the number of solo BAs migrating to BA syndicates, groups, and networks. In some jurisdictions, government incentives have stimulated high-net-worth individuals to become equity risk capital providers by reducing risk through tax relief and stimulating coinvestment between BAs to share risk, invest in larger deals, and pool experience and expertise to benefit the investee businesses.

In the United States, there is evidence of emerging coinvesting *between* BA groups and syndicates. BA investor Juliana Iarossi (see Chapter 2, p. 38) suggests that the BA community is evolving from individuals investing on their own or with a small and close community of friends and business partners to large networks across the nation that informally coordinate fundraising efforts within a community or across communities and states.

Regional and national syndication and coordination of BAs and BA networks enable emerging companies to raise more money from individuals through a more efficient process for entrepreneurs. This type of regional and national coordination also allows BAs and BA networks with low deal flow to participate with groups that may have higher deal flow but insufficient capital to support the local deals they wish to fund.

Time will tell whether or not BAs in other jurisdictions invest further afield or indeed across national borders, and this may be a trend in the future as emerging economies strengthen regulations and legal structures to protect foreign investors. The rise of equity-based *crowdfunding* may also play a role in dispersing BA investment more widely and is discussed later in this chapter.

Although the financing partnership between entrepreneur and BA investor is focused on producing a healthy financial gain for the parties, there are wider effects that include bringing innovations into the market, generating new employment, and stimulating a new cycle of entrepreneurs who become BAs themselves and invest in future entrepreneurs. Healthy and growing economies are best served by the unimpeded flow of capital with as many people as possible willing and able to deploy their capital to entrepreneurs who are creating viable and sustainable businesses.

In the United States, recent changes in Security Exchange Commission (SEC) regulations allow start-up ventures to pitch for investment *publicly* instead of being restricted to pitching in private meetings. Investors will still need to be accredited (see Appendix A), but entrepreneurs will be required to file disclosures about their public pitches in advance to the SEC, which may include additional details on how they will use the money. A venture that fails to file the form could be banned from conducting a similar offering for a year.

While these SEC regulations appear designed to prevent fraud (especially as it relates to *nonaccredited* investors), one concern relates to the need for entrepreneurs to disclose and file information on businesses that typically don't have much information to disclose, given their stage of development. Some BA investors have voiced their concerns that more regulations could drive up the cost of capital through increased reporting requirements as well as narrowing the definition of who can be a BA investor. Time will tell how such new regulations will affect the flow of investment to entrepreneurs.

For entrepreneurs operating locally in small markets such as Scotland, there may be limits to raising sufficient BA capital—as the sole source of risk capital—to grow world-class companies.[8] Concerns were raised earlier in the book over the "drip feeding" of investee ventures with small BA investment rounds that can take too long. Further, raising enough capital to accelerate high-growth ventures is more difficult in the absence of VC or where there is little coinvesting between BAs and VCs.

In theory, more successful BA exits will attract more BA activity as well as VC interest in coinvestment opportunities and prospecting for larger deals. However, VCs are unlikely to coinvest if they are dealing with a hostile BA investment community, and BAs are unlikely to coinvest if the terms and conditions favor the VC at the expense of the earlier BA investor. This identifies the challenge in providing sufficient equity risk capital to accelerate venture growth in smaller markets.

Trends in Entrepreneurial Venturing and Financing

We mention a few emerging trends and market conditions, which may provide future investable business opportunities for entrepreneurs. One observed trend is changing buyer preferences in emerging markets, where standard, unsophisticated, mass-produced products and services for a large low-income consumer market are giving way to a rising middle class demanding higher-quality goods and services. Taking the concept of user involvement, are there opportunities to empower customers and users in emerging markets to express themselves within the value proposition and engage with others who share similar perspectives and user profiles?

Another observed trend is making new technologies more relevant and user-friendly for different segments of the consumer market. Technology has overwhelmed many groups in society who are challenged or unable to absorb the different benefits that technology provides through products and services. This includes opportunities for "technology inter-connectedness" that allows consumers or businesses to have integrated use and access to mobile, Internet, PC, personal and shared data, monitoring and measurement options, and so forth that are easy to use and self-manage. Customers will also be attracted by high functionality that can be delivered for less cost.

We now look at three trends in the risk capital market that are likely to affect entrepreneurs going forward: early exits, super angels, and crowd-funding.

Early Exits

In this book, we suggested that BAs are increasingly seeking opportunities where the "path to exit" is more evident at initial investment. Regular exits are critical in releasing capital that allows BA investors to reinvest in new ventures and support local entrepreneurial venturing. Without evidence of regular investment returns, BA syndicates and groups are less likely to attract new investors or build their reputations to attract promising new ventures seeking investment.

More emphasis on BA exits has coincided with a trend toward strategic exits, particularly amongst web-based ventures. Large companies such as Google and Facebook are seeking to acquire ventures with distinctive skills and capabilities and are typically less interested in fully developed, profitable business models, as discussed in Chapter 6.

Strategic acquisitions are also happening earlier in a new venture's development cycle, resulting in some exceptionally high exit values after only a few years. Examples include:

✓ Instagram sold for $1 billlion at 2 years.
✓ YouTube sold for $1.6 billion at 2 years.
✓ Club Penguin sold for $350 million at 2 years.
✓ Playfish sold for $275 million at 2 years.
✓ Flickr sold for $30 million at 1.5 years.

In Chapter 6, we suggested an important distinction between how the venture prepares for a financial sale exit and a strategic sale exit. For a financial sale exit, the emphasis is on a fully developed business model, high growth in sales, and recurring profits. For a strategic sale exit, the emphasis is on creating distinctive capabilities and know-how, which offer competitive advantages and new profitability for the buyer. Preparing for a strategic sale exit suggests identifying those potential buyers that are growing by acquisition and are seeking new capabilities and assets of the investee venture.

For the BA investor, identifying a potential strategic exit at investment might favor getting the new venture to a break-even position as quickly as possible to minimize the capital needed, then building business value rapidly to become an attractive acquisition target. Initial valuations might be kept low to reach the target exit valuation. This trend suggests that entrepreneurs may be subjected to more questions from BA investors about likely exit options during the screening and due diligence process.

"Super Angels"

An increasing emphasis on early exits and strategic exits has given rise to the "super angel," a term that refers to BAs who raise an investment fund, invest in early-stage ventures, and attempt an early exit. Super angels share characteristics of both BAs and VCs, as they are typically traditional BAs but who invest other peoples' money, similar to a VC. The size of super angel funds is smaller than VCs, typically less than $10 million, with investments in the $500K–$2 million range.[9]

What appears to distinguish super angels from many BA syndicates and groups is that they make a high number of smaller investments (typically around $100k) and seek to invest in ventures that can get acquired quickly. Super angels thus seek to benefit from the leveraging effect of portfolio investing, which has been shown to provide higher investment returns. For example, one study of BA exits found that the median expected return increases by more than 50% among portfolios of 5–10 companies, and by more than 100% among portfolios of 5–20 companies.[10]

With VCs moving further up the "funding escalator," by investing later in the venture life cycle, super angels appear to be filling the equity gap between larger BA syndicates/groups and solo BA investors. Although super angels appear to invest in more deals than syndicates/groups and provide more investment per deal than individual BA investors, further evidence is required to determine whether or not a bias toward early and strategic exits results in superior investment outcomes and returns.

CrowdFunding

"Crowdfunding" (CF) has emerged as an alternative financing mechanism for entrepreneurs, but it remains unclear to what extent this new entrant in the early-stage funding market will find a place on the *equity* funding escalator. Its significant growth and potential future impact on entrepreneurial venturing and financing warrants its inclusion in our discussion.

Crowdfunders raised approximately $1.5 billion in 2011 to finance over a million projects, ranging from scientific research projects to community projects.[11] One of the main contributors to this total was U.S.-based "Kickstarter," which launched in 2009 and by 2013 had funded over 50,000 projects and raised over $800 million in donations from approximately 5 million people.[12] The United Kingdom's innovation foundation NESTA predicts that CF could provide £15 billion of finance per year in the United Kingdom by 2015.[13]

CF originated as a "donor-based" funding channel, which allows people to donate money to social or creative projects in which they have a particular interest or need to support. In return, donors receive "non-financial" rewards which range from small rewards to larger rewards depending on their level of donation.

Although the concept of CF is not new—whereby many people donate small amounts to fund a single project—the leveraging of the World Wide Web through a platform website is allowing entrepreneurs to expose their ideas, projects, and schemes to the widest audience and to interact with potential donors. Proponents of CF suggest that it has multiple benefits for entrepreneurs that include proving a concept, demonstrating market demand, preselling a product or service, building a brand or raising awareness, and in the case of social ventures, building a community of proponents and supporters.

More recently, "equity-based" CF has emerged, which has generated much debate among investors, entrepreneurs, regulators, and others. In theory, use of the web provides an additional route to raising capital, particularly for those who are not able to access more traditional risk capital sources, such as BAs and VCs. CF platforms can also provide an opportunity for investors to search for investable opportunities in their specific areas of interest and expertise and to access opportunities well beyond those available via traditional channels and personal networks.

However, equity-based CF raises a number of practical questions, which we briefly discuss here. Will equity-based CF entrepreneurs be able to solicit crowdfunders (i.e., investors) through the website or otherwise? Different countries have regulations that restrict solicitation of investors, which is construed to influence their investment decisions. The difference between the type of solicitation allowed in BA or VC fund raising and in equity-based CF will have implications for how investment "crowds" will be developed.

CF investors will be making investment decisions based on the review of documentation provided online and without face-to-face interaction. In the absence of personal, face-to-face interaction between entrepreneur and investor, this may reduce the effectiveness of screening and due diligence. Entrepreneurs could provide a video and the use of online media to engage with potential investors, but the level and detail to inform the investor of the business opportunity may weaken the basis of an investment decision. Will CF make the use of business plans obsolete?

If CF investors are drawn from the general public, will they require certification, similar to BA investors in many jurisdictions or be regulated, as is the VC market? CF investors who are drawn from the general public are unlikely to have entrepreneurial or industry expertise to make informative return-on-investment decisions. The CF venture may have hundreds of silent shareholders who add no strategic value to the business.

In comparison to donation-based CF investors, equity-based CF investors will have expectations of growth and return. Investors are likely to demand more information from the entrepreneur regarding the financial status of their investment. Some existing equity-based CF platforms require that investors remain silent partners, which also reduces a key benefit of BA investing, which is exposure to investor experiences, expertise, and contacts.

Equity-based CF does appear to offer particular advantages for the entrepreneur, including level of exposure to potential investors, speed in raising investment, and reduction in investment costs and procedures. Equity-based CF introduces the potential for more competition for deals that may benefit the entrepreneur and provides the entrepreneur with a regular platform for introducing new business opportunities.

With over 400 portals and growing in 2013, equity-based CF appears to be gaining acceptance and legitimacy as a funding source, but this differs by jurisdiction, as different regulatory bodies attempt to catch up with this fast-rising phenomenon. The world's first equity-based CF platform received regulatory approach by the United Kingdom's Financial Services Authority in 2012, and various countries have followed suit in providing various levels of regulatory approval. Canada, by comparison, has yet to approve equity CF, although one of its provinces, Ontario, approved equity CF that is restricted to Ontario-based "accredited" investors only.[14]

Equity-based CF also has the potential to revolutionize the prescreening of opportunities, which currently demands a significant commitment of time by solo BAs and the executive teams of BA groups and syndicates. In one sense, CF can build a portfolio of investable businesses with small amounts of seed funding, allowing entrepreneurs to test markets and for BAs and VCs to then pick winners. Will CF gain wider acceptance from BAs or VCs and be complementary or integrated into their more traditional investment activities, or remain as an alternative funding source?

Whether or not an effective regulatory balance is established for equity-based CF to flourish—that protects the entrepreneur and investor while preserving the ethos of CF—will be revealed over the coming years.

Final Thoughts

We sincerely hope that you have benefitted from reading this book. The purpose of the book was to provide an informed perspective for entrepreneurs seeking to raise business angel investment and to understand how an investor might see their business. We also hope that the approach taken in presenting material—using practical and evidence-based perspectives—has been effective in better understanding some of the key concepts related to entrepreneurial venturing and entrepreneurial finance, focusing on BAs.

One limitation of the book is the bias toward a "Western perspective" on entrepreneurial venturing and financing. We require much more knowledge about entrepreneurial venturing and BA investing in other parts of the world. Different jurisdictions will have variations in how entrepreneurs raise BA investment and how BA investment, as a distinctive private equity asset class, is acknowledged, created, and supported.

Appendix A

Tax Relief for BA Investors: The U.K. Enterprise Investment Scheme (EIS)

The U.K.'s Enterprise Investment Scheme (EIS), launched in 1994, is meant to increase the pool of U.K. informal investors. EIS provides a range of tax reliefs for investors who subscribe for qualifying shares in qualifying companies. To become a business angel (BA) investor in the United Kingdom required the individual to be either: (1) a certified high-net-worth individual or (2) a self-certified sophisticated Angel Investor.[1] To be a **certified high-net-worth individual** requires that one of the following applies:

✓ In the financial year immediately preceding the certification date (CD), an annual income of £100,000 or more.

✓ Held, throughout same period as above, net assets to the value of £250,000 or more, which do not include primary residence property or pension benefits, and so forth.

To be a **self-certified sophisticated Angel Investor,** one of the following must apply:

✓ Membership of a BA network or syndicate for 6 months prior to the CD.

✓ Made more than one investment in an unlisted company for 2 years prior to CD.

✓ Worked in a professional capacity in the private equity sector or in the provision of finance for small and medium enterprises for 2 years prior to CD.

✓ Worked as director of a company with an annual turnover of at least £1 million for 2 years prior to CD.

By comparison, **in the United States**, the Security Exchange Commission (SEC) definition of an **"accredited investor"** is as follows[2]:

- A natural person who has individual net worth, or joint net worth with the person's spouse, that exceeds $1 million at the time of the purchase, excluding the value of the primary residence of such person.
- A natural person with income exceeding $200,000 in each of the two most recent years or joint income with a spouse exceeding $300,000 for those years and a reasonable expectation of the same income level in the current year; or
- A trust with assets in excess of $5 million, not formed to acquire the securities offered, whose purchases a sophisticated person makes.

EIS makes it possible for an angel investor to have a tax-efficient diversified portfolio of unquoted investments without hands-on involvement. Where EIS relief is available, the BA will qualify for the following tax benefits:

1. Thirty percent income tax relief on up to £1 million of investment per tax year (plus the possibility of carrying back income tax relief to the previous tax year)
2. Exemption from capital gains tax on disposal of EIS shares at the end of the 3-year relevant period
3. Allowing losses on the disposal of the EIS shares to be set off against either income or capital gains
4. Unlimited capital gains tax deferral in respect of the disposal of other assets, on amounts reinvested in EIS shares
5. Inheritance tax relief for EIS investments

The relief from loss is more important for BA investors financing early-stage ventures. If EIS shares are disposed of at any time at a loss (after taking into account income tax relief), such loss can be set against the investor's capital gains or his or her income in the year of disposal or the previous year. Relief on losses is at the highest personal rate. To be eligible for EIS, the BA investor requires:

- ✓ A minimum investment of £5,000 in any one company
- ✓ A maximum combined investment in all companies of £1 milllion during one tax year

The more recent U.K. **Seed Enterprise Investment Scheme (SEIS)** is similar to EIS but is targeted at first seed rounds only and only up to £100k. SEI provides 50% income tax relief at the point of investment (to allow exemption from capital gains on disposal of SEIS shares after 3 years). With both EIS and SEIS, the requirement is ordinary shares (common stock) in an eligible company. As noted earlier, this is a potential disadvantage for U.K. BA investors, compared to their U.S. counterparts, in being able to secure preferred shares and other preferences.

BA syndicates or networks are exempted from legislation governing investment advisory services so long as they do not make any investment recommendations. This means that executive team members cannot advise BA investors on their investment decisions. If a BA syndicate or network is charging "success fees" and makes a profit from this activity, then they would be required to be authorized; in effect, they would be regulated similar to the venture capital market.

Research finds that 80% of U.K. BAs have taken advantage of the tax incentives under EIS, suggesting that it serves as a major incentive to stimulate early-stage investments.[3]

See HM Revenue & Customs.[4]

Appendix B

Traditional (Comprehensive) Business Plan Structure[5]

I. Executive Summary	Description of business concept and the business opportunity and strategy; target market and projections; competitive advantages; costs; economics, profitability, and harvest potential; the team; the offering
II. The Industry, Company, and Product(s) or Service(s)	The industry; the company and the concept; the product(s) or service(s); entry and growth strategy
III. Market Research and Analysis	Customers; market size and trends; competition, competitive edge; estimated market share and sales; ongoing market evaluation
IV. The Economics of the Business	Gross and operating margins; profit potential and durability; fixed, variable, and semi-variable costs; months to break even; months to reach positive cash flow
V. Marketing Plan	Overall marketing strategy; pricing; sales tactics; service and warranty policies; advertising and promotion; distribution
VI. Design and Development Plan	Development status and tasks; difficulties and risks; product improvement and new products; costs; proprietary issues
VII. Manufacturing and Operations Plan	Operating cycle; geographical location; facilities and improvements; strategy and plans; regulatory and legal issues
VIII. Management Team	Organization; key management personnel; management compensation and ownership; other investors; employment and other agreements and stock option and bonus plans; board of directors; other shareholders, rights, and restrictions; supporting professional advisors and services
IX. Overall Schedule X. Critical Risks, Problems, Assumptions	
XI. Financial Plan	Actual income statements and balance sheets; pro forma income statements/forma balance sheets; pro forma cash flow analysis; break-even chart and calculations; cost control; highlights
XII. Proposed Company Offering XIII. Appendices	Desired financing; offering; capitalization; use of funds; investor's return

Appendix C

Essential Documents for Financial Section of Business Plan

Document	Description
Statement of cash flows	Provides information on changes in cash account through inflows and outflows associated with daily operations of business. Tracks actual cash receipts and disbursements. Cash flow statement is derived from income statement items and linked to balance sheet. Allows entrepreneur or investor to see the cash flow position of the business and identify the key sources of cash inflow and outflow (e.g., sales, account receivables, cost of sales, operating expenses, etc.).
Income statement (profit–loss)	Records the flow of resources over time and projects the earnings for a specified period of time (e.g., earnings = net sales minus costs of goods sold minus operating/nonoperating expenses and taxes). Revenues and expenses are recorded in the income statement when transaction occurs, whether or not money has been received (or expended). Allows entrepreneur and investor to track revenues and expenses and depicts when business will cover its costs and begin to make a profit.
Balance sheet (statement of financial position)	Provides information on assets, liabilities, and shareholders' equity (e.g., Assets = Liabilities + Shareholders' equity). Shareholders' equity is the estimate of the value of total equity investment in the business. Allows the entrepreneur and investor to see the financial "health" of the business at a single point in time (vs. cash flow and income statements that review a period of time).

Appendix D

Tech Coast Angels: Summary of Screening Criteria[6]

Screening Process

Over 900 companies per year apply on the website for Tech Coast Angels (TCA) funding. Approximately 25% make it to the screening process, and 10% make it into due diligence. TCA typically funds between 10 and 20 new ventures per year. The general process is as follows:

1. **Web application**

   The first step is to fill out an application with overview of company, including a summary of financials and also upload an investor Power-Point presentation.

2. **Initial review**

   TCA staff and industry-specific investor panels perform an initial screening of the application to ensure it is within the scope of interest. If it passes the initial review stage, the entrepreneur will be invited to present at a prescreening.

3. **Prescreen presentation**

   This involves an elevator pitch of between 8 and 15 minutes, followed by Q&A. The audience is a small group of TCA members who have domain expertise in the technology or market on a web conference call or at a separate meeting. The purpose of this meeting is to determine if the entrepreneur is ready to present to the larger group, and to provide constructive feedback to improve the presentation. The entrepreneur receives feedback and is told whether or not he/she passed the prescreen and will be able to present at a screening session.

4. **Screening presentation**

   Three to four companies are invited to present at a bimonthly screening session, which consists of 15 minutes of PowerPoint presentation and 15 minutes of Q&A. After each presentation, the entrepreneur is asked to leave the room while TCA members discuss whether there is enough interest to move forward into due diligence. The entrepreneur is then invited back into the room and given immediate feedback. Presentations are usually videotaped so that members who are not present can participate later online on the member-only secure website. The goal of a screening session is to get significant interest from TCA members and attract a "deal lead" that will coordinate the due diligence and be the entrepreneur's point of contact throughout the due diligence and funding process.

5. **Due diligence**

A due diligence team from members who were at the screening. Due diligence consists of verifying representations by the entrepreneur, speaking with customers, reviewing agreements and patents (if any), checking references, backgrounds, and so forth. Results of the due diligence process are posted on the TCA website (in the members-only section). If results are positive, the venture moves forward to a monthly lunch or dinner meeting, depending on the network.

6. **Monthly lunch/dinner meeting**

Companies that pass due diligence present at monthly lunch/dinner meetings and are introduced by the "deal lead," who led the due diligence team. This allows the entrepreneurs to present to members who may not have seen their initial presentation. This is the final opportunity for entrepreneurs to garner enough interest from members to secure funding. Typically, a signed term sheet is available when a company presents at this stage. TCA members' terms of investment follow "standard" terms for financings developed over the years by venture capitalists (VCs) and other sophisticated investors.

7. **Funding**

Funding occurs after there has been enough interest generated through dinner meetings and internal communication from the entrepreneur and deal lead. Members invest in deals individually; however, everyone invests based upon the same term sheet. Thus, only a small percentage of members need to participate for the venture to secure funding. Typically, the minimum individual TCA member's investment amount is $25,000.

Appendix E

Sample Outline of *Preferred* Investment Term Sheet[7]

The Offering

Issuer: [____], a corporation incorporated under the laws of ...

Securities: Class A Preferred Shares (the **"Preferred"**)

Amount of the offering: $[____]

Price per share: $[____] per share (the "**Initial Price**"), based on premoney valuation of $[____] and attached capitalization table

Investor(s): [____] and other accredited investors, acceptable to corporation

Closing date: Initial closing on or before [____]

Terms of the Preferred

Liquidation preference: Preferred will have the right to receive (x) initial price from a sale, liquidation, balance paid to common shareholders, and so forth.

Conversion: The Preferred may be converted at any time, at the option of the holder, into Common Shares, and so forth.

Automatic conversion: Each share of Preferred will automatically convert into common shares upon...and so forth.

Shareholders' Agreement

Information rights: The Corporation will provide to each holder of at least [____%] of Preferred unaudited annual and quarterly financial statements and an annual business plan, and so forth.

Protective provisions: Consent of majority of Preferred is required to approve any asset sale, merger, change in number of directors, and so forth.

Preemptive rights: Each of the major investors will have a right to purchase its *pro rata* share of any offering of new securities (e.g., to maintain proportionate ownership), and so forth.

Co sale rights: If any shareholder proposes to sell their shares to a third party, shares will be offered on the same terms. Existing shareholders may sell their pro rata share of the amount to be purchased by third party, and so forth.

Election of directors: Provision agreeing to elect board members, as designated by the Preferred, founders, common shareholders, and so forth.

Sale transaction: Refers to any merger, reorganization, consolidation, or other transaction involving the Corporation or the sale, exchange, or transfer of all or substantially all the Corporation's assets, and so forth.

Other Matters

Option pool: Number of common shares reserved for Corporation's stock option plan, and so forth.

Share purchase agreement: Corporation and investors will enter into a share purchase agreement containing standard representations and warranties, over the period of ___ years.

Founder matters: Each founder will have transferred all relevant intellectual property (IP) to Corporation, entered into an employment agreement, and signed agreements with respect to voting and vesting their Founders' shares (e.g., vesting of all shares on completion of a trade sale or IPO), and so forth.

Expenses and fees: Corporation will reimburse investor for legal fees and disbursements, up to a maximum of [____]

Expiration date: These terms are valid until [__], and will expire on [__]

Binding terms: For a period of X number of days, the Corporation agrees not to solicit offers from other parties for any financing. Corporation will not disclose these terms to anyone other than directors, key service providers, and other potential Investors in this financing.

This Term Sheet may be executed in counterparts, which together will constitute one document. Electronic signatures shall have the same legal effect as original signatures.

[*CORPORATION NAME*]   **[*NAME OF INVESTOR(s)*]**

_____   _____

Signature   *Signature*

Notes

Chapter 1

1. Davis (2003).
2. High-growth firms experiencing growth rates of 20% or more over at least a 3-year period (National Angel Capital Organisation, 2011).
3. Aernoudt and Erikson (2002).
4. Elston and Audretsch (2011).
5. Sohl (2007).
6. Ernst and Young (2013).
7. Mason and Harrison (2010); Petty and Gruber (2011).
8. Brush, Edelman, and Manolova (2012).

Chapter 2

1. Burns (2008).
2. Bhide (1994).
3. Bhide (1994).
4. Stinchcombe (1965).
5. Alverez and Busenitiz (2001).
6. Elston and Audretsch (2011).
7. Story and Greene (2010).
8. Bhide (1992).
9. Shane (2009).
10. Branscomb and Auerswald (2002).
11. Elston and Audretsch (2011).
12. Murray (1999).
13. Denis (2004).
14. Krugman (2009).
15. Gompers, Kovner, Lerner, and Scharfstein (2009).
16. Small Business Administration (2009).
17. Robinson (2013).
18. Mulcahy, Weeks, and Bradley (2012).
19. Kaplan and Stromberg (2001).
20. Denis (2004).
21. Roberts and Barley (2004).
22. Branscomb and Auerswald (2002).

23. Shane (2009).
24. Shane (2012).
25. Sohl (2008).
26. Wiltbank (2009); Pierrakis and Mason (2008); Sohl (2008).
27. Mason (2009).
28. Lindstrom and Olofsson (2001); Wright, Westhead, and Sohl (1998).
29. Ernst and Young (2013).
30. Umesh, Jessup, and Huynh (2007).
31. Coveney and Moore (1998).
32. Lindsay (2004).
33. Wiltbank and Boeker (2007).
34. Centre for Strategy and Evaluations Services (2012).
35. Benjamin and Margulis (2005).
36. Wong (2002).
37. Centre for Strategy and Evaluations Services (2012).
38. Gregson, Mann, and Harrison (2013).
39. Halo Report (2013).
40. Tyebjee and Bruno (1984).
41. Payne (n.d.).
42. Arthurs, Hoskisson, Busenitz, and Johnson (2008).
43. Wiltbank and Boeker (2007).
44. Roberts and Barley (2004).
45. Lumme, Mason, and Suomi (1998).
46. Frye (2003).
47. Gompers and Lerner (1999); Lerner (2002).
48. Gregson, Mann, and Harrison (2013).
49. Mason (2009); Harrison, Mason, and Robson (2003).
50. Berger and Udell (2002).

Chapter 3

1. Schumpeter (1934).
2. Kim and Mauborgne (2005).
3. Porter (1980).
4. Astebro (2003).
5. Chesbrough (2010).
6. Paul Atkinson interview.
7. Adapted from Osterwalder and Pigeuer (2010).
8. Blank (2013); Reis (2011).
9. Bhide (1994), p. 150.
10. Blank (2013).

11. Timmons and Spinelli (2009).
12. Bhide (1994).
13. Roberts and Barley (2004).
14. Cassar (2012).
15. Collewaert and Vanacker (2012).

Chapter 4

1. Tyebjee and Bruno (1984).
2. Gompers, Kovner, Lerner, and Scharfstein (2009).
3. Dimov, Shepherd, and Sutcliffe (2007).
4. Gregson, Carr, and Harrison (2013).
5. Gregson (2011).
6. Gregson (2011).
7. Riding, Madill, and Haines (2007).
8. Mitteness, Baucus, and Sudek (2012).
9. Smith, Mason, and Harrison (2010).
10. http://www.angelcapitalassociation.org/entrepreneurs/faqs/
11. Smith, Mason, and Harrison (2010).
12. Carpentier and Suret (2013).
13. Mason and Harrison (2002).
14. Benjamin and Margulis (1996), p. 221.
15. Villanueva (2012).
16. Kollmann and Kuckertz (2009).
17. Champenois, Engel, and Heneric (2006).
18. Amis and Stevenson (2001); http://berkonomics.com/?p=1214
19. Ernst and Young (2013).
20. Chaplinsky (2005).
21. Ernst and Young (2013).
22. http://www.lincscot.co.uk/

Chapter 5

1. Gregson (2011).
2. Chaplinsky (2005).
3. Denis (2004).
4. Halo Report (2013), p. 11.
5. Wong (2002).
6. McKaskill (2009).
7. Kaplan and Stromberg (2001).

8. Gregson (2011).
9. Pirnay, Surlemont, and Nlemvo (2003).
10. Clarysse, Wright, Lockett, and Knockaert (2007).
11. Clarysse, Wright, Lockett, and Knockaert (2007).

Chapter 6

1. Gregson, Carr, and Harrison (2013).
2. Demsetz (1988).
3. Mason (2009); Gregson, Carr, and Harrison (2013).
4. Gompers and Lerner (1999).
5. Brettel (2003).
6. Dashboards are used to monitor the major functions of a business and to highlight particular key performance indicators (KPIs), similar to the dashboard of an automobile. Often they are presented using chart, graphics and other visual indicators that would allow the investor to monitor and interpret the investee's performance in the context of projected and agreed-upon milestones.
7. Kaplan and Stromberg (2003).
8. Roberts and Barley (2004).
9. Smith (2005).
10. Kaplan and Stromber (2003).
11. Aghion and Bolton (1992).
12. Gompers (1996).
13. Denis (2004).
14. Riding, Madill, and Haines (2007).
15. Shane (2009).
16. Mulcahy, Weeks, and Bradley (2012).
17. Markman and Gartner (2002).
18. DeTienne (2010), p. 204.
19. Mason and Harrison (2002).
20. http://www.tommckaskill.com/
21. http://www.basilpeters.com/
22. McKaskill (2009).
23. Bruno, McQuarrie, and Torgrimson (1992).
24. Shane (2009).
25. Kim and Weisbach (2005). The sample involved almost 17,000 IPOs across 38 countries.
26. Certo, Holcomb, and Holmes (2009).
27. PWC (2012).
28. Helwege and Liang (2004).

Chapter 7

1. Burkart, Gromb, and Panunzi (1997).
2. Drucker (1954), p. 37.
3. Chesbrough (2010).
4. Edwards (2010).
5. The Standard & Poor 500 is a stock market index which is based on the market capitalization of 500 large firms that are publically traded on the New York Stock Exchange.
6. Cambridge Associates (2013).
7. Wiltbank (2009).
8. Gregson, Mann, and Harrison (2013).
9. Knowledge@Wharton (2010).
10. Sim Simeonov, CEO of FastIgnite, Inc. ran a Monte Carlo simulation on data from the Kauffman Foundation Angel Investor Performance Project (2007), which had data on 56 business angels with exits in 112 companies.
11. Baeck, Collins, and Westlake (2012).
12. http://www.kickstarter.com/help/stats?ref=footer
13. Baeck, Collins, and Westlake (2012).
14. Ontario Securities Commission (2013).

Appendix

1. British Business Angel Association (2012).
2. http://www.sec.gov/answers/accred.htm
3. Wiltbank (2009).
4. http://www.hmrc.gov.uk/eis/
5. Timmons and Spinelli (2009), p. 276.
6. See http://www.techcoastangels.com/for_entrepreneurs/screening-process-2
7. Adapted from MaRs sample term sheet; http://www.marsdd.com/

References

Aernoudt, R., & Erikson, T. (2002). Business angel networks: A European perspective. *Journal of Entrepreneurial Finance 5*(4), 277–286.

Agarwal, R., & Bayus, B. L. (2002, August). The market evolution and sales take-off of product innovations. *Management Science 48*, 1024–1041.

Aghion, P., & Bolton, P. (1992). An incomplete contracts approach to financing contracting. *Review of Economic Studies 59*(3), 473–494.

Alverez, S. A., & Busenitz, L. W. (2001). The entrepreneur of resource-based theory. *Journal of Management 27*(6), 755–793.

Amis, D., & Stevenson, H. (2001). *Winning angels: The seven fundamentals of early stage investing*. Great Britain: FT Press.

Arthurs, J., Hoskisson. R., Busenitz, L., & Johnson, R. (2008). Managerial agents watching other agents: Multiple agency conflicts regarding underpricing in IPO firms. *Academy of Management Journal 51*, 277–294.

Astebro, T. B. (2003). The return to independent invention: Evidence of unrealistic optimism, risk seeking or skewness loving? *The Economic Journal 13*, 226–239.

Baeck, P., Collins, L., & Westlake, S. (2012). *How the UK's businesses, charities, Government, and financial system can make the most of crowdfunding*. London, UK: NESTA.

Bank of England. (2001). *Financing of technology-based small firms*. London, UK: Domestic Finance Division, Bank of England.

Benjamin, G. A., & Margulis, J. B. (1996). *Finding your wings: How to locate private investors to fund your business*. New York, NY: John Wiley & Sons.

Benjamin, G. A., & Margulis, J. B. (2005). *Angel capital: How to raise early stage private equity financing*. Hoboken, NJ: John Wiley & Sons.

Bhide, A. (1992, November–December). Bootstrap finance: The art of start-up finance. *Harvard Business Review* 109–117.

Bhide, A. (1994, March–April). How entrepreneurs craft strategies that work. *Harvard Business Review* 150–161.

Blank, S. (2013, May). Why the lean start-up changes everything. *Harvard Business Review* 3–9.

Branscomb, L. M., & Auerswald, P. E. (2002). *Between invention and innovation: An analysis of funding for early-stage technology development*. Gaithersburg, MD: National Institute of Standards and Technology.

Brettel, M. (2003). Business angels in Germany: A research note. *Venture Capital: An International Journal of Entrepreneurial Finance 5*, 251–268.

British Business Angel Association. (2012). *Business angel investing: A guide to the legal, tax & regulatory issues*. London, UK: BBAC.

Bruno, A. V., McQuarrie, E. F., & Torgrimson, C. G. (1992). The evolution of new technology ventures over 20 years: Patterns of failure, merger and survival. *Journal of Business Venturing 7*, 291–302.

Brush C. G., Edelman, L. F., & Manolova, T. S. (2012). Ready for funding? Entrepreneurial ventures and the pursuit of angel financing. *Venture Capital: An International Journal of Entrepreneurial Finance 14*, 111–129.

Bruton, G. D., Filatotchev, I., Chahine, S., & Wright, M. (2010). Governance, ownership Structure and Performance of IPO firms: The impact of different types of private equity investors and institutional environments. *Strategic Management Journal 31*, 491–509.

Burkart, M., Gromb, D., & Panunzi, F. (1997). Large shareholders, monitoring, and the value of the firm. *Quarterly Journal of Economics 112*, 693–728.

Burns, P. (2008). *Corporate entrepreneurship: Building an entrepreneurial organisation.* New York, NY: Palgrave Macmillan.

Cambridge Associates. (2013). *U.S. Venture Capital Index and selected benchmark statistics.* Boston, MA: Cambridge Associates.

Carpenter, G. S., & Nakamoto, K. (1989, August). Consumer preference formation and pioneering advantage. *Journal of Marketing Research 26*, 285–298.

Carpentier, C., & Suret, J.-M. (2013). Entrepreneurs' experience and angels' decision process: A longitudinal analysis. Retrieved March 31, 2013, from SSRN: http://dx.doi.org/10.2139/ssrn.2253289

Cassar, G. (2012). Industry and startup experience on entrepreneur forecast performance in new firms. *Journal of Business Venturing 29*(1), 137–151. Retrieved from http://dx.doi.org/10.1016/j.jbusvent.2012.10.002

Centre for Strategy and Evaluations Services. (2012, October). *Evaluation of EU member states' business angel markets and policies: Final report.* Kent, UK.

Certo, S. T., Holcomb, T. R., & Holmes, R. M. (2009). IPO research in management and entrepreneurship: Moving the agenda forward. *Journal of Management 35*(6), 1340–1378.

Champenois, C., Engel, D., & Heneric, O. (2006). What kind of German biotechnology start-ups do venture capital companies and corporate investors prefer for equity investments? *Applied Economics, 38*(5), 505–518.

Chaplinsky, S. (2005). *Valuing the early-stage company.* Charlottesville, VA: University of Virginia Darden School Foundation.

Chesbrough, H. (2010). Business model innovation: Opportunities and barriers. *Long Range Planning, 43*, 354–363.

Christensen, C. M., Suarez, F. F., & Utterback, J. M. (1998). Strategies for survival in fast-changing industries. *Management Science, 44*(12), S207–S220.

Clark, C. (2008). The impact of entrepreneurs' oral pitch presentation skills on business angels' initial screening investment decisions. *Venture Capital: An International Journal of Entrepreneurial Finance 10*, 257–279.

Clarysse, B., Wright, M., Lockett, A., & Knockaert, M. (2007). Academic spin-offs, formal technology transfer and capital raising. *Industrial and Corporate Change, 16*(4), 609–640.

Collewaert, V., & Vanacker, T. (2012). *Forecast bias of entrepreneurs in venture capital-backed companies*. Brisbane Australia: ACERE Conference.

Coveney, P., & Moore, K. (Eds.). (1998). *Business angels: Securing start-up finance*. Chichester, UK: Wiley Press.

Dane, E., & Pratt, M. G. (2007). Exploring intuition and its role in managerial decision-making. *Academy of Management Review 32*, 33–54.

Davis, C. (2003). Venture capital in Canada. In D. Cetindamar (Ed.), *The growth of venture capital: A cross cultural comparison* (pp. 175–206). Westport, CT: Praegar.

Demsetz, H. (1988). The theory of the firm re-visited. *Journal of Law, Economics, & Organization 4*(1), 141–161.

Denis, D. J. (2004). Entrepreneurial finance: An overview of the issues and evidence. *Journal of Corporate Finance 10*, 301–326.

DeTienne, D. (2010). Entrepreneurial exit as a critical component of the entrepreneurial process: Theoretical development. *Journal of Business Venturing 25*, 203–215.

Dimov, D., Shepherd, D., & Sutcliffe, K. M. (2007). Requisite expertise, firm reputation, and status in venture capital investment allocation decisions. *Journal of Business Venturing 22*(4), 481–502.

Drucker, P. (1954). *The practice of management*. New York, NY: Harper.

Edwards, E. (2010). *Start-up: The complete handbook for launching a company for less*. Cincinnati, OH: Essential Books.

Elston, J. A., & Audretsch, D. B. (2011). Financing the entrepreneurial decision: An empirical approach using experimental data on risk attitudes. *Small Business Economics 36*, 209–222.

Ernst & Young. (2013). *Global venture capital insights and trends 2013*. UK: Ernst & Young Global Limited.

Frye, M. (2003). *The evolution of corporate Governance: Evidence from IPOs*. University of Central Florida, Working Paper.

Gompers, P. A. (1996). Grandstanding in the venture capital industry. *Journal of Financial Economics 42*, 133–156.

Gompers, P. A., & Lerner, J. (1999). *The venture capital cycle*. Cambridge, MA: MIT Press.

Gompers, P., Kovner, A., Lerner, J., & Scharfstein, D. (2009). Specialisation and success: Evidence from venture capital. *Journal of Economics and Management Strategy 18*(3), 817–844.

Gregson, G. (2011). *Investment negotiation between academic entrepreneurs and private equity investors: Examining factors affecting investment deal outcomes* (pp. 1–15). Frontiers of Entrepreneurship Research, Babson College.

Gregson, G., Carr, J., & Harrison, R. (2013). *The entrepreneur-business angel investor relationship: How does it influence initial and follow-on investment decisions and investment outcomes?* Lyon, France: BCERC Conference.

Gregson, G., Mann, S., & Harrison, R. (2013). Business angel syndication and the evolution of risk capital in a small market economy: Evidence from Scotland. *Managerial and Decision Economics 34*, 95–107.

Halo Report. (2013). *Angel group update: 2012 year in review.* SVB Financial Group, Angel Resource Institute, CB Insights. Retrieved from https://www.svb.com/halo-report/

Harrison, R. T., Mason, C. M., & Robson, P. J. (2003). The determinants of long distance investing in business angels. In W. D. Bygrave et al. (Eds.), *Frontiers of entrepreneurship* (pp. 116–129). Babson Park, MA: Babson College.

He, L. (2008). Do founders matter? A study of executive compensation, Governance structure and firm performance. *Journal of Business Venturing 23*, 257–279.

Helwege, J., & Liang, N. (2004). Initial public offerings in hot and cold markets. *Journal of Financial and Quantitative Analysis 39*, 541–569.

Kaplan, S., & Stromberg, P. (2001). Financial contracting meets the real world: An empirical analysis of venture capital contracts. *Review of Economic Studies* 1–35.

Kaplan, S., & Stromberg, P. (2003). Financial contracting theory meets the real wold: An empirical analysis of venture capital contracts. *Review of Economic Studies* 281.

Kim, C., & Mauborgne, R. (2005). *Blue ocean strategy: How to create uncontested market space and make competition irrelevant.* Boston, MA: Harvard Business Press.

Kim, W., & Weisbach, W. S. (2005). *Do firms go public to raise capital?* (Working Paper 11197). Cambridge, MA: National bureau of economic research.

Knowledge@Wharton. (2010). *VC super angels: Filling a funding gap or killing the next Google.* Retrieved from http://knowledge.wharton.upenn.edu/article.cfm?articleid=2580

Kollmann, T., & Kuckertz, A. (2009). Evaluation uncertainty of venture capitalists' investment criteria. *Journal of Business Research 63*(7), 741–747.

Krohmer, P., Lauterbach, R., & Calanog, V. (2009). The bright and dark side of staging: Investment performance and the varying motivations of private equity firms. *Journal of Banking and Finance 33*(9), 1597–1609.

Krugman, P. (2009). *The return of depression economics and the crisis of 2008.* London, UK: W.W. Norton Company Ltd.

Lee, P. M., & Wahal, S. (2004). Grandstanding, certification, and the underpricing of venture capital backed IPOs. *Journal of Financial Economics 73*, 375–407.

Lerner, J. (2002). Boom and bust in the venture capital industry and the impact on innovation. *Federal Reserve Bank of Atlanta Economic Review* (4), 25–39.

Lindsay, N. (2004). Do business angels have an entrepreneurial orientation? *Venture Capital: An International Journal of Entrepreneurial Finance 6*(2–3), 197–210.

Lindstrom, G., & Olafsson, C. (2001). Early stage financing of NTBFs: An analysis of contributions from support actors. *Venture Capital: An International Journal of Entrepreneurial Finance 3*(2), 151–168.

Lockett, A., Murray, G., & Wright, M. (2002). Do UK venture capitalists still have a bias against investment in new technology firms? *Research Policy 31*, 1009–1030.

Lumme, A., Mason, C., & Suomi, M. (1998). *Informal venture capital: Investors, investments and policy issues in Finland.* Dordrecht, Netherlands: Kluwer Academic Publishing.

Markman, G. D., & Gartner, W. B. (2002). Is extraordinary growth profitable? A study of Inc. 500 high-growth companies. *Entrepreneurship Theory and Practice 27*(1), 65–75.

Mason, C. (2009). Public policy support for the informal venture capital market in Europe: A critical review. *International Small Business Journal 27*(5), 536–556.

Mason, C. M., & Harrison, R. T. (2002). Is it worth it? The rates of return from informal venture capital investments. *Journal of Business Venturing 17*, 211–236.

Mason, C. M., & Harrison, R. T. (2010). *Annual report on the business angel market in the United Kingdom: 2008/09.* Department of Business, Innovation and Skills, HM Revenue & Customs Report. Retrieved from http://www.ukbusinessangelsassociationorguk/sites/default/files/media/files/bbaa_annual_market_report_2008-2009pdf

McKaskill, T. (2009). *Raising angel & venture capital finance.* Melbourne, AUS: Breakthrough Publications.

Min, S., Kalwani, M. U., & Robinson, W. T. (2006). Market pioneer and early follower survival risks: A contingency analysis of really new versus incrementally new product-markets. *Journal of Marketing 70*, 15–33.

Mitteness, C. R., Baucus, M. S., & Sudek, R. (2012). Horse vs. Jockey? How stage of funding process and industry experience affect the evaluations of angel investors. *Venture Capital: An International Journal of Entrepreneurial Finance 14*(4), 241–267.

Mulcahy, D., Weeks, B., & Bradley, H. S. (2012, May). *We have met the enemy… and he is us: Lessons from twenty years of the Kauffman Foundation's investments in venture capital funds and the triumph of hope over experience.* Kaufmann Foundation, SSRN.

Murray, G. (1999). Early stage venture capital funds, scale economies and public support. *Venture Capital: An International Journal of Entrepreneurial Finance 1*(4), 351–384.

Mustar, P., Wright, M., & Clarysse, B. (2008). University spin-off firms: Lessons from the years of experience in Europe. *Science and Public Policy 35*(2), 67–80.

Ontario Securities Commission. (2013). *Securities law & instruments.* Retrieved from http://www.osc.gov.on.ca/en/SecuritiesLaw_ord_20130620_215_mars-vx.htm

National Angel Capital Organisation. (2011). *Investment activity by Canadian Angel Groups: 2010 report.* Ottawa, Canada: NACO.

Nelson, T. (2003). The persistence of founder influence: Management, ownership, and performance effects at initial public offering. *Strategic Management Journal 24,* 707–724.

Olleros, F. (1986). Emerging industries and the burnout of pioneers. *Journal of Product Innovation Management 1*(1), 5–18.

Osterwalder, A., & Pigeuer, Y. (2010). *Business model generation.* Hoboken, NJ: John Wiley & Sons.

Payne, W. (n.d.). *Side car funds and angel groups.* Retrieved from http://angelnetwork.com/images/docs/SidecarFundsAndAngelGroups.pdf

Peters, B. (2009). *Early exits: The first book on exits for entrepreneurs and angel investors.* Canada: Meteor Bytes Data Management Corp.

Petty, J. S., & Gruber, M. (2011). In pursuit of the real deal: A longitudinal study of VC decision making. *Journal of Business Venturing 26*(2), 172–188.

Pierrakis, Y., & Mason, C. (2008). *Shifting sands: The changing nature of the early stage venture capital market in the UK* (Report No. SS/17). London, UK: NESTA Research Report.

Pirnay, F., Surlemont, B., & Nlemvo, F. (2003). Towards a Typology of University Spin-offs. *Small Business Economics 21,* 355–369.

Porter, M. (1980). *Competitive strategy.* New York, NY: First Free Press.

PWC. (2012). *Considering an IPO? The costs of going and being public may surprise you.* Delaware: PWC.

Reis, E. (2011). *The lean start-up.* New York, NY: Portfolio Penguin.

Riding, A., Madill, J., & Haines, Jr., G. (2007). Investment decision making by business angels. In H. Landström (Ed.), *Handbook of research on venture capital* (pp. 332–346). Cheltenham, UK: Edward Elgar Publishing.

Roberts, M., & Barley, L. (2004). *How venture capitalists evaluate potential venture opportunities* (Case 9-805-019). Boston, MA: HBS Publishing.

Robinson, D. (2013). Do private equity fund managers earn their fees? Compensation, ownership, and cash flow performance. *Review of Financial Studies 26*(11), 2760–2797.

Schumpeter, J. (1934). *The theory of economic development.* Cambridge, MA: Harvard University Press.

Shane, S. (2009). *Fool's gold: The truth behind angel investing in America.* New York, NY: Oxford University Press.

Shane, S. (2012). The importance of angel investing in financing the growth of entrepreneurial ventures. *Quarterly Journal of Finance 2*(2), 901–942.

Small Business Administration. (2009). *The small business economy.* Washington, DC: Government Printing Office.

Smith, D. G. (2005). The exit structure of venture capital. *UCLA Law Review 53*, 315–356.

Smith, D. J., Mason, C. M., & Harrison, R. T. (2010, November). *Angel investment decision making as a learning process* (Working Paper 10–05). Hunter Center for Entrepreneurship. University of Strathclyde.

Sohl, J. E. (2007). The organization of the informal venture capital market. In H. Landström (Ed.), *Handbook of research on venture capital* (pp. 347–368). Cheltenham, UK: Edward Elgar Publishing.

Sohl, J. E. (2008, March). *The angel investor market in 2008: A down-year in investment dollars but not in deals.* University of New Hampshire, Centre for Venture Research.

Sohl, J. E. (2013, April). *The angel investor market in 2012: A moderating recovery continues.* University of New Hampshire, Centre for Venture Finance.

Stern, S. (2004). Do scientists pay to be scientists. *Management Science 50*, 835–853.

Stinchcombe, A. L. (1965). Social structure and organizations. In J. G. March (Ed.), *Handbook of organizations* (pp. 142–193). Chicago, IL: Rand McNally.

Story, D., & Greene, D. (2010). *Small business and entrepreneurship.* Harlow, UK: Financial Times/Prentice-Hall.

Timmons, J., & Spinelli, S. (2009). *New venture creation: Entrepreneurship for the 21st Century.* Singapore: McGraw-Hill.

Tyebjee, T. T., & Bruno, A. V. (1984). A model of venture capitalist investment activity. *Management Science 9*, 1051–1066.

Umesh, U. N., Jessup, L., & Huynh, M. (2007). Current issues faced by technology entrepreneurs. *Communications of the ACM 50*(10), 60–66.

Villanueva, J. (2012). *Does it matter how you tell it? On how entrepreneurial storytelling affects the opportunity evaluations of early-stage investors.* Graduate School, University of Minnesota. Retrieved from http://conservancy.umn.edu/bitstream/144342/1/Villanueva_umn_0130E_13414.pdf

Wang, S., & Zhou, H. (2004). Staged financing in venture capital: Moral Hazard and risks. *Journal of Corporate Finance 10*, 131–155.

Wiltbank, R. (2009). *Siding with the angels: Business angel investing – promising outcomes and effective strategies.* London, UK: NESTA.

Wiltbank, R., & Boeker, W. (2007). *Returns to Angel investors in groups.* Kauffman Foundation and Angel Capital Education Foundation.

WIPO. (2013). *What are intellectual property rights?* Retrieved from http://www.wipo.int/about-ip/en/index.html

Wong, A. Y. (2002). *Angel finance: The other venture capital.* Working Paper, University of Chicago.

Wright, M., Vohora, A., & Lockett, A. (2004). The formation of high-tech university spin-outs: The role of joint ventures & venture capital investors. *Journal of Technology Transfer 29*, 287–310.

Wright, M., Westhead, P., & Sohl, J. (1998). Habitual entrepreneurs and angel investors. *Entrepreneurship Theory and Practice 22*, 5–21.

Zacharakis, A. L., & Shepherd, D. A. (2007). The pre-investment process: VCs' decision policies. In H. Landstrom (Ed.), *The handbook of research on venture capital* (pp. 177–192). London, UK: Edward Elgar.

Index

OTHER TITLES IN OUR BABSON COLLEGE ENTREPRENEURSHIP RESEARCH CONFERENCE COLLECTION

Andrew "Zach" Zacharakis, Babson College, Editor

FORTHCOMING IN THIS COLLECTION

• *Strategic Bootstrapping (6/1/2014)* by Matthew W. Rutherford

The Babson College Entrepreneurship Research Conference was founded by Babson College in 1981, and is considered by many to be the premier entrepreneurship research conference in the world. Frontiers of Entrepreneurship Research papers contain the proceedings of the conference are the most comprehensive collection of empirical research papers on entrepreneurship. The Entrepreneurial Research Conference was established to provide a dynamic venue where academics and real-world practitioners, through spirited dialogue, could link theory and practice. Each year, the Conference attracts more than 350 entrepreneurial scholars who come to hear the presentation of more than 220 papers. Business Expert Press is proud to be affiliated with Babson and BCERC.

Announcing the Business Expert Press Digital Library

Concise E-books Business Students Need
for Classroom and Research

This book can also be purchased in an e-book collection by your library as
• a one-time purchase,
• that is owned forever,
• allows for simultaneous readers,
• has no restrictions on printing, and
• can be downloaded as PDFs from within the library community.

Our digital library collections are a great solution to beat the rising cost of textbooks. e-books can be loaded into their course management systems or onto student's e-book readers.

The **Business Expert Press** digital libraries are very affordable, with no obligation to buy in future years. For more information, please visit **www.businessexpertpress.com/librarians**. To set up a trial in the United States, please contact **Adam Chesler** at *adam.chesler@ businessexpertpress.com* for all other regions, contact **Nicole Lee** at *nicole.lee@igroupnet.com*.